PENGUIN CANADA

SONG OF THE AZALEA

KENNETH ORE is a first-time author in his seventies who was born in Hong Kong. During the 1950s, '60s, and '70s, he was a secret recruiter for the Chinese Communist Party within British-controlled Hong Kong. He married a Party-approved woman, had one daughter, and emigrated to Canada with his family in 1974.

JOANN YU is a first-time author who works as a projects specialist and technical communicator in the information technology field. They both live in Vancouver.

SONG OF THE AZALEA

MEMOIR OF A CHINESE SON

KENNETH ORE

WITH **JOANN YU**

PENGUIN
CANADA

PENGUIN CANADA

Published by the Penguin Group

Penguin Group (Canada), 10 Alcorn Avenue, Toronto, Ontario, Canada M4V 3B2
(a division of Pearson Penguin Canada Inc.)

Penguin Group (USA) Inc., 375 Hudson Street, New York, New York 10014, U.S.A.
Penguin Books Ltd, 80 Strand, London WC2R 0RL, England
Penguin Ireland, 25 St Stephen's Green, Dublin 2, Ireland (a division of Penguin Books Ltd)
Penguin Group (Australia), 250 Camberwell Road, Camberwell, Victoria 3124, Australia
(a division of Pearson Australia Group Pty Ltd)
Penguin Books India Pvt Ltd, 11 Community Centre, Panchsheel Park, New Delhi – 110 017, India
Penguin Group (NZ), cnr Airborne and Rosedale Roads, Albany, Auckland, New Zealand 1310
(a division of Pearson New Zealand Ltd)
Penguin Books (South Africa) (Pty) Ltd, 24 Sturdee Avenue, Rosebank, Johannesburg 2196,
South Africa

Penguin Books Ltd, Registered Offices: 80 Strand, London WC2R 0RL, England

First published 2005

1 2 3 4 5 6 7 8 9 10 (WEB)

Copyright © Kenneth Ore, Joann Yu, 2005

Manufactured in Canada.

LIBRARY AND ARCHIVES CANADA CATALOGUING IN PUBLICATION

Ore, Kenneth, date
Song of the azalea : memoir of a Chinese son / Kenneth Ore ; with Joann Yu.

ISBN 0-14-301770-5

1. Ore, Kenneth, date. 2. Zhongguo gong chan dang—Party work.
3. Hong Kong (China)—History—20th century. 4. Ex-communists—Canada—Biography.
5. Hong Kong (China)—Biography. 6. Chinese Canadians—Biography. I. Yu, Joann II. Title.

DS796.H753073   2005   951.25'04'092
C2004-907446-6

Visit the Penguin Group (Canada) website at **www.penguin.ca**

*In memory of my mother,
those who died in the fight,
and those who struggled to exist,
I write this book*

*I alone am responsible for the contents of this book,
including the historical and geographical background.
Many names have been changed for the protection of the
innocent and the guilty. Nevertheless, the story still reflects
the true experiences of my life and of those around me.*

—KENNETH ORE

CONTENTS

PREFACE

The China my mother was born into coincided with the biggest shift in Chinese history. In 1912, after 267 years of rule, the Qing Dynasty crumbled and Pu Yi, the last emperor of China, abdicated the throne. In the years preceding, China had opened its doors to foreigners, only to be coerced and exploited. By the early 1900s, China had been carved and divided: the Russians had Outer Mongolia; the Japanese controlled Inner Mongolia, Manchuria, the Liaodong Peninsula, Shandong province, and Taiwan; and the Portuguese had Macau. Many cities—Lüshun, Dalian, Guangzhou, Nanjing, Tienjin, Shanghai, and many others across China and, undoubtedly, much of Southeast Asia—were taken and divided into concessions by foreign powers, including France, the United States, Germany, and the Netherlands.

At the same time, in the early 1900s, Kuomintang Nationalists and the Chinese Communists fought each other for power and control. With the Chinese preoccupied, the Japanese were able to occupy Manchuria in 1931. On July 7, 1937, Japan declared war by storming over Lugouqiao (Marco Polo) Bridge into Beijing. By 1940, northern and eastern China, including Beijing, Shanghai, and the Yangtze Valley south to Nanjing and Guangzhou, were occupied and administered by the Japanese. The Kuomintang Nationalist government established its war capital in Chongqing. In 1941, the Japanese simultaneously attacked Hong Kong, Pearl Harbour, and Southeast Asia.

Many intensely patriotic Chinese wanting to fight the Japanese and serve their country joined the Communists. I was one of them. We wanted change, and Mao Zedong and the Communists appeared to have the solutions. They told us that the Kuomintang Nationalist government led by Chiang Kai-shek was corrupt and offering no resistance to the Japanese invasion.

We had witnessed the endemic and systemic corruption of the Kuomintang government and found it untrustworthy. Many high officials had shifted state properties, including monetary funds, into their own pockets. The soldiers, poorly equipped with tattered clothes, straw shoes, and outdated World War I rifles, often marched to the front lines starving. The Americans supported the Nationalists as its bulwark against Communism and sent truckloads of aid—powdered milk, canned food, uniforms, weapons, medicine—that found their way to the black market and, eventually, into the hands of Communist guerrillas.

At the same time, the Communists painted a beautiful picture of China's future, making us believe—and we wanted to believe—that to save China and alleviate the deep affliction of its people, we must depend on the Communists and the Communists alone.

We had to believe them. But once we joined, we saw from the inside, with horror, its true face. It was difficult to see one's own people slaughtered by the enemy, but a hundred times more heartbreaking was to see them murdered by one's countrymen. It happened then, and it continues. Even now, despite impressive buildings and massive structures in the major cities, mostly along the coast, China's villages and rural areas remain backward and poor.

After half a century, I fear the facts reveal our efforts have been in vain. Carrying this painful burden of knowledge and searching for a solution, I have walked a long way.

Amid all the hopelessness I lived and grew up with, there are still things to remind me of humanity's dignity. My own mother's life was a shining example of strength, resourcefulness, willpower, and courage.

On many occasions, Mama could have been killed by the Japanese, or by thieves or thugs. We would have starved to death if she hadn't found rice. We could have been arrested at any of the checkpoints on the road of retreat if not for her quick thinking. Mama persevered, so that I, one of the fortunate, can live to tell the tale.

PROLOGUE

1917   Chiu Yeung, near the port of Swatow,
Guangdong province, China

What does a child know of money? A bit of silver buys her candies and toys, embroidered slippers and sticky rice cakes. The smallest gift lights up her eyes, her shiny black eyes. Bring home real rice—the fluffy white polished kind—and you'll feel her arms embrace you. No more hunger, no more chalky wild yams, she cheers. And if you can afford an egg, a whole egg every year or two, then you're the best father in the world.

But a father? Well, fathers are men and a man needs much, much more than trinkets. The same silver that delights his child barely fetches him a dream or two, a whiff of an opium pipe, no more.

At least that's the way Chau saw it. Chau was a stevedore slaving on the docks of Kowloon, a peninsula north of Hong Kong's Victoria Harbour. Baptized in sweat, Chau and his gang of coolies strained and grunted for mere pieces of silver a day. Heavy burlap sacks and cumbersome wooden crates carved their sun-roasted hides. Their bruises, their blood made Hong Kong a major port. How else could China ship her goods to the world? Fancy lace tablecloths and gowns. Citrus fruits and spices, oolong tea and incense, salty dried clams and sandalwood fans. The heady perfume tickled their noses and churned their stomachs as it mingled with the stench of rotting fish and rat urine.

Work came irregularly on these wharves. But whenever silver came their way, Chau and his fellow coolies celebrated with man-sized bowls of rice, roast goose, and other delicacies to strengthen their wiry frames. Jugs of spicy wine soothed their aching muscles. And, in dimly lit backrooms, opium fuelled their dreams.

Who could begrudge a stevedore his dreams? Dreams that take him to a world without problems, or at least to a world that offers more than just back-breaking labours—a kinder, gentler world.

Chau would grope his way through dark lanes and corridors to a familiar faded curtain, smudged with the grease of countless hands and drooping across a doorway barely wide enough for a man to squeeze through with his lady friend. Not that Chau could afford to caress silk-clad curves while he chased down his opiate dreams with tea and ginseng. He was content to lounge alone.

Weariness and tension drained from his shoulders as he stepped across the door's threshold. He slipped off his shoes as easily as he shrugged away the image in his mind of his daughter's coal-black eyes. He curled up on a wooden platform and reached hungrily for the bamboo pipe. A few deep breaths and the world was sweet—for a short while.

Through his opiate haze, Chau watched black smocks float by. Here, a wide, flowing sleeve; there, a low mandarin collar. Coolies and clerks, bankers and thieves filled the backrooms of the opium den. The den's masters wore smocks, tailored in the traditional martial arts style with the cuffs rolled back to reveal the white cotton underneath.

"Beware, foolish one," warned the cuffs, "our owner, the loan shark, will crush your skull should you fail to pay for your indulgences."

But Chau did not heed the cuffs' warning. One day, when he had no jobs lined up, Chau bought a few dreams on credit. It is easy for small sums to add up quickly, and before long, his stevedore's wages could not cover even the interest on the loans. As his debts mounted, the black-smocked thugs visited Chau's flat across from the wharf, at the corner of Canton and Haiphong roads.

"Pay now," they threatened, "or you'll pay with your arm, or your life."

Like many other parents of his time and in his situation, Chau decided to sell his daughter in order to repay his debt. The stevedore had two daughters to sell, but he knew the youngest, still an infant, wouldn't fetch much. His first-born, however, was a capable and attractive girl. Whenever some small thing delighted her, dimples kissed her cheeks and her eyes crinkled into upside-down smiles. Who cared that she had a firm, masculine jaw, so long as her teeth and gums were healthy? Her young hips already looked strong enough to bear many sons. Wai Chi was eight years old.

The loan sharks preferred to take girls as inventory for their prostitution division. It was an effective accounts receivable system. Chau refused, however, to give his daughter to the goons. Instead, a broker put him in touch with Ore K.W., a wealthy lace merchant who was in the market for a concubine. Ore could have picked up a beggar girl for nothing more than table scraps and rags but, as luck would have it, Chau came from the same village as Ore—Chiu Yeung, near the port of Swatow. They had both left their families behind there and ventured to Hong Kong to make their fortune. They were, in a sense, neighbours.

The Ore family honour required a price to be paid so as not to lose face: three hundred silver pieces for Chau's eldest daughter.

A few days later, Chau was staring out the window of his cramped bachelor's flat, where he lived while away from his family, when a messenger boy arrived with a promissory note. After the broker's commission, the stevedore would receive one hundred pieces of silver. Chau sat down on his narrow cot and studied the cockroaches on the walls. The flat's putrid air choked him. Could he have made a mistake? His finger traced a path through the dust and grime on what passed for a washstand. It was the right thing to do. Daughters were liabilities.

Resolutely, he stood up, reached under the cot, and pulled out his satchel, a navy blue square of cotton gathered into a hobo's bundle. He packed his mandarin jacket, trousers, and sandals and slung the bag over his shoulder. Then he headed back to Chiu Yeung village. It took him three days by steamship from Hong Kong to Swatow and then a few hours' walking from Swatow.

When he arrived home, he found his eldest daughter babysitting her siblings. He watched from the doorway as his three sons played on the dirt floor. Wai Chi hoisted the baby onto her hip, took wild yams from a charred clay pot sitting on the stove, and began feeding her bits of the boiled orange vegetable. Chau could imagine his wife's bitter reproach: "This is all we've got to survive on. While you burn silver smoking opium, we grub for yams."

Months of this sparse diet had whittled any remaining baby fat off Wai Chi's slender frame. One braid bounced over her shoulder as she turned to stare at him. Her eyes, as dark as the soot on the clay pot, were solemn, but in their depths shone the trust a child reserves for her father. Her look made him pause.

Wai Chi approached her father and reached for his arm. It hung limp. He did not smile back when she smiled her welcome. He swallowed the guilt that rose like bile in his throat with a muttered curse. Then he took Wai Chi by the hand, led her over the dirt path to the Ore household, and left her there.

When his wife returned home, she knew at once why her eldest daughter was missing. "How could you?" she hissed. "How could you sell your own daughter?"

"We have three sons," was his laconic reply.

"What's going to happen to your daughter?"

"The old man wanted another concubine," said Chau, reaching for his tea. He stared at his cup, refusing to meet his wife's accusing glare. "Some comfort in his old age, maybe. His wife fought him on that one. She wants a maid."

"A maid? A concubine. You want your daughter to nurse some aging bastard? *Kwa char luk!" May you be stuffed in a coffin like a dead man and be sawed with it into short pieces!* That was enough of an insult for the man of the house. Chau leapt from his chair and, as was his way, silenced her with his fists.

For days afterward, his wife haunted the Ore doorway. She begged them not to use Wai Chi as a maid or concubine. "The girl would make a perfect daughter-in-law," she pleaded. Finally, Ore gave in. He assigned Wai Chi to his first son, Yick Ting.

⁂

What happened to Wai Chi wasn't that unusual in 1917 China, but it scarred her nonetheless. As an adult, she rarely mentioned her father or her early years in the Ore household. "I was little better than a servant at first," she once said. "I stood on hot bricks to stir a wok big enough to boil me in."

Like the other women in the household, she ate only what was left over from the men's dinner. None of the women dared sit down for a meal until the men had finished eating. Since Wai Chi had been bought into the family, her status was the lowest. All the women and even the servants gossiped and looked down on her. But whatever happened during those years made her strong. She learned to endure pain and never complain.

Yick Ting was a silent fellow. Years earlier, his mother had hanged herself, after Ore had taken his first concubine. Following his wife's suicide, Ore had promptly taken a second wife. In this huge household, filled with the children of his stepmother and his father's concubine, no one noticed Yick Ting. For his part, the eleven-year-old cared more about books than marriage, but if his father had decreed this girl to be his future wife, so be it.

Yin Lee—a rather progressive sort—was the eldest child in Ore's family and had assumed much of her deceased mother's authority. She and Yick Ting were Ore's only two children by his first wife. Ore yielded to Yin Lee's wishes most of the time, perhaps partially out of guilt for his wife's suicide.

Eventually, Yin Lee saw Wai Chi's intelligence and realized the injustice of her future sister-in-law slaving over a wok. And so, that autumn, when Yin Lee moved to Guangzhou to attend school, she took Wai Chi, by this time eleven or twelve years old, with her. At first, Ore grudgingly paid for Wai Chi to attend junior high school. But he soon ordered Yick Ting to take over the payments for his future wife—a wife Yick Ting did not choose and whom his strong-willed older sister insisted on having schooled.

Yick Ting had no choice. At age fifteen, he quit senior high school to work in the family business. His salary paid for Wai Chi's tuition all the way through medical school. They married after Wai Chi graduated, and then settled in Swatow. Wai Chi fulfilled her role as a good wife and bore Yick Ting two sons and a daughter.

I am their second son.

In many ways, my father was progressive, too. He made sure his new wife no longer had to eat the leftovers at the second sitting. He didn't object to her working for the local dairy company. She rode in a fancy rickshaw, usually owned only by rich people, promoting baby formula to young mothers in Swatow and the surrounding countryside. To warn people to get out of the way as she rode down the street, all she had to do was step on a pedal that rang a bell. This in itself was a luxury—most rickshaws had no bell, the puller shouting his way through crowds.

My father never had the chance to finish high school. He remained a clerk most of his life. But if it weren't for him, he always pointed out, Mama wouldn't be making four times his salary.

In her last years, Mama let drop bits of family history the way she had once dropped slithers of salted fish into my rice bowl—sparingly, but enough to make me curious. Gleaned from Mama's scraps and Father's journals, our family story reminds me of a tapestry with most of the threads plucked out.

I sift through my old photos and letters. I ruthlessly interrogate myself, cursing the feeble light of memory. But, in time, the answers come. Images and conversations, faces and voices, thoughts and feelings. Vivid and troubling, they fill my mind. And they fill in the tapestry. As I wrestle with my past, I see that Mama's story, and Grandfather's, are inextricably woven with my own.

My mother often grieved for her own mother, my grandma Chau, who had committed suicide long before I was born. My grandmother was tired—tired of going hungry, of getting sick, of being beaten.

"Never forget," Mama often reminded me, "how fortunate you are to have a mother." She was right, but that took me a lifetime to learn.

I always meant to talk with Mama so that she could understand who I was. She must have wondered what I did with all the money I earned at my many jobs. Was she disappointed that she couldn't depend on me?

Can you hear me in heaven, Mama? This is my story ...

SONG OF THE AZALEA

1

IRON SOLDIER

1941 Kowloon, port of Hong Kong, British colony

Real soldiers have no mothers. Not the hush-a-bye, cradle-you-when-you're-sick kind, anyway. Soldiers are rugged and strong, and gloriously brave. This I knew. I saw it in movies; I heard it at school.

"China is our mother," declared Mr. Soong, who taught me physical education. His muscles rippled as he strode across the platform. *Just like a general,* I thought. And we, obedient and loyal students of Dao Kwun Primary School, standing in neat rows across the courtyard as we did every morning, formed an invincible army. I stood straighter. My head rose a touch, if only to see above my classmates' shoulders. Our commander's voice rang out: "We must be ready to fight alongside our brothers."

Like the famous Big Sabre Troop our teacher always told us about. On moonless nights, this troop would strip naked and noiselessly slip into enemy camps. Anyone wearing clothes must be Japanese. Snap. The Big Sabre soldier would break the enemies' necks. *How brave, how exciting. Someday that will be me. Yes, Mr. Soong, I will fight. I will be a man.* We shouted the lyrics to "March of the Volunteers"—all two hundred of us boys and girls—loudly enough for the Japanese emperor to hear.

1

Arise! Thousands of hearts unite ...
Face the enemy's fire—march!

Chests swelling, we dared his men to set foot among us. We would tear them to shreds. *I* would tear them to shreds.

So what if I was only eight years old? I could learn. If only we hadn't moved to Kowloon. If we were still in Swatow, I could run away and join the Chinese army. Our teachers assured us that the Kuomintang, China's governing Nationalist party, would save our country. Generalissimo Chiang Kai-shek and his Nationalists would chase the Japanese out of Manchuria and the occupied territories. The Kuomintang had even made peace with the rebels in central China, the Communist Eighth Route Army. Now they fought the Japanese together. Kowloon, though, was part of the British colony of Hong Kong. Here, we had the King's troops to protect us. We didn't have to fight—yet. Instead, we pooled our lunch money and cracked open our piggy banks to buy rifles and planes for the Chinese army.

"Bam! Bull's eye!" yelled K.K., my older brother, as he fired his slingshot at a pebble. "That's another one for me. I'll wipe out an entire squadron by myself."

Another shot bounced and stung my shin. I bit down hard—soldiers don't cry. Not even eight-year-old ones. Instead, I yelled, "Hey! You hit your own troops. Don't you remember what we just sang?" Marching stiffly with an imaginary rifle, I reminded him, "We are iron soldiers."

Aim the gun outward, forward we march together.
Do not kill fellow citizens, do not hit our own people.

"Of course, I know that. You're a Jap."
"Am not."
"Are too. Nyah, nyah, Kee Ngai is a Jap."

I looked up at my big brother. *Hmm.* Two years made a huge difference. While he was built like a water buffalo, I looked more like a monkey. Time to switch tactics. *Vrooom!* I was an ace pilot. *Ratta-tat-tat. Ratta-tat-tat. Shreeee-keboom.* I bombed my big brother to smithereens. Song or no song.

Not that I had anything against K.K. In fact, since we had moved to Kowloon, I talked to him more than to anyone else. This was a big city, with buses, taxis, and lots of people who didn't know you. It was bigger even than Swatow. That's what I remembered of Swatow, anyway, which wasn't much. We had left when I was four. All I recalled of the trip was throwing up on the ship.

Father didn't join us in Kowloon until a year later. Shortly after, he left to go to Taishan, some hundred miles away. Even though he was a simple bank clerk, he had an important job there, transferring documents to Wuzhou, where they would be safe from the Japanese.

We didn't see much of Mama either. Her patients kept her busy. Our baby sister, Mei Mei, was only four, too young to know anything. We had a nanny, but she was too old. At least forty, even older than Mama. Besides, all she cared about was keeping our school uniforms clean. So that left my brother for company. We loved to talk about the war. He wanted to join the Kuomintang army. The air force intrigued me more. For now, though, we couldn't join either. We had to go to school.

It was Monday, December 8, 1941, 8 A.M., and we were running late for school, as usual. K.K. bounded down the street ahead of me. Although it was December, the days were still warm. We wore our summer uniforms—a short-sleeved white shirt that absorbed the sweat trickling down our backs and light brown shorts that left our legs free to race. A rattan bookbag banged against my hip. My black leather shoes slipped from time to time on the pavement as I struggled to catch up with my brother.

Street vendors squatted here and there with their charcoal stoves. They grinned at me over their steaming pots and tempted me with treats. Rolled rice noodles and porridge. Brown sugar rice cakes. Foot-long doughnuts. But there was no time to stop—I had to get to school on time; otherwise, the headmaster would make me sit on an imaginary chair, back straight, thighs taut, until fire coursed up and down my legs. That had happened to a classmate the week before, and I didn't want it to happen to me.

About four blocks from home, I heard the sirens. No one paid any attention at first. We were used to air-raid drills. Then came the explosions, and people around me began to panic and run in all directions. "The Japanese bombed the airport," someone shouted.

Kai Tak Airport was only five miles away. Rushing home in fear, I ran into Nanny. "Go home quickly," she said. "Where is K.K.?"

"I don't know."

"I'll keep looking for him. You go home to your mother."

Home was 166 Fa Yuen Street, a three-storey concrete building. The ground floor consisted mostly of shops, with a few people living in the rear quarters. Two flats, side by side, made up the second and third floors. We lived in a second-floor flat with two tenant families: Mr. Hung and his daughter, and Mr. Chu and his wife. From the crowded street, I could see Mama pacing our balcony. Spotting me, she leaned over the railing to greet me. I raced up the stairs. Her eyes, usually sharp and bright, were clouded with worry. "Where could K.K. be?" she fretted, continuing to pace.

My brother came home half an hour later, smug and full of bravado. He had made it all the way to school, like a hero who made it through enemy territory. The administration, however, had ordered everyone to go home immediately. Little did we know then that we would never see our classmates or teachers again.

It was December 8, 1941. The attack on Kai Tak Airport was just the beginning of a long and bitter occupation of Hong Kong by the Japanese. Japan had also bombed Pearl Harbor, the Philippines, and Malaya in a series of simultaneous surprise actions. In one daring stroke, Emperor Hirohito's generals blew the Pacific theatre wide open.

Almost a year before the attacks, Winston Churchill had said, "If Japan goes to war with us, there is not the slightest chance of holding Hong Kong or relieving it." Of course, none of us knew about Churchill's statement at that point. Not me. Not Mr. Jung next door. Not the naive young recruits called in from Canada to help defend us. Some of them had never held a rifle or thrown a grenade. All we were told was that the British were defending Hong Kong and reinforcement was on the way.

All we knew was the need to hide. While bombers flew overhead, we crouched in the flat's only sheltered spot: a crawlspace beneath the stairs leading to the third floor. All of us—Mama, kids, Nanny, and the two tenant families—jammed in to share that precious space. All of us except Father. How I missed him. He might as well have been halfway across the mainland. Like Mei Mei, I wrapped my arms around Mama.

We cowered in silence. Chins dug into shoulders, elbows found midriffs. My nose rubbed on Mama's silk cheongsam—a gown with delicate floral patterns that made her look so elegant. The dress smelled comfortingly of sandalwood. The scent of Nanny's camphor and eucalyptus rub wafted by. Somebody passed gas. We struggled to ignore each other's body odours as the hours went by.

"It stinks," Mei Mei complained.

"Shh," we whispered back fiercely.

When the droning overhead died down, we crawled out. Soon there was knocking on our door. Families began to drift in, parking themselves in our living room and under the stairs. The Lums, with their daughter Sukyee, whom I played with, the Kos, the Mahs, and all their servants moved in to stay with us. Many friends turned to Mama in times of crisis: Mama always kept her head. Now, they felt safe with Mama; she would know what to do. And so the population of our one-thousand-square-foot flat swelled to fifty. Our guests occupied the bedrooms, the living room, even the hallway, where the children slept.

Mama had helped all these people before in one way or another. But how could we feed so many? We had a few cans of fish and preserved vegetables on hand, but not much rice. For many years, Mama had set aside money for emergencies. That afternoon, despite the frantic confusion in the streets, my mother headed out alone to a friend's store.

It seemed that all of Kowloon had rushed out to hunt for food. Many people had already bought what they could and were rushing back into hiding. Looters had emptied some stores; only those grocers with metal shutters were able to protect their goods. A desperate crowd jostled outside the friend's store, clamouring for rice. When he opened the shutter a crack to do business, Mama called out, "Ah Dong! Ah Dong! It's Lao Chau. Will you please sell me some rice?"

Ah Dong charged her three hundred Hong Kong dollars, a year's salary. Mama had only much larger bills, plus a few small ones. But in times of war, no one haggles over prices. Nor do merchants make change.

Once home, Mama proudly displayed her prize: a two-hundred-pound sack of rice for five hundred dollars. We congratulated her on her coup. "Remember Lee Choi Moon, the coolie?" she asked. "He's my patient. Luckily, he was there and helped me carry the rice home. Otherwise, people on the street would have torn the bag apart or robbed me."

The next day, the Japanese shelled Kowloon from the New Territories, lying to the northwest. I began to worry that we were in very real danger. They could hit us. I wanted to yell, "*We* haven't done anything! Don't bomb our homes!"

Wheeee-boom! *Wheeee*-boom! My ears hurt as shells ripped into the flats across the street. The explosions roared so loudly that the world seemed to go silent for a moment. Then the noise cracked my skull, like the clanging cymbals and booming drums at the dragon dances that scared me when I was younger. Except this time, the drummers had gone crazy. Our building shook. Windows shattered. Furniture crumpled. Bowls and dishes smashed, striking jarring chords and discordant notes amid the blasts. Mrs. Mah screamed and wailed. I wanted to, but had forgotten how. Terror had struck me dumb.

Then things started to go out of control. The police stopped patrolling the streets—the shelling and gunfire made it too risky. Ordinary citizens, clerks, tailors, and coolies among them, broke into army hospitals and warehouses. The British had abandoned these buildings months earlier when the air-raid drills began. The mobs now seized canned food, uniforms, and other supplies.

That's how Lee Choi Moon got the butter, he bragged. The tall, reedy twenty-year-old coolie swaggered in with a case of it on his shoulder, and stayed. He probably figured the butter gave him the right to live with us. I had to admit that butter was a nice change from soy sauce on our rice, even though it tasted a bit strange. Before long, there was a queue for the bathroom. Maybe that's why the men eventually kicked him out.

At dusk, we heard shouts of "Victory! Victory!" *Have the Kuomintang come to rescue us?* Fists pounded on doors.

"Let us in!" The voices sounded hoarse. "We have come to protect you. We are the Friends of Victory. Open the door." Crowbars smacked iron gates. "We need support. Give us cash."

Who are the Friends of Victory? Do war heroes demand protection money? We heard screams and cries for help reverberating in the street. The voices haunted us in the twilight hours. "Please, sir, spare us. Gods in heaven, somebody help us."

The Friends of Victory turned out to be ordinary thugs, like the ones who hung outside gambling dens and kicked you for looking at them. Without a police or army presence, people were doing whatever they liked. *What will happen to us?*

The darkness didn't help. At night, the city snuffed out its lights. We had practised this many times before, during the air-raid drills. Even our balcony was shrouded in blankets. Only the flames consuming a few bombed-out buildings lit the streets. As I squatted in the dark, every horrible scene I had ever seen at the movies or heard about at school replayed itself in my mind. The reality of war seemed more menacing than my fantasies, and yet … *Bam, bam!* As pistol shots rang out, I wondered, *What do real guns look like?*

"Victory! Victory!" The shouts seemed farther away now. We hushed our voices, waiting for the echoes to fade. *Perhaps no one noticed us. Perhaps we're safe.*

But the sound of bullets and cannon shells returned with dawn. By noon, curiosity got the better of me. I crawled onto the balcony. Through the railing, I could see pale-faced soldiers in helmets dodging down our street. Rumour had it that Canadian soldiers had come to strengthen the colony's defence. *Were these Canadian soldiers?* They used the pillars of the buildings on the street to shield their retreat. A few ran beneath our balcony. They had round cheeks with pimples, like the boys at the local high school. *Didn't soldiers have tanned, leathery faces and square jaws?*

Just as the soldiers retreated, scampering from pillar to pillar, a Japanese scout unit advanced, also using the pillars as shields. The invaders wore cloth caps rather than metal helmets. The shots firing back and forth sounded like firecrackers, sometimes popping my ears, sometimes echoing far away. It vaguely occurred to me that I could be hit by a stray bullet, but that didn't matter. *This*—deep, giddy breath—*this is like being a real soldier. Good thing Mama didn't notice me crawling out here. Otherwise, I would get a sound bamboo lashing.* Puzzled and awed by the soldiers, I finally went back inside our flat to play with Mr. Lum's daughter. We recited our favourite rhyme:

Round and round we spin, in a pretty garden,
Fried rice cake, sticky rice dumplings,
Mama called me, the dragon boats to see,
No, no, I won't go!
I'll watch my chicks, watch them grow.

We turned a scrap of lumber into a make-believe piano and sang jolly tunes for the rest of the afternoon. But at dinnertime, we again heard loud chants, this time from under our balcony. "Victory! Victory!" The Friends of Victory had returned. They stomped up the steps. "Open up," they shouted at the Jungs, who lived in the flat beside us. When there was no response, the gang pried open our neighbour's iron gate and wooden door.

"Help! Spare us!" Mrs. Jung shrieked. "Please stop. Don't take that! Pity us."

"Be quiet or we'll kill you. Where's the money? You must be a traitor!" shouted the thugs.

The other children and I looked at each other in fear. K.K. whispered that he wasn't afraid of anything. Still, all of us, adults and kids, trembled and huddled inside the flat. We would be next.

Clank! Bang! went our gate and door. Without a word, our tenants retreated to their bedrooms, locking the doors. Mr. Lum, the lawyer, looked at Dr. Ko. The doctor wheezed and glanced uncomfortably at his toes, twisting his hands atop his vast belly. Neither moved toward the door. Their wives turned anxious eyes toward Mama.

Clank! Bang! went the gate again. "Open the door! Let us in! You must be traitors!"

Mama swiftly counted some bills, then planted them in her pockets. "Yes, yes, I'm coming. Please don't frighten the children," she called out as she motioned the men to hide under the stairs. Then she opened the door a little, placing herself between it and the gate so that the thugs couldn't see into the flat.

I couldn't resist peeking out from behind her. *What do real gangsters look like? Mean and ugly, with scars?* I was disappointed. Only four or five men wearing unbuttoned Chinese jackets and loose grey trousers and brandishing thick iron rods and wooden sticks. Maybe more of them were waiting below. These ones didn't sport any scars and they didn't even look that ugly. They looked more like a pack of greedy wolves. At least the leader had a pistol stuck in his waistband. Through the gate, one of them pushed a dagger against Mama's stomach. "Let us in," he shouted. "We're men of integrity. Support us. Our brothers need food and supplies. We're here to keep order and search for spies."

"We're all Chinese patriots here. I love my country, too," Mama immediately replied.

The shouting subsided, although a couple of the men continued to call out, "Open the gate. We have no time to waste." The leader seemed more reasonable. "We need money. How much could you donate?"

"How much do you want?" Mama asked. I tried to guess how much the Lums' jewellery and cash added up to. We had a lot of money in the flat to give. Or that the thugs could grab if we didn't give them it.

"Two hundred dollars."

"We don't have that much money. You said you were patriots too …"

"Don't waste time," another said. "Open the gate, or we'll pry it open. Don't say I didn't warn you."

"If you come in," Mama measured her words carefully, holding the leader's gaze, "you'll scare everyone. We're all seniors and children. No men here. If you come in and seize our belongings, I'll have to join you to take from others."

"Don't talk to her! She's wasting our time. Just break open the gate." The others began banging on the gate again and on our half-open door. The leader looked annoyed for a moment—since he had the pistol, shouldn't he be giving the orders?

Mama caught the look. "Please, don't frighten the children," she pleaded. "My elderly patients will die of panic. I respect you. You're doing good for our people. You must be a strong leader. A man of honesty and integrity wouldn't terrorize the weak and helpless."

The man with the pistol paused and then said, "All right, just give me what you have." They agreed on a sum of fifty dollars. Mama searched her pockets for the bills she had planted—just the right amount. Taking the money, the men turned to go.

"Oh, no! You can't just leave us like that. Please, sir!" My mother reached through the gate and grabbed ahold of the leader's jacket.

"What?" He spun around and glared at her.

"What if others come asking for a donation?" Mama said. "How can we prove we've already paid?"

"What do you want? A receipt?"

"They won't recognize a slip of paper," my mother pleaded.

Another pause. "All right. I'll post two of my men outside your door for the night. That's the best I can do." His voice was gentler. He and his men shifted uneasily. They seemed different somehow. After talking with Mama, these ragtag bandits began to see themselves as noble resistance fighters. She thanked them and wished them luck. "Victory!"

After the gang left, Mrs. Jung called out for help: the Friends of Victory had stabbed her husband in the abdomen. Mama fetched her doctor's bag and went to treat his wound. We were lucky the two "guards" didn't take advantage of Mama opening the gate and force their way into our flat. Mr. Jung's wound wasn't deep, maybe half an inch, and the knife hadn't punctured any organs. Nevertheless, the couple was shaking. *They are not brave like my mama.*

That evening, with calming words and a meal, my mother secured the guards' respect. They didn't even ask to use our toilet. Early the next morning, the two thugs knocked on the door and politely said goodbye. Later, friends down the street told us that they had been visited by two or three gangs that night.

On Friday, December 12, Kowloon fell to the Japanese. The fighting had lasted only five days. We feared being shot by Japanese soldiers standing guard on the street if we went outside. So we stayed in, carefully rationing our rice, and having no idea when the Japanese occupation would end, if ever.

Like the Friends of Victory, Japanese soldiers pounded on doors. "Where are the flower girls?" they bellowed.

From our balcony, I could hear doors smashing and women screaming for help. I knew what flower girls were. In movies, victorious enemy soldiers always killed babies and grabbed women. These women became their "flower girls." Surrounded by the pitch black of night, we jumped at the sound of every gunshot. Women in neighbouring flats shrieked. Others sobbed and begged for mercy. I had never seen a woman being raped or killed, but I could imagine their fingers clawing at Japanese eyes. Just like in the movies. I tried not to hear. Or see. Or feel. Footsteps came and went, the soldiers in their army boots stomping noisily. Rattling gates and banging on doors, they demanded their "prize." Sometimes we heard nothing at all. That was even worse. I could hardly breathe then.

After the soldiers had rampaged for several days, the Japanese imposed martial law. Teams of soldiers searched the city, flat by flat, to flush out spies and restore order. They were efficient exterminators.

Heavy knocks on our door. "Open up." I obeyed. Two soldiers and a translator stood there. The soldiers' uniforms—from their woolen caps and winged collar tabs down to their crisp trousers—fit snugly. They held their rifles loosely. I stared into a broad face with a pencil-thin moustache over tightly drawn lips. Whack. A palm smacked me across the face. I stumbled back, dizzy and terrified. The room buzzed and spun. I didn't cry or feel pain. But it took all my strength to remain on my feet, to keep from landing on the floor.

Mama came to my rescue, reasoning with the men until they left without searching our flat. That confused me. The soldiers seemed reasonable when they left, but I was still steaming over the slap. *How dare he?* No one had ever slapped me before. Even parents didn't slap their children like that. At least, I'd never heard of such a thing. Slaps on the palm or rear end, yes, but never the face. But my world had changed. Soldiers slapped, and not just boys like me but also grown men and old women. The humiliating sting of the Japanese palm earned the lasting resentment of every Chinese person in occupied territory.

Our new masters did as they liked. We froze for curfews anytime, anywhere. As soon as a soldier blew his whistle, everyone on the street crouched on the spot. It might be for hours or even all day. It was like a schoolyard game, except it wasn't fun. No food, no water, no washroom. We cringed for fear of being shot. The invaders with their bayonets patrolled the streets. We tried to avoid going out, but we needed to buy food. Mama sometimes took K.K. and me with her to the warehouse, where we picked up cigarettes and canned vegetables to sell on the street corner. Many times we had to stay squatting at our makeshift stall for four to six hours at a stretch, at the soldier's whim. But we made a little bit of money, and Mama saved every penny of it. When my birthday came, I didn't receive an egg, dyed red for good luck and a long life, as was Chinese tradition. It was too expensive.

A few days later, on December 25, the Japanese took control of Hong Kong. In some ways, martial law gave the city a sense of stability. Our live-in guests returned to their homes. After the initial shock of the invasion, each family sought the security of daily routine to provide a normalcy of sorts within a far-from-normal world.

Even with fewer people around, Mama worried about feeding us. To save the rice, we ate only yams and beans. When these ran out, we boiled a handful of rice in water until it thickened into a gel. Set with a bit of edible lye, the mixture formed a clear tofu-like brick, which we called fairy cake. Strips of fairy cake made for a tasty bowl of noodles in broth. After a few weeks, though, our knees and feet began to swell from malnutrition. It hurt to squeeze our swollen feet into our shoes. Eventually, even getting up in the morning became difficult.

That's why, one February day in 1942, Mama and I ventured out to find food. She always took one of us along for errands. I was sorry she was not wearing her pretty silk cheongsam that I so loved. Instead she wore a rough black cotton smock and wide peasant trousers that belonged to Nanny. Her hair fell in a short tangle around her shoulders. She wrapped a dark scarf over her head like an old woman, tying it under her chin. Smudges of charcoal on her face completed the costume. She had turned into an aging widow from the countryside with a grandson in tow. No one would want her as a flower girl. Or so she hoped.

Fa Yuen Street was only three blocks from Nathan Road, Kowloon's main street. Despite the Japanese occupation, walking along the familiar street lifted my spirits. We were heading for my uncle's flat, the flat where Grandfather Chau once lived. I knew the route well. We cautiously made our way down Nathan Road, took a right-hand turn onto Jordan Road, and then a left onto Canton Road. With my hand firmly in Mama's, I felt safe. This was familiar territory. To my right lay the wharf where, I had been told, Grandfather had worked years ago. To my left was a terrace about four feet above street level. I had strolled along it dozens of times, often staring at the tourists as they gawked at the camphor-wood chests and embroidered linens. The curio shops were closed now, but the memories made me smile. I even kicked a pebble or two. Then I saw the barricade.

They had closed Canton Road, near the Haiphong Road intersection, just before my uncle's flat. Barbed wire stretched across the road, leaving a small opening about a foot and a half wide. An enemy soldier stood in front of this opening, aiming his bayonet at the heart or belly of each pedestrian wanting to pass through. We knew the procedure. First, we would have to bow to him—a respectful, ninety-degree bow. If, for whatever reason, he didn't like or trust us, or if our bow wasn't low enough, he could run that bayonet through our bodies in an instant.

I pulled back, but Mama told me to stay calm. "Don't run. Don't turn your head. Just be polite and do what I do."

The soldier didn't look evil. Even though I knew he could kill me, I thought he looked just like one of us, only tense and grim. And with Mama next to me, there was no need to be nervous. The soldier pointed his rifle at my mother and scanned our faces, then let us pass. I sighed softly in relief.

That's when I glanced toward my uncle's flat. Maybe I would see Uncle's friendly face grinning at us from the window. Instead, to my horror, I saw two men tied to the gate of the shop directly below the flat, hanging there like strips of cured pork.

What did they do? Fail to bow? Run away in panic? They looked like Lee Choi Moon or maybe the Friends of Victory, uneducated coolies. They were barefoot and stripped to the waist, their loose peasant trousers belted with string. Mud was smeared across their chests. Their arms were threaded between the thick iron bars, twisted behind them, and tied. They tried to look up at us as we passed, but couldn't. Their heads and backs hung forward. Around each neck was wrapped a wire as thick as a coat hanger. At the end of each wire was a rough granite block, the kind used to build retainer walls. Slowly, ever so slowly, pulled by the weight of the block, the wire sliced into the men's flesh. Blood dripped down their necks and faces.

I quickly looked away. My face flushed and blood thundered through my veins like the ocean surf. I began to shake and feel nauseous. Afraid of getting my own head chopped off, I tried to run, but my mother held me fast. She looked straight ahead, forcing me to continue walking at the same steady pace as she. Her palm wasn't sweaty; her fingers didn't tremble. *Keep moving, don't look nervous, don't be afraid, stay calm,* her grip said. To run, or even hesitate, could be fatal.

We turned the corner onto Haiphong Road and hurried up the stairs to Uncle's flat. *What was wrong with me?* I couldn't think or see clearly. I had trouble breathing. I hated them. *Hated them.* Yet what could a nine-year-old do? In my mind, I heard K.K. taunting me, "Coward!"

Mr. Soong's voice echoed through my muddled brain: "We must defend our people. We must deliver them from unspeakable suffering. We are iron soldiers." *Where is my sabre? I'm a soldier. Yes, Mr. Soong, I will fight. I'll kill them all.* As soon as the nausea faded, that is. For the first time in my life, the word "enemy" had a human face. The enemy, an enemy who looked just like us, had come to destroy our people—and I could only cling to Mama.

2

RUN. DIVE. RUN.

1942 Hong Kong, British colony; to Taishan, Guangdong province; to Wuzhou, Guangxi province, China

As the queue wound its way down the Hong Kong–Macau pier toward the barbed-wire fence, each person bent over as he or she reached the front of the line. One by one, at gunpoint, the men, women, and children ahead of us showed their bared bottoms to the Japanese soldiers manning the barricade.

"What are those people doing, Mama?" I gasped.

"Nothing. Don't look."

"Why are their bums in the air?"

Mama ignored me. She was irritable, as we all were. My brother, K.K., my sister, Mei Mei, and I had been waiting with my mother in line for hours for the steamship to Macau, the nearby Portuguese colony. From there, we would go to Taishan to join Father. Since there wasn't enough food in Hong Kong, the Japanese didn't care if we locals left.

A dozen soldiers, most of them wearing spectacles, strolled about. Some lounged against the fence, wiping their brows. Although it was only spring, the heat was sweltering, and the overcast skies provided no relief. My cotton shirt already clung to me, limp and damp. Sweat beaded on the backs of my bare legs. I was tired. I wanted to go home. My tummy growled for food, even if only for fairy-cake noodles. When I complained, Mama told me not to whine.

I continued to stare at the people passing through the barricade. All of them bowed, then dropped their pants or lifted their skirts. *Why would grown-ups show their private parts in public?* Mama had always told me not to do that. *Don't those people know better?* A few of the soldiers pointed and grinned at the rear ends on display. Then I noticed the men in white coats holding glass tubes. They were inserting the foot-long tubes partway into each person's rear—it didn't matter if the person was male or female, infant or elderly. The sound of crying children was making me nervous. "What are those men doing?" I persisted. "Will we have to stick out our bums, too?"

We shuffled forward a few steps, drawing closer to the barricade. K.K. grunted as he dragged our bags along. Mama fussed over Mei Mei and didn't look at me, but I could see her lips tighten. "They're doctors," she said. "They need to test each of us for disease before we leave."

"Will it hurt?"

"No," she lied.

The cold, hard glass stretched my anus. Then the doctor poked around inside me. *Ouch.* Still, I refused to cry. *Only babies cry.* But I didn't see the doctors do anything with the tubes. *How could they test anything without taking a sample?* Nor did they use a new tube for each person—just the same one, over and over again. It was a final violation and humiliation for the Chinese people escaping the occupation. Then, though, all I knew was that my abdomen was twisting in cramps. While resolutely ignoring my quivering innards, I hoisted up my shorts and marched through the barricade. *Who cares why the Japs want to poke our bums?* We're free. At least, we would be soon.

Aboard the steamship, Mama bought us barbecued pork with rice. We gobbled the thick slices of the tender meat, glazed in a sugary crust and nestled in steaming mounds of fluffy white rice, the sauce staining our bowls red. It was a feast. It had been a long time since we'd seen meat and whole grains of cooked rice.

We arrived in Macau around dinnertime. Mama left Mei Mei and me with K.K. while she looked for a place to stay for the night. Standing with legs spread apart and arms crossed, my brother took the job of guard seriously, never letting the baggage or us out of his sight. That's when I noticed how many bags we had—ten in all. Since Father was not here to help, poor K.K. had had to haul all of them. The canvas duffel bags, stuffed with our bedding, stood taller than me. Tilted on their side, though, they made comfortable seats. I perched on one while Mei Mei plopped down beside me. "Hurts," she whimpered, pointing at her knee. It was swollen.

When Mei Mei had first bumped her left shin on the stairs a few months earlier, the skin didn't break. Father was still with us then and had warned, "There is no bruise, but it is slightly warm to the touch. Keep watch." A month or two later, the shin became red and swollen. By that time, Father had left for Taishan. Since Mama was licensed to practise medicine only in China, she couldn't operate in any of the Hong Kong hospitals. She found a local surgeon to cut out the infection, but he was unable to book an operating room. Just three days before the Japanese invasion, the surgeon cut out the infected part from Mei Mei's shin at his clinic. A week later, the shin reddened even more and became painful; it was still infected. My mother took Mei Mei back to the clinic, but the surgeon was gone. As the situation in Kowloon and Hong Kong grew increasingly turbulent, doctors left their practices and, like other citizens, went into hiding or tried to get out of the colony. Mama couldn't find any surgeons, and in a few weeks' time, the redness had spread from Mei Mei's shin to her knee. Now, the knee looked red and puffy. Squatting on the street, waiting for Mama to return, all we could do was give Mei Mei candy and gently rub her knee.

"Don't run around on the streets," Mama had warned us. "Someone may kill you and chop you up into wonton." She was serious. We had heard that thugs had followed a fat woman down a back lane and butchered her. They then sold her flesh to a restaurant. I gulped. *What if someone decided to slaughter the three of us?* Even K.K. might not be strong enough to fight them off. We stayed put, and I felt a sense of relief when I saw a Chinese policeman, in a Portuguese uniform and round cap, stroll past us.

Before we left Kowloon, Mama sold most of her valuables—her silk fabrics, woolen textiles, gold and diamond rings. Now, she could afford to buy us food and a place to stay, and later, to pay for many unpredictable expenses. Safe in a hotel suite that night, we forgot all about human won ton as we stuffed ourselves with rice and soup. Mama hoped that the warm food would help Mei Mei's infection. After dinner, K.K., Mei Mei, and I stared out the window at the waterfront for a while, then ran around the room. Even Mei Mei, with her sore leg, joined in the game. Over the chair, under the tables, on the beds—this trip was great fun. Each of us had our own bed to sleep in, for once not having to lie crosswise in the same bed. It was like being on holiday, except we had to go to bed early. The next day, Mama said, would be a long one.

In the morning, we left Macau. Mama had five coolies shoulder our luggage and, together, we crossed over to the border town of Zhuhai, and a second Japanese checkpoint. Mama was fearless. She spoke to the translator and showed the soldier her document from the Hong Kong Japanese authority. The translator and soldier looked bored, just like the ones in Macau, and waved us through.

From Zhuhai, we trekked through Zhongshan County, which was Japanese-occupied territory, toward the Tam Kong River. Local peasants carried our luggage along narrow paths beside the rice fields while a coolie carried Mei Mei and me in baskets, hung on the ends of a bamboo pole that he shouldered. The two of us dangled on either side of him like sacks of grain. The baskets were hanging so low that, when we crossed a narrow bridge, we almost touched the water.

Ahead of us on the farm road, three soldiers watched as we approached. They wore Kuomintang uniforms and held rifles. *But we're in Japanese-controlled territory. Is it the Japanese, trying to trick us?* Only later did I learn that there were pockets of Kuomintang and Communist guerrillas in the area.

Mama's nerve never left her. Telling us to wait, she went ahead to face the danger and negotiate with those aiming the barrels of their rifles at us. "We have nothing for you to search for," she said calmly. "How could a woman with three children have anything in her luggage worth bothering about? And please don't frighten the children."

The Kuomintang soldiers at the checkpoint let us pass in exchange for money and cigarettes. They didn't check our luggage.

A little while later, we came upon a checkpoint marked by a red flag stuck in the ground on the side of the road. The three men holding rifles wore uniform tops and coolie trousers. The soldiers in my picture books didn't wear coolie trousers. These men were part of the Communist Tung Kong Battalion. "Native thugs," we called them, though not within earshot, of course; face to face, we were loyal supporters of their cause. Going up to the men at the checkpoint, Mama praised them for fighting the Japanese. We were comrades, she said. Offering cans of food and cigarettes, she persuaded them to let us pass. They hungrily took the items and waved us on.

The peasants kept us walking on a small path until noon, when we arrived at a small fishing boat moored on the Tam Kong River. The owners of the boat, a family of four, took money in exchange for a promise to smuggle us past more checkpoints. Our luggage was loaded on-board, covered with a tarp, and baskets of fish placed on top. The parents and one of the sons each used a thick bamboo pole to push against the riverbank and the river bottom and manoeuvre the boat upstream; the other son rowed with an oar. The sons were only a few years older than K.K. If the Japanese caught us, we would likely all be shot. Without a permit, it was illegal to travel outside of one's city, town, or village, and we might be considered spies or smugglers.

It was dusk when we finally pulled ashore for dinner. After a simple meal of rice and preserved vegetables, the father announced, "We'll have to stay here until dark. There's a Japanese checkpoint upstream. Safer to hide here, among the trees and shrubs, until it is darker."

We arrived at the Japanese checkpoint about midnight. Our guide knew that the Japanese soldiers were afraid of attacks and would likely stay inside the guard tower that stood eight feet above us, overlooking the river. "Don't make a sound. Keep dead silent," he whispered. We hid among the bags beneath an oiled canvas canopy stretched across the middle of the deck. The boat hid behind the trees and the tall reeds of the riverbank. Our guide pushed the boat upstream with the pole. It slipped quietly through the water without a splash. *Would the guards notice us in the dark? What would we do if they caught us?* The memory of the two coolies with granite blocks dangling from their necks haunted me even as, our boat safely past the checkpoint, I nodded off to sleep.

When I awoke, I was relieved to find all parts of my body intact. K.K. and I poked our heads outside our canopied quarters to see that the murky river had taken on a golden sheen in the morning light. We had left the trees and reeds—and their shade—far behind. K.K. leaned over the side of the boat to reach for something in the river. "Hey, look," he shouted. I stared at what looked like a bloated pig, a pale blue blob against the yellowy brown water flowing past us. With a shudder, I made out fingers and hair.

"Poke it," my brother urged. "Are you scared? I'm not. Watch me. Look, there's another one."

Part of me wanted to look. But I couldn't bear to, at least not for long. I didn't dare touch these corpses floating past the boat, one or two at a time. Some were naked; most drifted face down. I couldn't tell whether they were men or women. *Maybe,* I kept hoping, *they're only animals.*

There wasn't any blood in the water, and the corpses didn't smell rotten. The only odours were of dried grass and mud, dead fish, and our own salty dampness. After a while, the bloated forms bumping against the boat didn't shock me as much as they first had. *Who were they? Did they have children?* I tentatively stretched a finger toward one that drifted near the boat, but then drew back swiftly.

As we continued upstream, we were stopped by a riverside Communist guerrilla checkpoint. The guerrillas waved their rifles at us to stop the boat. Mama spoke with them and gave them money and cigarettes. Again, Mama had persuaded these men to let us continue.

It took us the rest of the day to reach Chek Kum, a small town where a friend of my father lived. We stayed with him for the night. In the morning we packed a lunch of dried rice cakes, dried sweet potatoes, and water and, leaving our luggage behind, trudged onto the road again. If we didn't find Father, we would return to Chek Kum to continue on to Kuomintang-controlled territory, also known as Free China. Unburdened by luggage, we were able to travel more quickly, and we felt safer, too, walking through the Japanese-occupied territory. We hoped to reach Taishan by late afternoon.

As we walked, the weight of the humid air made us feel like we were in a steamer. I tugged at the shirt plastered to my chest. K.K. nudged me in the ribs. "Look!" He pointed to the side of the trail. More bodies. These ones, mostly men, were thin and dried up. I could make out the skeletons of a few, which were naked to the waist. Despite the heat, these corpses didn't stink either.

When I kept plodding on in silence, K.K. teased me. "Too scared to talk? Dare you to poke these ones," he said.

I wasn't scared, really. Just not interested in these wizened remains.

We passed two more Communist guerrilla checkpoints on our long walk and, both times, Mama negotiated our safe passage. By early evening, we reached Japanese-occupied Taishan. We crept quietly away from the river's edge to the outskirts of town, holding Mama's hand, watching for soldiers. Mama had an address for Father from four months before the Japanese invaded Hong Kong. She had since lost contact with him, as parts of Guangdong province were occupied and mail could not get through.

Mama led us into the small town. It was quiet, with what few people there were on the streets going about their business. Mama asked a vendor for directions, and about the situation in Taishan. "We have a lookout for Japs," the vendor replied. "If you hear our metal washbasins clanging, run with the locals to our hiding places. We haven't seen any Japs recently, but you never know."

Armed with the vendor's directions, we headed down the street. At last, Mama found the address we were looking for—Father's flat. She knocked. A woman opened the door and stared at us uncomprehendingly. As we followed Mama back down the stairs to the street, my legs began to ache. K.K. shifted Mei Mei's weight on his back. *Where could Father be?* We knocked on a few other doors, but soon learned that Father had left Taishan for the security of Wuzhou, three hundred miles to the west, in Free China.

Had we come one hundred miles for nothing? Mei Mei wept with disappointment. The day's journey had been hard on her knee. Mama, as usual, said little but simply found us lodging for the night. The next day, we fetched our luggage from Chek Kum and continued westward, determined to find Father. After taking a small boat from Chek Kum to Guangzhou, we boarded a huge junk, along with five hundred other passengers.

From the tiny square windows near our bunks, I watched barges loaded with cargo drift down the Pearl River. Hundreds of fishing boats and junks bobbed on the water. Our ship, which we dubbed "Tao," or "Island," towered over them. A towboat pulled us westward up the river.

Two days later, now in Free China—far west of Hong Kong, and even farther from Japan—our ship arrived in Wuzhou, a city divided by Sai Kong, the West River. Wuzhou was much smaller than Hong Kong. The provincial high school and university, with their dormitories, occupied the south bank of the river. The city core and the main residential area were north of the river. Bai Shan, or North Mountain, with its many different trees and bamboo groves, could be seen farther north of the small business centre. Wuzhou had no public transit, no taxis, and few bicycles. There were a few wooden carts on the streets, and many locals carrying huge bamboo baskets laden with fruit, fresh dates, and small logs on their backs. The north shore sloped from the lowlands in the east to the highlands in the west. Every year, the West River flooded the east side of the city, and the children had great fun swimming in the water-filled streets. Somewhere in this city, Father was working diligently on his accounts and watching over bank documents.

When we arrived in Wuzhou, Mama asked one of the locals to go to the Bank of China to let Father know we had arrived. We didn't have to wait long. Father was working and couldn't come to greet us but had given the messenger his address. We found the flat and moved our luggage in. The apartment building, on the east side of the city, had six units on each of the three floors. Each unit had a six-hundred-square-foot living area, much smaller than our flat on Fa Yuen Street in Kowloon. The building, like most in the city, was made of wood and brick. A set of stairs sat at each end. The ground-level units were occupied by grocery stores.

Father had hired a maid to help with household chores and had furnished the one-room flat with a few simple items. A bamboo table and six chairs filled the makeshift study and dining area. The four wooden planks lined along the wall and protected with mosquito nets were to be our beds. On the wall beside three of the beds hung a clip with a bundle of thirty brand-new one-dollar notes. Father later told us that he had prepared these for our monthly allowance money. If we made an effort to save pocket money at the end of the month, Father would reward us dollar for dollar.

By the time Father came home from work, the maid had dinner ready. As soon as Father walked through the door, Mei Mei wrapped herself around his leg. He peeled her off and tossed her playfully in the air. I wished I could wrap myself around him too, but his hand on my shoulder was enough. The look in his eyes assured me that I had taken good care of Mama.

There was no tearful reunion, no hugs or kisses. In fact, my parents rarely hugged or kissed me. But they did always show their love through food—and there was plenty of food that night. While my mother sipped her tea, she explained to Father in detail our trip from Kowloon to Macau to Taishan and then to Wuzhou. Father told Mama how the bank had ordered him to Wuzhou because of the advancing Japanese.

Father looked the same as I remembered him, except for an extra strand or two of grey hair. His slicked-back hair revealed a broad forehead and fierce eyebrows. His eyes, deep-set in his angular face, seemed mild though as he gazed at us over the dinner table. The relief in their depths hinted at months of worrying about his family.

Mama's face showed few traces of strain. Months of bombings, anarchy, occupation, and the burden of dragging three young children, one nearly crippled, along with a mountain of luggage, through enemy territory had only firmed her jaw slightly and sharpened the lines around her mouth. It was as though surviving war demanded no more courage from her than bandaging a broken arm.

As for me, I felt neither relief nor overwhelming joy over the reunion with Father, since we had been taught to stifle our emotions; just a quiet comfortableness that this was the way the world should be, with all of us sitting around the table, just like being home in Kowloon. Seeing my parents together again reminded me of the years before the war, before Father went to Taishan. I remembered how Father took care of us when Mama was recovering from tuberculosis.

Father had rented a room in a nearby building where Mama could recover without being bothered by us children. Antibiotics for tuberculosis weren't available then. Instead, a long needle was used to inject air into the rib cage to shrink the infected lung and stop it from functioning. Father made sure our maid served Mama healthy meals—expensive cow's milk, precious eggs, chicken soup. He brought fresh flowers—gladioli and ginger lilies—to Mama every day. I remember the fragrant lilies vividly. In the evenings after dinner, Father sat by the table and watched as we did our homework. Once we finished, he taught us Mandarin. We learned the forty Mandarin phonetics and practised our conversations. When we didn't pronounce correctly, he would rap our knuckles. That's why K.K. and I spoke perfect Mandarin. Now, it came in useful on the road of retreat.

Mama always told us that Father was a good and honest man; that we should learn from him and his frugal living, his kindness and generosity to the poor, and his defending of the defenceless. Nevertheless, K.K. and I were scared of Father in those days, particularly when he rapped our knuckles with his chopsticks at the dinner table or used a rattan whip on our palms when we were too rambunctious. Still, we respected Father. He was always so serious. He stood so straight, which made him seem even taller than he was. "A man must hold his head high," he used to tell us. "Never compromise your principles." Father would take us to the park on Sundays, which he said was his "sons' day." My brother and I would push Mei Mei along in a baby carriage while he lectured us. "Be honest, be kind. Always remember the poor and help others."

It was comforting to resume our walks in Wuzhou. One Sunday, Father, K.K., and I hiked up a mountain path. Mei Mei, whose knee had swollen so much that the leg now looked shorter than the other, stayed with Mama at the flat. Even Mama, a doctor, wasn't sure what was wrong with Mei Mei's knee, and had no equipment with her with which to check. And since it was wartime, any doctor practising Western medicine had long since fled.

It took us forty-five minutes to reach the foot of North Mountain. The odours of salted fish and preserved vegetables, of dust and sweat, faded as we climbed. The lighter air and the fresh scent of the mossy forest awakened our senses. We were welcomed by a gentle breeze, and with it, the music of hundreds of birds. K.K. and I playfully chased each other around the huge trees.

"When you walk in a rural area in a pitch dark night, remember this: Black is soil, white is stone, and bright is water." Father wanted us to remember this should we ever need to retreat again. I was to find those words useful, not only on the road of retreat but also during moonless nights of air raids in Wuzhou.

Father continued to teach us. "This," he said, pointing to a towering Chinese parasol tree, "bears a lot of nuts. When you press the nuts, you get tung oil. Remember how we burned tung oil when the electricity went out? Did you know Wuzhou has another name? It means sky-high parasol tree."

There were so many types of trees. Along the way, Father showed us bamboo, willow, pine, banyan, and pagoda trees. With each came a different lesson. Our heads swam with facts. We eagerly walked toward the teahouse, a bamboo hut set against the hillside, overlooking the forest we had hiked through.

Father taught us many things: our table manners, how to save money, and even how to tie down our luggage so that the flimsy suitcases and canvas bags didn't fall apart when handled roughly and tossed about during transport. He spoke many Chinese dialects and even knew some English. But, he told us, when he first went to Hong Kong to attend school, he felt "deaf and mute." He didn't understand a word of Cantonese. The other students teased him, and the teachers didn't help, as they spoke only Cantonese. Father studied diligently, and by the end of the school year, he was among the top five students in his class. Two semesters later, he was the top student. He often reminded us to study hard and not waste our education.

Now, in Wuzhou, he didn't seem so much stern as kind. As we sat in the teahouse drinking sweet, warm soymilk and eating long Chinese doughnuts and steamed buns, we told Father about our new teacher in Wuzhou, a fat, old-fashioned schoolmaster. We had missed enrolment for the regular school semester, so we went half days to listen to him. We sat with his other students on stools in an open classroom, one big room with five rather primitive long wooden tables. In the traditional style, our teacher had us memorize Chinese classics: in singsong voices, we recited endless lines of literature every day.

We bought tofu *ja* to take back for Mama and Mei Mei. *Ja* was the residue left after the soybeans were pressed dry. In peacetime, tofu *ja* was used as pig feed. The teahouse owner explained how these cakes of fermented soybean dregs, excellent when stir-fried with pork and snow peas, could be made only in Wuzhou, because, in all of China, only here did two rivers meet. The clear Lay Kong River and the yellow West River flowed side by side for miles without meeting, until eventually joining just west of the city. Only water taken from this point was suitable for making tofu *ja*.

As we climbed the steps to our flat, the aroma of sizzling chili peppers made me sneeze and my eyes water. At the top of the stairs, Father pushed open the trap door to the third floor. We climbed through into the corridor. To our left was a row of doors that opened into the flats facing the main street. To our right, another row of doors opened into the kitchen and bathroom for each flat. Shih Yee, the sixteen-year-old who lived with her deaf older brother and another family in the flat next to ours, was in the hallway, armed with a basket of food on her way to her kitchen. Seeing me, she grinned and waved. "Uncle," she nodded at my father and smiled.

As we entered our flat, I saw Mama at the table, drinking tea. She had just come back from visiting a friend in our building whom she had given medical advice to. Three other Bank of China employee families lived here also. The bank provided for all our needs in Wuzhou, so Mama had extra free time to visit with the wives of Father's colleagues, to chat or play mah-jong. Sometimes they summoned her for medical help. The rest of the time she took care of Mei Mei.

"Mama," K.K. and I chimed respectfully before flopping onto our beds.

"Be careful," she warned. "Don't stain the covers."

Guiltily, I kicked off my canvas runners, which had collected dirt from the trail and orange dust from our floor tiles. The glazed surface of the clay tiles had worn down, leaving a layer of powder beneath our feet. Clouds of orange dust floated up when I bounced off my bed. Dashing back to the table, I told Mama about our walk. "We saw bamboo groves. Did you know we get chopsticks, hats, bed mats, baskets, chairs, beds, carrying rods, and walls from the stalks? Do *you* wrap rice bundles in the leaves for the May festival? Father says people do. Bamboo also makes good raincoats and roofing," I blurted in one breath. My mother smiled, seemingly impressed with my newfound knowledge.

All our commotion woke up Mei Mei. Her knee was still swollen and lumps had begun to show around her neck. She also had a slight fever. But without medicine or a firm diagnosis, there was little my mother could do. "We'll have to take her to the herbalist tomorrow," she said.

"You wouldn't have to if you had taken better care of her in the first place," Father muttered. "And you're supposed to be a doctor." Father was referring to his warning to Mama to monitor Mei Mei's shin carefully when it had first been wounded.

Mama didn't answer.

"Going to the herbalist is good. It is better than doing nothing." Father gave his consent as we sat down to the dinner our maid had brought in. I savoured the chewy tofu *ja,* which had absorbed the flavour of the stir-fried peppers and green onions. I picked up a second piece, then nearly dropped it as air-raid sirens blasted out. It didn't matter whether we were eating, bathing, or sleeping—the by now all-too-familiar wailing meant we had to head for the bomb shelter.

The Japanese fighter planes and bombers from Guangzhou were on their way to Guilin and the war capital, Chongqing. They bombed the industrial areas and airfields around Wuzhou on their way to attack the Nationalists and the Americans. The 14th Air Squadron "Flying Tigers"—a volunteer American air force unit stationed in Guilin—often ascended high into the clouds to attack the Japanese flying in below. Japanese bombers, desperate to lighten their payload quickly so that they could escape faster, would aimlessly drop their bombs in and around Wuzhou. At times, they flew extremely low with open canopies, gliding and floating down near the ground.

Stuffing another piece of tofu *ja* into my mouth, I scrambled for the door. Mama grabbed biscuits and a thermos of water. Father piggybacked Mei Mei. In the hallway, Shih Yee and her brother, and most of our other neighbours, were filing out from their flats. A few people, though, stayed put, not bothering to leave their dinners. In the fading glow of sunset, we shuffled through the streets like rumpled ghosts, a dark stream of shadows flowing toward the mountains.

At the edge of the city, I glanced back. "Traitors! Traitors!" a crowd was shouting as people pointed at two or three men waving bright torches to help guide the Japanese. Our teacher had told us that the Japanese had planted their fifth column in Wuzhou. I wanted to run back and punch these men who signalled the enemy with torches at night and mirrors by day. But the siren blasts had become short and insistent. The bombers were here.

Mama gripped my hand and led me toward the entrance to a series of cave-like tunnels burrowed into the hillside. A wash of cool, damp air hit me as we entered. We managed to find seats, carved out of the dirt walls, near the back. More and more sweaty bodies pushed their way past us. Ripe odours filled my nostrils. *Why can't they find another shelter?*

A baby began to sob. "Quiet," someone whispered.

"Shut the kid up," came another fierce whisper. "Do you want to get us all killed?"

The mother muffled her child's cries with her chapped hands. By the eerie glow of a few weak light bulbs, I could see the baby's face turn purplish red as it struggled and kicked. Voices echoed loudly in the tunnel: "The enemy pilots can probably hear us if we're noisy. If they suspect we're here, they'll bomb us for sure." I glanced at my brother, stared at the baby, and then turned back to K.K. He looked away.

Silenced by our fear, we waited for the droning of the bombers and the explosions to subside. After about an hour, we were able to return to the city, a city lit by firelight. Our building luckily had been spared, and we happily went inside, back to our dinner. As we filed in, I peeked out the kitchen window at the street behind us. Flames consumed the wooden frames of buildings and left behind blackened bricks. Despite the fires, young and old alike searched the fiery debris for their belongings. Volunteers came with manual water pumps. Suddenly, I heard explosions coming from all directions. As I watched, I saw bodies being torn apart. I turned away, but couldn't help but hear the screams and cries for help. And the shouts of warning about the toy-like objects that were lying in the streets.

It was a part of life in Wuzhou—the air-raid sirens, fires, bombs, and severed body parts. Perhaps the maid would reheat my tofu *ja*.

The next afternoon while Father was at work, we set out to the herbal-ist, K.K. and I taking turns piggybacking Mei Mei. The herbalist's shop was a small room at the front of his flat. I was fascinated by the stacks of drawers and glass jars filled with strange-looking roots and dried animal parts. I wanted to pull them out to feel and sniff them. The old man peered at the lumps on Mei Mei's neck as he listened to Mama explain about the swollen knee. He pulled mysterious leaves and powders out of the drawers, then left the room, returning with a black ointment that smelled like manure. Mei Mei made a face when he smeared it on her neck. "Bring her back in a few days," he ordered.

By the next visit, the skin had broken and pus oozed out. "It hurts," Mei Mei sniffled. To soothe her, we gave her maltose, a sticky liquid sugar that came in pots. Often we wound it around a chopstick like taffy. This time, Mei Mei sucked on a wad of it stuck to a cookie while the herbalist poked at her neck. He pinched each wound and squeezed the lumps out, one by one. They looked like pink olives. Mei Mei cried and kept sucking on her maltose.

About two weeks later, new lumps developed where the old ones had been. So we kept taking Mei Mei back to the herbalist—visits she hated. During the day while Father was at work, Mama, K.K., and I took turns holding Mei Mei to force her to drink the bitter brews the herbalist had us make for her. Mei Mei hated the foul-smelling and -tasting concoctions and the stinky ointments. She hated staying with Mama or the maid while K.K. and I played outside. She hated everything. She hated us. Some days she would turn against Mama, perhaps beginning to believe what Father said about it being all Mama's fault. She would often be rude to Mama and, even many years later, we frequently found the lace sofa covers with scissor snips in them.

Almost anything could trigger a tantrum: the dust and heat, her vegetables, the herbal brews. About ten more lumps grew in her neck before the lumps finally subsided. Mama could do nothing for Mei Mei except give her better food and bigger portions than the rest of us. I hoped that Mei Mei would be healthy soon and her fun-loving self once again. She'd forget all the pain and smelly brews.

When K.K. and I weren't busy helping Mama, we were memorizing long passages our teacher had assigned as homework, or playing together; that is, when K.K. wasn't with the older boys in our building. They had no use for someone so young.

"Bet I could beat you at knives today," I challenged my brother. We each had a small blade, maybe five inches long, which we practised throwing. I tossed mine first and drew a line where it stabbed the ground. My brother did the same. "Let's see if you can hit between those lines," he said.

I did. So did he. The two new lines created a narrower target. We continued throwing our knives until mine, as always, finally missed the ever-shrinking target. K.K. grinned. "Just wait," I said. "I'll beat you next time. I'll be good enough for the Big Sabre Troop."

In the summer, we discovered new games. We were delighted to play in the flood water of the West River. The locals had warned us that the lower part of the city, where we lived, would flood. And it did, the city streets filling, inch by inch, with water. Those living on the ground floor of our building—indeed, in all the buildings near us—

were forced to move to higher ground. As shops were covered with water, resourceful vendors steered long sampans along the city's new canals, creating floating markets from which Mama and the maid bought fish and vegetables.

Even more exciting was that we could dive from our third-floor flat into the murky water only a few feet below. We waited until Mama was visiting friends across town—having hired one of the boats now operating like a water taxi to take her—then hoisted open our six-foot-high front windows. Even though we didn't know how to swim, we jumped in, gulping the murky water and waving our arms frantically in a struggle to keep afloat. The local children laughed and came to our aid, showing us how to work with the water. Before long, we could spin and twist in the flood water as well as any of them.

"I'm an American air carrier," I hollered.

"I'm a submarine. Watch me dive! Watch out for my torpedoes!" K.K. plunged beneath the water's surface.

I pretended to strafe the water. "My fighter planes will gun you down when you surface."

"Hey, I'm an Ally!"

"No, you're not. You're a Jap!"

"Am not."

"Are too."

We kicked and squirted each other in mock battles, then followed our new friends, swimming through the corridors and stairwell of our building. When we reached the top of the stairs, we pushed open the trap door, made our way to our flat, and dove out the window again. Kowloon had been nothing like this.

The floods lasted a month or two. By August, it was time to start school again. I was placed into primary four and K.K. in primary five. Our neighbour Shih Yee sometimes helped me with my homework. With brush and ink in hand, we worked on my Chinese calligraphy. Holding my hand in hers, Shih Yee patiently guided my clumsy strokes. Row after row of characters danced on my copybook. "Hold your brush straight," she said. "Think of it as one flowing river of ink. Never go back to fill in your strokes."

After an hour or so of homework, we sang. Shih Yee knew all my favourites, all the sad, patriotic ballads. "On the Shung Far River" described how the Chinese people endured Japanese rule after Chiang Kai-shek, China's leader, conceded three resource-rich northeastern provinces to Japan on September 18, 1931. It became a day to remember as thousands of refugees fled to unoccupied territory.

Wandering! Wandering! Unceasing wandering! All these days,
What month? What year? When can I return to my beloved home?

I often cried when I thought about the displaced refugees. After more than ten years of wandering, they still could not return home. Tears ran down Shih Yee's cheeks, too, when she sang. Her brother, however, didn't care for our songs. One day, he came over and smashed the table with his large fist. I jumped. He towered over me, gesturing wildly. He flushed red and grunted. Because of his deafness, he couldn't speak properly. Shih Yee touched him on the shoulder, using hand signals to figure out what he needed. With all our singing, we had forgotten about eating.

Even after Shih Yee left to make lunch, I couldn't stop thinking about the refugees we had been singing about, and the foreign enemy who had taken over and caused this suffering. I hoped that the Kuomintang government could save us.

At school, we studied *Public Truths,* a collection of essays describing the root of social problems. This book, I believed, held the answer to everything. It told us that the foreigners—the Japanese, the Europeans, and the North Americans—had enslaved China, had made us dependent on their goods, and had made us forget what a great nation we were. They even destroyed our culture by importing their religions.

"Don't you hate foreigners?" I asked K.K. one day after reading *Public Truths.*

"Yeah."

"Remember those students demonstrating the other day? They told everyone to boycott foreign goods. I wish I could do something more."

"Join the army."

"I know, but I can't join until I'm eighteen. What can we do now?"

"I'd go now, if they'd let me."

"Hey, what about that Baptist church? Foreigners started that. We could plaster posters all over it."

Poster paper was not easy to find so we used the pages from our exercise books for our posters. We spent several evenings, after school and before Father came home, copying phrases from *Public Truths* onto fifty sheets:

The imperialists burned down the heritage palaces and mansions.

The imperialists robbed by asking huge compensations, for gold,
    silver, and our antiques.

The imperialists kept concession areas inside China.

The imperialists took all our internal and external custom duties.

We were very proud of our work. On Friday afternoons, the church doors were opened to distribute milk powder to anyone who came. By the time we arrived, the church was empty but the doors were still unlocked. While I kept a lookout, K.K. glued our posters on the walls inside. Then we glued some on the outside walls. A few people on the street were looking at us curiously, so we glued the remaining posters onto a nearby electricity post and quickly left.

See, everyone, we love our country. We're exposing the foreigners.

Just before Sunday service, we waited near the church to see how people would react to our brazen act of defiance. Those passing by seemed impressed. People were pointing at our posters and asking each other who had put them up. I wanted to shout, "We did! We did!" But I knew better than to take credit for it so merely nudged K.K. and grinned. We left before the service began, not staying to see the congregation's reaction. We beamed all the way home, savouring this one small victory for our homeland.

At school we studied other material besides *Public Truths*. Still, while the teachers drilled us in everything from mathematics to history to physical education, they mostly concentrated on telling us about the war, about how Generalissimo Chiang Kai-shek and the Kuomintang would lead us to eventual victory.

I got along with most of the local kids, even though I spoke a slightly different dialect. However, Bing, who sat behind me in class, made my life miserable for a time. When the teacher asked quiz questions, he would pinch me relentlessly until I gave him the answers.

"Ore Kee Ngai, do you have a question?" The teacher frowned at us.

"No, sir." Pinch, pinch. My arm was growing sore from Bing's pinches. I whispered the answer to him.

Finally, I told K.K. about Bing's bullying. That day after school, K.K. grabbed Bing and pinned him against a wall. "Go ahead, Kee Ngai. Punch him out."

I stood frozen.

"Don't worry," K.K. said. "I'll hold him tight. Hit him hard."

I couldn't do it. K.K. snorted in exasperation and slammed Bing against the cement wall until blood ran down the boy's face. I knew that from then on, I would go to class in peace. My brother backed up his direct approach to life with his muscles—play by the rules or else.

I guess I was lucky that he took care of me. As we walked home from school one afternoon, the air-raid sirens began wailing, then immediately switched to short blasts, signalling an emergency. The planes had arrived. There was no time to run to the bomb shelter. Some people didn't bother to run anywhere at all—attacks earlier in the week hadn't caused much damage. But we weren't going to take any chances. We ran toward the riverbank, only six blocks away, thinking to hide in the wrecked boats. As we ran, I pointed at a bomber flying by. "Look, K.K. It is coming in low. It's loaded."

"Stay away from the buildings."

I nodded. It was only common sense to stick to the centre of the street to try to avoid being hit by debris from explosions. I heard blasts as the plane dropped clusters of silver-grey bombs. We knew these bombs were bigger and heavier than we were.

"Hit the ground," K.K. yelled as nearby buildings collapsed in smoke.

I flattened myself, hugging the road. As the bomber retreated, I shook my fist. "Stupid Japs! I'm not scared of you!" We began running again toward the boats, but our reprieve was short-lived. As we heard more engines approach, we realized that the fighter planes were circling overhead, looking for human targets. Then the familiar staccato of machine gun fire. Someone beside us screamed. A woman cried, "Help me!" but we had to keep running. We passed a man lying silent at the edge of the road but we had no time to stop. The river was only a thousand feet away.

Over the curb, down the dirt slope, onto the riverbank we scrambled. Others had had the same idea. There were about ten of us struggling in the foot-deep mud that sucked at our feet as we ran and stumbled and ran again toward the water. A spray of bullets cut in front of us. We dove into the mud. The fighter plane zoomed past us, and we got up and made another dash for the boats. The plane circled back. We turned to flee, trying to outrun the plane. *Run, dive, run. Run, dive, run.*

"Bastards! Dogs!" people swore. The pilot was toying with us, playing with his prey. Some people had given up trying to outrun the plane. Short of breath and exhausted, they looked around, seeking some semblance of cover. Suddenly, K.K. stopped. I did too. We turned to face our enemy. We would be heroes, would not give in to fear. That's when I saw the pilot. He wore a brown leather hat, like a swimming cap. Leaning out of the cockpit, he peered down at us through his goggles. He looked determined, cruel. Was he smiling even? We shook our fists at him, then once again began running.

"Follow me, Kee Ngai," my brother said. He dodged the bullets as he leapt zigzag lines in a crooked advance toward the river. Every so often he paused. "A plane can't zigzag," he wheezed, catching his breath. "He can't hit you. His machine gun can't swivel. He has to turn his plane around to aim at you."

But by now, the fighter had circled back. Only six of us left. The other four lay where they had been shot. From somewhere behind me, I heard screams and the dull thud of bodies falling. I didn't know if it was fear that made my breath come in ragged gasps. I only knew the clarity and fierceness of my hatred for the Japs. My lungs felt ready to burst as I ran even faster, running from death. I saw the machine gun bullets, longer than my finger. My heart pounded harder, my cheeks burned, my fists clenched and unclenched. *I'm not scared. I'm not scared of the mean Japs. Where can we hide?* I scanned the beach frantically but saw no refuge, only remnants of shipwrecks and junks littering the riverbank.

"Let's run for that wooden boat," K.K. called. "As soon as we reach it, jump into the water." I noticed a boat jutting out of the mud at the river's edge, about five hundred feet away.

"Okay, I'm behind you. But I can't run that fast. Wait for me!"

"Hurry! You run like a turtle, Kee Ngai. *Come on!*"

The plane roared behind us. Fists clenched, we turned around to challenge the pilot again. Only one other person left on the beach. A tanned young man, muscles bulging, raced toward us.

Ratta-tat-tat. Ratta-tat-tat. Horrified, I heard the bullets piercing him from behind. His intestines—a whitish rope smeared with blood—burst from his stomach. He didn't even seem perturbed. *How can he look so calm?* The man picked up his intestines and stuffed them back in. I stood rooted in the mud, staring. His black trousers were soaked with what looked like blood. He appeared so focused, so intense. He ran toward us, slowly now. The plane too seemed to be flying in slow motion. Every so often, the man bent over and picked up his innards again. No horror, no panic—he might as well have been tying his shoelaces. Then, just ten feet away from us, he dropped to the ground.

About two hundred feet past us, the plane circled back. *We will be next*. We made a mad dash for the river.

"Quick, Kee Ngai," K.K. shouted. "Dive! Dive!"

The muddy river enveloped us. Cool, soothing, safe. I was thankful for our swimming practice during the summer. We plunged into the depths, coming up from time to time for air. The current sent us downstream, past the log jams, to the east end of town. We had escaped.

We stayed in the water until the sirens announced with one long burst of sound that it was safe to return home. Then we swam to the riverbank, where bodies and parts of bodies—organs, brains, and orphaned limbs—soaked the ground with blood. Clothes dripping wet, we made our way through the city. We were a long way from home. I had seen bombed-out buildings and corpses before, but nothing prepared me for the carnage I was to see.

Arms and legs hung from electricity poles and buildings. Homes, offices, and warehouses were burning, flames bursting through holes where windows once had been. Volunteer firefighters desperately tugged at their carts and manual pumps, but they could do nothing to halt the destruction. All that remained of many buildings were bare, charred, brick frames. In stunned silence, we dodged corpses on the street. Many of the wounded were lying about, groaning.

"Watch out for those mine bombs," warned a grey-bearded man. "They're not toys." The shiny, extra-large metallic bottles with fins did look like toys. I was tempted to pick one up but knew that it would explode and kill me. I had seen it happen to other people.

Finally we reached our block. Our building was the only one left standing. My heart skipped a beat. *Are Mama and Mei Mei still there? What about Father? Did they blow up the bank, too?* Panicked, K.K. and I picked our way through the rubble to reach the stairway. What a relief it was to have Father greet us at the door. Mama and Mei Mei turned to us as we came in. After keeping silent all the way home, K.K. and I now couldn't stop talking.

"We stood there and shook our fists at him," we bragged.

"Don't do that next time," said Mama, her brow furrowed. "You should go to the shelter where we always go. I was so worried about you."

"But the emergency siren went off right away," K.K. said. "We didn't have enough time to reach the shelter."

"How did you run in the mud? Wasn't it hard to swim for so long?" Proud of her big brothers, Mei Mei wanted to know everything. "Weren't you scared?"

I could not remember being frightened. I was past being shocked. We were numb. Numb from the air raids, from seeing people dying, corpses and body parts, burning buildings. Our daring gesture of defiance against our enemy, just like brave soldiers, filled my mind. There was no room for fear. But the image of the man with his intestines falling out stayed with me.

3

SHIH YEE

1943 Wuzhou, Guangxi province, China

Near the end of 1942, we began to feel more secure. The air-raid sirens rarely went off, and the family was still together. The Japanese air offensive into Free China had been dealt a major blow after a Japanese air force major general was killed in action, gunned down by a fighter pilot of the American 14th Air Squadron. That January, my parents sent K.K. to Guilin to study in a naval academy where one of my uncles taught. As the air battles quieted down, there seemed to be little risk that we would have to flee again.

Without K.K., I was lonely for someone to play with. Shih Yee noticed and took a greater interest in helping me with my homework. She also often took me out with Kit, one of my father's young colleagues. Sunlight streamed between two buildings, casting a dusty spotlight on us, as I planted my elbows on my favourite street vendor's crudely made table and surveyed the people strolling by. Some toted newspapers, others browsed in shops. Across from me, Shih Yee and Kit were chatting and joking. Her braids gleamed with golden highlights, while his backlit face took on a reddish halo. I began to eat with relish the bowl of noodles with beef brisket the noodle seller handed me. Suddenly, a roaring laugh exploded from deep within Kit's belly.

Looking up, I saw Kit's stool tilted back and his body shaking with laughter. The hawker glanced up from his steaming pots, then went back to boiling noodles.

Whatever the joke was, I had missed it, but I enjoyed the music of Shih Yee's soft chuckles blending in with Kit's good-natured laughs. Even I could see how right these two were together. Still, at that moment, a budding romance was far less interesting than the allure of mounds of flat rice noodles, topped with steaming brisket, soaking in a fragrant broth. Bits of fat melted on my tongue and slid, gooey and rich, down my throat. Meanwhile, I strained every drop of juice from the meat. I chewed patiently, meditatively, as the tender chunks of beef released their hearty flavours.

Every so often, I glanced up. Shih Yee looked so pretty that day. She didn't have the sculptured cheekbones and large eyes of movie starlets, but a round baby face, with eyes that crinkled when she laughed. Her lips always looked so full, so pillowy. I caught Kit glancing at their flower-petal softness. The real reason that Kit came so often to our flat was finally dawning on me. He didn't come just to spin Mei Mei in the air until she squealed with delight, or to show me how some clerks stole bills from the bank's stacks using chopsticks. We enjoyed his easy-going nature, and we all liked him; I hadn't noticed he was more interested in Shih Yee than in me.

Because Shih Yee spent so much time with me, I naturally became their chaperone. Although I didn't pay them much attention when I had a bowl of beef brisket in front of me, at least my presence somehow made their dates socially acceptable. A nice single girl wasn't supposed to be alone with a man, even a nice man. Kit didn't seem to mind having me around. He told me once about Yuet Sai Lau, the most famous restaurant in Wuzhou, known for its Fried Paper-Wrapped Chicken. He told me how the chef marinated the chunks of chicken in top-grade soy sauce, a little sugar, and a splash of rose liquor before wrapping them with rice paper. How he fried the wrapped chicken until the rice paper was brown. And how, when you sunk your teeth into the wrap, the fragrance of the meat juice with rose liquor wafted up enticingly, and the tender chicken almost melted in your mouth. My mouth was watering just listening to Kit's description.

Now, having finished my soup, I tried to follow Kit and Shih Yee's conversation. The couple was no longer joking around. Kit, in fact, looked grim as he explained what had happened when he and a few friends went to Yuet Sai Lau Restaurant the night before. "The restaurant was full. Well, it's full every night. A few rich refugees. Mostly officers in uniform."

"How could you tell they were officers?" I interjected.

"Their shoes. Officers and their personal guard wear leather military boots. All nicely polished. Ordinary soldiers go barefoot. Or they twist together straw sandals for themselves. Just look at the injured veterans begging on the street."

I knew about the beggars. Everyone ignored these wounded soldiers wandering the city in groups of three or four, asking for food and money. Because I was seldom allowed to go outside at night, I knew nothing of the nightlife that Kit was describing.

"Every night, the city's best restaurants are filled with officers in uniform," continued Kit. He described how they enjoyed lavish banquets—platter after platter of hard-to-find delicacies such as roast duck, abalone with shiitake mushrooms, crispy fried prawns, and roasted suckling pigs. Wine was poured endlessly. But most of the officers were too drunk to have much of an appetite for the obscene amounts of food they ordered.

"That food could have saved a village from starvation," Kit said indignantly.

"But why did they order so much if they weren't going to eat it?" I asked. Such waste made no sense to me.

It made no sense to Kit either. "Who knows? They wanted to have a good time. They certainly had enough prostitutes around to dance with."

Shih Yee made a motion and frowned. Kit quickly changed the subject. "Do you know where the officers get the money, Kee Ngai?"

"Where?"

"They steal it from their own men. They collect rations for soldiers they don't have. Not just that. They even take rations from the soldiers they do have."

"How could they?" asked Shih Yee in disbelief.

"Even worse," Kit added, "our men on the front lines often go without food. Why? So their commanders can gorge on roast duck and throw out their wasted leftovers here in Wuzhou, where it's safe, away from real danger."

I struggled to understand. Drunken officers, raucous parties, stolen rations—the soldiers in movies weren't like that. Of course, I believed Kit. I always did. But could he have misunderstood? Weren't our soldiers all glorious and brave?

On the way home, Kit was still outraged. "Starving. The men on the front lines are starving. The ones who come back wounded are starving. What's the use of raising relief funds? The officers steal that, too."

I was troubled by the thought of a commanding officer stealing from his troops. Surely, it was impossible that China's brilliant commanders could be corrupt. By the time we entered my flat, however, our mood had lifted and we were singing a song Shih Yee had taught me about Lugouqiao Bridge—the Marco Polo Bridge in Beijing. She explained that on July 7, 1937, the day after the Japanese had stormed the bridge, Chiang Kai-shek declared war. Japan had destroyed the garrison and breached China's historic strength and dignity. As we always did with every patriotic ballad, Shih Yee and I finished the song in tears. Lost in visions of noble battles, I forgot Kit's words.

But I remembered them again when I saw the veterans begging on the street and noticed that their sandals were simply wisps of straw twisted together and tied to their feet. And again when K.K. came home in June and told us how officers in Guilin, seemingly unworried about the war, threw wild parties every night. K.K. didn't understand it either.

As flood season came and went, news from the front lines filtered into the city. Although Japan's air force had weakened, its ground troops had not. The battlefront was steadily edging toward us. Wuzhou was no longer safe. Father needed to follow the all-important bank documents to Chongqing, the war capital, where these documents would be secure—assuming we won the war, that is. The bank provided for Father and his co-workers to leave for Chongqing right away, and made arrangements for the employees' families to leave as well. Two weeks after Father left, it was our turn to go. But I didn't want to. I argued that I should stay with Shih Yee.

"Don't be silly," Shih Yee tweaked my ear affectionately. "You're only ten. You must go with your family."

"What about you?" I whined. "Why can't you come with us?"

"I'm not family."

"You're like my sister."

"You've been a good little brother, too, but I have my own family. I must take care of my real brother, and we'll have to move back to the village to be with our parents, who are old, in case anything happens."

In case anything happens. *What if the enemy captured Wuzhou?* Shih Yee wouldn't be safe and might be forced to become a flower girl like the girls in Kowloon. Shih Yee would scream, and I would be too far away to hear or help her.

Brusquely, Shih Yee said, "Enough tears, Kee Ngai. You're a man, remember? We'll see each other again when all this is over."

As I boarded the junk, she told me to remember her, to be brave. Still, I cried.

The bank had hired three junks to take us, along with about forty other employee families, out of the city. Ten soldiers escorted us, in case we came across robbers or enemy soldiers. We passengers had to stay under the broad awning that stretched across the middle of the ship. The people who worked on the boat occupied the deck space at either end. At the back, the women cooked our meals and cleaned up. At the front, the men leaned and twisted, using sails and poles to move the ship upstream and westward toward Chongqing, and Father. When the river narrowed and the waters grew rough, these peasants— stripped to the waist and with turbans on their heads to provide a touch of shade and catch their dripping sweat—waded ashore and pulled the boats with long ropes. I watched as the ropes gouged their straining shoulder muscles.

As town after town slipped by, the colours of the water changed. The yellow mud around Wuzhou gave way to clearer water. Just outside Hengxian, our first stop, I peered over the side of the boat and I could see to the river bottom. *If I jumped in, would the swift current carry me back to Shih Yee?*

Some of the girls on-board wore long, pale blue gowns like Shih Yee had, and they reminded me of her, but they didn't play with me or teach me calligraphy. No one here knew the lyrics to "On the Shung Far River" or "Lugouqiao Bridge," and they didn't care to learn. I tried to sing, but the songs sounded dull and wispy without Shih Yee's accompanying voice.

About a week later, we reached Bose, where we disembarked and stayed for two weeks. Rumours spread among the families that the bank manager was awaiting funds from the Bank of China to cover our expenses. The next leg of the journey would be on foot, and so Mama decided to sell some of our clothing and other belongings that were too cumbersome to carry. The first few times, Mama took K.K. and me with her when she went to the nightly town market, but soon we were going by ourselves. My brother handled the duffel bag holding our items to sell while I was responsible for the mat and kerosene lamp.

Vendors jostled for prime locations to hawk their wares—tooth-brushes, soap, clothes, leather shoes, groceries, clocks, ivory chopsticks, and jewellery. As usual, the market was busy as refugees mingled with locals, and shoppers edged past each other. Looking for a place to set up, we spied a small clearing and staked out our spot. I unrolled the mat and arranged the clothing we wanted to sell. K.K. pumped air into the kerosene drum, forcing out a blue-white mist. The lantern lit a brilliant circle around us.

"Hey, K.K." Pui Ming, a teenage boy from our Bank of China group, strolled up to us. "Did you hear the latest? In June, General Chen Chang fought off the Japanese on the lake outside Yichang. The Japs lost twenty-five thousand soldiers and more than a hundred battleships. Chongqing will still be safe when we get there."

"Where'd you hear that?" Both K.K. and I jumped up, eager to hear news of any victory. Yichang, in Hubei province, was situated on the Yangtze River, only 375 miles from Chongqing.

"I've got my sources. You guys should come to the market earlier just to circulate. This is the best place to sniff out news. The whole country is here. There are refugees from the Northeast, from Shanghai, from Hong Kong."

"Careful," K.K. warned. "Some of them must be spies and traitors."

"Well, we know what we'd do if we caught them, eh?" Pui Ming pounded his fist into our limp bag before sauntering off.

A local man came over to our mat to look at the trousers I had set out. He wore loose Chinese-style pants although he didn't look like a peasant. Anxious to sell the pair that had a small hole before selling the others, I reached for the defective trousers. K.K. stifled a snort and moved back a few steps, pretending not to know me.

"Here, sir," I did my best impersonation of a cheerful, engaging urchin. "Buy this pair. Heavy wool. You don't often see such good-quality Western trousers around here."

"How much?"

"Thirty yuan."

K.K. remained ominously silent. In Wuzhou, thirty yuan had been our allowance for a month.

"That's too much," the man cried.

"But look at the rich brown colour. And all the pockets and buttons." I thrust them into his hands. He stroked the fine wool, not seeing the hole. Then he held the trousers against his own, lining up the waistband to check the length.

"I haven't seen anyone here wear anything like them," I urged.

"Five yuan. That's all they're worth."

"No, sir. At least twenty-five. We're not starving. We can take them with us."

After some haggling, we struck a price. The moment the customer left, K.K. whirled around. "You cheat! How could you be so sneaky? He'll have us both arrested! You're going to get it someday—just you wait." The pride I had felt for my salesmanship turned to worry that the buyer might return. We began to stuff the clothes back into the bag as fast as we could. Picking up the mat and lantern, we raced away. When we arrived home, out of breath, K.K. stuttered incomprehensibly to Mama, who looked at us suspiciously.

"Look, Mama." I handed over our earnings before K.K. could tattle on me. "See what someone was willing to pay for Father's trousers with the hole."

My mother scanned our faces, but didn't quiz us. She had enough on her mind. Although she no longer worried about transportation or food—the bank arranged all that—she had unofficially become our group's doctor, and people were starting to come down with malaria. Mama had run out of quinine to treat the disease, so she had asked the bank manager in charge of our group to find some.

In the morning we left Bose and began walking the twenty miles to Kou Chau, a border town between Guangxi and Guizhou provinces. Our ultimate destination was Chongqing, but to avoid the congested main route, we took a quieter southwestly route. Local farmers were hired to carry the sick, small children, and our luggage in their carts, pulled by cows. With forty families, averaging four people in each, we were a long line of refugees walking on the road.

Many of us children had fun walking through the paddy fields and forested pockets along the way. We played, picked up small stones in the creeks for souvenirs, and chased each other about. At lunchtime, each family was given cold steamed buns. We reached Kou Chau at dusk. There were no shops or restaurants, so we bought vegetables and meat from the locals to prepare a meal. We drank sweet-tasting water from the town's shallow creek.

By the time we reached Kou Chau, the sweating attacks that Mama had begun to experience during the day were accompanied by a high fever. At times, she would stiffen and tremble with cold. Attacks of these malaria symptoms lasted a few hours at a time. Then Mama would seem healthy for two or three hours, before the symptoms started up again. Whenever she began shaking, K.K. and I piled quilts on her, but they didn't stop the cold that seemed to reach deep inside her.

With Mama so ill, I had to help treat her patients, the family members of the bank employees. Some of them lived with us in the rice-wine brewery, a spacious warehouse that accommodated nine families comfortably on the second floor, where rice used to be stored. Others lived with local families in the town. While K.K. did the work he preferred—loading luggage and fetching barrels of fresh water—I made the most of my chance to play doctor. The malaria made Mama's hands shake too much to give injections, so that task fell to me. At first, I wasn't too keen on it, but Mama let me poke her skin until I figured out how to find a vein. She watched as I rubbed alcohol on a patient's skin, then blew lightly on the spot while inserting the needle—so deftly that the patient didn't feel more than a pinch.

"There you go, Mrs. Chan. All done. Here's something for the fever," said Mama, taking pills from her doctor's bag. "Take two with meals three times every day." I counted out the pills and handed them over to the patient.

Two days later, checking on Mrs. Chan's progress, I shook the thermometer and wiped it carefully with alcohol, just as Mama had taught me. "Are you still getting diarrhea from the local water? Any vomiting? How about cramps?" My examination complete, I reported back to my mother. "She says her stomach hurts."

Mama didn't respond. She lay trembling violently, perspiration coating her face and neck. When the attack subsided, she gritted her teeth and sent me back to Mrs. Chan with different medicine. While the other malaria patients—there were about five of them at the time—buried themselves in blankets all day long, Mama's steely resolve kept her practising even when she was deathly ill. I felt proud to help.

When I wasn't poking people with needles or delivering medicine, I helped K.K. take care of Mei Mei. Only scars remained of the lumps she had had on her neck, but she continued to lose weight. Her injured leg was becoming wasted, even though the original wound had healed. The knee was still bloated, though, and we all wondered if the swelling was because of our malnutrition during the occupation of Kowloon. But now, with our family allowance from the bank, we ate well. *Why wasn't Mei Mei getting any better?*

K.K. and I cooked Mei Mei the most nutritious meals we could—minced pork with salted vegetables, steamed fish with garlic and black bean sauce, chicken breast with ginger and green onion, pig liver stewed in wine. Girls from the other families helped us with the food preparation by shopping for groceries and sometimes lighting our wood-and-charcoal stove, a task that took some skill. Each family had set up its own cooking spot on the balcony. The stove was a can about ten inches in diameter and twelve inches high, with a small opening near the bottom. We placed a wine bottle in the centre of the can and packed sawdust, our only fuel, around it. From the opening at the bottom, we tunnelled through the sawdust and then took away the wine bottle, creating an air passage. Then we lit the sawdust. If the sawdust was not compacted properly, it produced a lot of black smoke but insufficient heat for cooking.

A local herbalist advised us to feed Mei Mei house geckos. Catching these tiny house lizards and cooking them was bad enough, but then we had to get Mei Mei to eat them. We also boiled barks, roots, and leaves as prescribed by the herbalist. And just like in Wuzhou, we had to hold her down and pinch her nose so that she would open her mouth and down the terrible brew. I hated having to hold her down but I knew the medicine would make her better.

Of course, we had time for fun, too. Even Mei Mei had friends. Sometimes, on days her leg wasn't hurting, she hopped around, teasing the others, giggling and chortling the way she used to, before the war.

The older children loved to swipe haw cakes, treats one of the villagers made from hawthorn berries. "They're delicious," K.K.'s friend Pui Ming assured me, smacking his lips loudly. I craved one. As Pui Ming and his brother, Foo Ming, had done, I stole a palm-sized, bamboo-leaf packet from the bundles behind the villager's house. Inside, the haw cake sparkled with what looked like burgundy jelly but felt much firmer. Into my mouth it popped. Sweet as cherries. I quickly sneaked another one, then refolded the packet. No one would be able to tell that the packet was now hollow. I felt the thrill of a well-executed crime.

A week later, it was time to move again, this time to Anlong, in the mountains of Quizhou, across Guangxi province's border. There we would wait, along with the staff and their families, and the documents, merchandise, and machinery, of many of the country's national institutes, until transport was available to take us farther. The military had priority over all types of transport, whether it was truck, rail, or ship. The autumn air cooled noticeably as we climbed behind the locals who packed our belongings on their backs, or on the backs of donkeys who had to be coaxed and pulled up mountain trails only wide enough for two. A villager piggybacked Mei Mei. Although Mama was recovering, she was weak, and K.K. carried some of her belongings. Arriving in Anlong after a long day's walk, we boarded with a local family in a roomy mud house.

My brother, who hated getting sweaty and grimy, took a bath as soon as we reached Anlong. The responsibility for ensuring our water supply—fetching it from a fountain on the mountainside—would be his during our time in Anlong, even after the early snows glazed the footpath with ice. K.K. headed out on the mountain path every morning with two buckets, which he dutifully filled with water.

We were curious about the customs of the locals, who seemed to never bathe. We learned that the locals took only two baths in their lifetime—once when they were born and once when they married. Their bodies were bathed again after death. This custom was common in many parts in China, simply because of a lack of hygiene education and poverty. Whenever the sun came out, they took off their clothes and tried to catch the fleas that stayed in their hair and clothes, which were shiny and hard with encrusted sweat. Foo Ming and Pui Ming had told me the men of Anlong always slept in the nude.

"You're not serious?"

"Go look for yourself," they responded. "Dare you."

So, early one morning, K.K. and I sneaked downstairs. We gently eased open the door to the servants' quarters. Three men were fast asleep on wooden planks. A musty smell filled the air. K.K. and I nodded at each other, and together yanked off the greasy grey quilt from our landlord's stableboy, Xian Lok. With a yelp, our victim jumped up, as naked as his horses. "What's wrong? Is there an emergency?" Xian Lok pulled a shirt over his bulging belly. When we explained why we had disturbed his dreams, he tossed his head back and laughed. The other men rolled over and snorted but didn't wake up. Rather sheepishly, K.K. and I trotted out of the room. At least we had answered one question.

I soon set out to answer another. I had never seen where pork came from, so one day I went over to a butcher's house, just a few blocks from ours. I watched while men led a pig to a bench. It took three of them to tie the four-hundred-pound animal on it, upside down. Its stomach rose in a fleshy mound. The hog screamed long, shrill screeches.

I turned away. *Did that fat woman who was butchered in the alley in Macau shriek like that?* The flower girls in Kowloon did. I remembered how the corpses we saw in the river had been swollen like hogs. I wanted to look again to see where the shrieks were coming from, but I worried that I might see fingers, hair. The blood trickled past me and covered the dirt floor. I remembered how the street soaked up the blood of the two coolies twisting on the gate below Uncle's flat.

Half an hour later, the cries stopped. I hadn't looked, nor had I left. I didn't ask to take a warm liver home the way Mama often did.

As I wandered home through the village, I noticed several soldiers. The Kuomintang had established a post just across a narrow bridge. Two hundred thousand soldiers of the national defence force occupied the surrounding area. The soldiers I saw looked sallow and gaunt. Some wore only half a uniform—a tattered military jacket—pulled over faded peasant trousers and flimsy straw sandals, even though the ground was covered in snow.

"Chiang Kai-shek is calling for students to join the army," K.K. told me when I arrived home. "A hundred thousand students makes a hundred thousand soldiers, he says. He is sending troops to Burma." K.K. was told that the Americans would provide uniforms with helmets, army boots, and rifles; training; and food. This unit would join the British in Burma to fight the Japanese.

"What a great chance," I said. "Can we join? Though I bet Mama wouldn't let us." But my brother appeared lost in thought and didn't seem to hear me.

That night, when Mrs. Mok came to visit us, she told us that her son Foo Ming had asked about joining the army, and that K.K. had already signed up and was waiting for his summons. I was shocked. My brother hadn't told me he was joining. Why hadn't he thought to take me?

He hadn't told our mother either. The next day, Mama marched over to the army post, her jaw set, her eyes glinting, and an embarrassed K.K. at her side. Much later she explained how she talked her way past the guards, past the junior officers, all the way to the commanding officer. The general—with a belly like the Buddha, Mama later told Mrs. Mok—could not withstand her onslaught of arguments. K.K., only twelve, was too young to join, though he looked older because of his broad build. Surely, the Kuomintang was not so desperate as to rely on child soldiers? Surely, a man so discerning as the general would not allow such a young boy to handle one of his rifles? Perhaps one of his junior officers had made a mistake. The general would, of course, ensure none of his men would allow K.K. to join his troop if he tried to again.

When Mama and K.K. came home, neither would tell me what had happened. K.K. refused to say anything at all. For days, my brother sulked. Then he got over it, as Mama knew he would; it wasn't in his nature to bear a grudge. Besides, like most children instilled with Confucian ideals, we respected our mother, knowing she had only our best interests in mind.

Once K.K.'s mood had improved, we scooted out to the weekly flea market, where vendors crowded into an open area with their mats and tables. Anlong had no real shopping streets and not even proper stalls in the market, but there was still much to observe. Peasants and soldiers milled about. It was a sunny day, warm for autumn, and many villagers had taken off their clothes to search for lice. Quilted jackets and bedsheets lay in heaps. The ripe smells of animal manure and unwashed bodies mingled in the air. We saw men in their faded white turbans exchanging rumours from the battlefront.

A farmer's wife waddled over, deftly swinging chicken eggs attached to a length of straw. I watched as she sat down to string more eggs, tying one end of straw firmly around the end of one egg, then looping the next section around another egg, and then another, until she had a batch of ten eggs to sell. She began to string together another batch. Surely, she would drop or smash an egg. But she didn't. When she realized we weren't buying, she chased us away. Her broad-rimmed bamboo hat bobbed as she waved her arms, plump with layers of cotton padding, and shouted at us in her mountain dialect.

I went over to a vendor who sold sticky rice. He scooped some out of a warm pot and rolled it into a ball the size of my fist. I dipped it into the bowls of seasoning, squishing on as much of the toasted black sesame, chopped peanut, and sugar as I could. I bit into it greedily, then choked, taken aback by the salty bitterness. K.K. laughed. "That's rock salt, dummy. Not sugar." He knew refined white sugar didn't exist in a town like this; indeed, even raw sugar was unheard of. Nor had these mountain villagers ever tasted sea salt, only rock salt. Their swollen necks were caused by a lack of iodine, which was absent in rock salt.

Thirsty now, I bought some tea, the same kind I had seen locals drinking—a tepid brew of dried fern leaves that tasted bitter and slightly burnt. Before I could finish it, I heard an old woman shouting. I followed K.K., who was pushing his way to the front of the crowd that was gathering. We saw an older woman wearing a patched jacket with holes that had no doubt seen as many market days as she had. She was clawing at two soldiers with her bony fingers. "Two yuan! Give me my two yuan," she yelled, quivering.

The soldiers stared at each other, clutching the vegetables they'd taken from her basket. They were probably peasants, too. Kit had told me that rich people paid peasant boys to enlist as substitutes for their sons. Once in the army, the boys earned barely enough for a few packs of cigarettes after their commanders skimmed off most of their pay.

The two teens, their grey uniforms as faded as the woman's jacket, stared hungrily at the vegetables. We all knew that the camp soldiers had barely enough rations to survive on. They got by on sticky rice and noodles that they sometimes bought, sometimes grabbed, on market day.

The woman persisted. "You lousy robbers. Come around here and steal our food. How dare you? Pay up."

"We don't have any money," came the blunt reply.

"If you can't pay, give me back the vegetables."

The soldiers looked down at the ground.

"Now, now, auntie," someone in the crowd called out. "Let them go. Here, let me pay the two yuan."

But the woman refused to be placated. Still hanging on to the two who had seized her vegetables, she cried, "Give me my money!"

The crowd parted as a general, followed by his bodyguards, marched toward the soldiers.

"Your men ..." the woman began.

Another villager spoke up. "It's just a small matter ..."

Both fell silent, though, when the imposing figure in the crisp uniform raised his hand. "Take them away." His voice rang out, clipped and curt. He turned on the heels of his polished black boots. His guards—they wore shiny military boots too, I noted—marched the teens to a nearby field. The crowd drifted after them. "What's going to happen?" I asked K.K. He shrugged.

I lost sight of the soldiers as they left the marketplace. Then two shots rang out in quick succession. I felt something fall away inside me. My stomach knotted in spasm. I ran toward the field and pushed my way to the front of the crowd. On the ground lay two bodies in faded grey uniforms. A bullet had hit one of the soldiers between the eye and temple. His face was blown apart but, like a turned page, a portion of the flesh was bound to his skull. The other body still had a face, although it was turned away from me. I saw a small hole in his chest. *How could a general do this to his own men?*

As the executioners left, they joked and swapped cigarettes. The crowd slinked away, shaking their heads. K.K. and I trudged home in silence. What could we say? He had seen it. I had seen it. We could not pretend otherwise. The refrain of a song, the one I'd chanted to K.K. back in Kowloon, began ringing in my head:

Aim the gun outward, forward we march together.
Do not kill fellow citizens. do not hit our own people.

How could our own officer murder our own soldiers, our comrades, our own iron soldiers?

When we got home, I felt too queasy to eat dinner. Mama glanced at my pale face but didn't question me. Halfway up the stairs to my room, I began to feel as though I couldn't catch my breath. There, at the top of the stairs, I saw it—the image of the soldier's face, his face-less face. My knees buckled.

"Are you all right?" Mama called up.

I roused myself. "Yes, yes," I mumbled.

For days, weeks even, that face leered at me every time I went up those stairs. At dinner, I had no appetite. Nothing made sense. *What if the general had sons? Would he have done the same to his own sons? Why did our own people kill these soldiers?* The questions haunted me for years afterward.

"It's the old woman's fault," I complained to K.K. "If she hadn't shouted so loudly and made such a fuss, nothing would have happened."

"Yeah. Over a few lousy vegetables. But she was poor too. She probably needed the money."

"Do you think the general is corrupt, like those officers in Wuzhou and Guilin?"

"Who knows? Maybe he needed to discipline his troops. Maybe it was an example for the other men."

"Well, he could've jailed them instead. Why did he have to kill them for a couple of vegetables? I bet he's never gone hungry. Did you see how fat and strong he looked? His belly was as big as Xian Lok's. Even his guards looked well fed."

Neither K.K. nor I had answers. Two lives for two yuan. It didn't make sense. Soldiers are supposed to die on the battlefront, not in a village market. "Be kind to the poor," Father had always told me. Perhaps there was no justice for the poor. It was then that I realized that an officer could callously sacrifice his own men. It was nothing but a show of his authority, his power to do whatever he wanted. But the crime didn't match the punishment. With such injustices within our own troops, who needed enemies? Our enemy didn't have to be Japanese or a foreigner—he could be Chinese. He could be a brave-looking general. Or a neighbour, or even a friend. He could be one of us.

4

SONG OF THE AZALEA

*1943–1945 Anlong, Quizhou province, to Chongqing,
Sichuan province, China*

Squatting among the other passengers in the covered army truck, I
shifted about, trying to find a pocket of breathable air. The forty Bank
of China families were divided among five trucks, about thirty adults
and five children in each, in a caravan travelling to Chongqing. We
would be safe there, rejoined with Father—unless China lost the war.

A grimy ochre dust swirled around us, sifting into our clothes, our
hair, our noses and throats. I could taste dry grit on my tongue. If it
had rained, we would have been mired in mud on these unpaved
roads. Instead, we could hear the fat tires of our army truck churning
the steep mountain roads into powder. And the truck's engine,
converted to burn charcoal rather than precious gasoline, spewed an
acrid smoke that choked me and stung my eyes.

Even my mind felt enveloped in a dry fog, where dreams and
memories floated past. I tried to look away from one that kept coming
into view—the image of a bloodied skull. I tried to reason with myself.
It was the fault of only one corrupt official, not the whole
Kuomintang. I must be careful not to generalize, not to make too
much of one incident. Still, those two soldiers in Anlong were hardly

older than K.K. What if K.K. had joined the army? What if it had been K.K. who had been a hungry soldier browsing in the market one moment, and the next, a corpse slumped in the mud, executed by a comrade? The movies, my teachers, my father had always told me Chiang Kai-shek's Nationalist government was China's only hope. But what about the two boys killed by their own army?

I stared at the captain and private whom the bank had hired to guard our truck. Perhaps they would die defending us against robbers. Perhaps we would all die. Some of the older boys had heard rumours that the Bank of China had worked out schedules with another bank for transporting employee families on these winding mountain roads, where we were vulnerable to robbers. They sent us in separate caravans so that one group might escape even if the other met with an unfortunate end. Everyone knew an ambush could happen anywhere, even if no one talked about it.

The robbers would have to first blast their way through the walls of luggage surrounding us, I thought. And with ten families and two guards packed together in the one truck, I was protected by other bodies, too. Still, bullets could always get through. People would scream. Would there be lots of blood? Maybe, maybe not. The soldier in Anlong had died with only a tiny hole in his chest.

I reached inside my shirt to finger the banknotes Mama had pinned there. Every time the bank issued our living allowance, Mama divided it among the four of us as a precaution. If the robbers attacked us, I might have to run away on my own. If I stole a rifle and hid, maybe I could rescue the others. Then again, maybe I would be scared, clutching my handful of banknotes.

The sun glared down on us as the truck made its way through the mountains. We fried like tofu *ja* in a wok, like the tofu *ja* we ate in Wuzhou. That life seemed so long ago now. Would Shih Yee remember me? I could see her, a basket of food on her hip, crossing the hallway to make dinner. Wouldn't she be surprised to see me in a caravan winding through the mountains, travelling with real soldiers with real guns?

My eyes darted to the captain in his neat, smart uniform and perfectly tied leggings, then to the pistol he carried in a holster at his side. I longed to run my fingers along its barrel. "Would you like to hold it?" Captain Tan's voice was soft, not like the coarse tones of the soldiers in Anlong. He spoke Mandarin without any trace of an accent. An intellectual, perhaps a university student. With a smile, he removed the bullets and handed me his weapon. I stroked the smooth wooden handle and the shiny barrel, so cool beneath my fingertips. Heavy, solid, real. I used both hands to hold it up and aim.

"It's a Mauser pistol," he explained.

K.K. also gaped in awe when his turn came to hold it. We were fascinated with guns and marksmanship. A Mauser sure beat our weapon, a slingshot. With these soldiers to guard us, the robbers wouldn't dare attack.

I edged my way to the back of the truck and peeked out at the road disappearing behind us. On one side, craggy cliffs rose five storeys; on the other, the ground dropped away—thirty, forty feet, or more. Behind us, other trucks creaked and groaned as they lurched and lunged up the hill. Every so often, the driver's assistant would jump out and stuff a wooden block behind the tires to keep our truck from rolling back and off the cliff.

As we rounded a bend in the road, a peculiar stench began to permeate the truck. The stink of rotting meat soon saturated the air, suffocating me. With a frown, Captain Tan straightened up, the muscles in his neck tautening as he loaded his pistol. From the back of the truck, he scanned the trees. Nothing. As the truck jostled us, I began to feel sick to my stomach. Another boy retched over the side of the truck.

When we finally pulled over at the next village, I scrambled off the truck, gasping for fresh air. But I couldn't escape the odour of decay. Then I saw the source of the sickening smell. About thirty bodies lay piled at the side of the road. Mats covered some; coffins made of thin wooden boards held others; still others lay in full view. Several coffins had burst from the swelling of the corpses. One coffin, its lid curving upward, contained the body of a pregnant woman. Flies buzzed about the smaller bruised and bloated bodies. Even K.K. wouldn't dare me to touch these corpses. He pinched his nose and set off to look for clean water to drink.

From what looked like a government building behind the makeshift graveyard came a village official. "Robbers," the man told Captain Tan. "They chopped down a tree to block the road. Set an ambush."

"How many?" Captain Tan spoke in a clipped, professional tone.

"Don't know. We heard machine guns. They just kept shooting until the screaming stopped. After they left, we pulled the bodies off the truck; they were under the luggage."

"Did you find anything else?"

"Just clothes, things like that."

"Money or bank documents?"

"No, sir."

After we got back onto the truck, Captain Tan told us the murdered group had been part of the other bank's caravan, filled with employee families like us. Robbers never left survivors, not even children. If they hadn't attacked that caravan, they would have murdered us. Glancing back at the bodies, I shuddered at the thought of what it would be like to be ambushed. There would be no chance to run. I would be flattened along with everyone else by machine gun fire.

The commander clenched his pistol until his fingers turned white. His thumb rubbed the handle in methodical strokes as his voice tightened. "Veterans. Must have been veterans. Who else would have machine guns?" He wouldn't look at us. "This is what happens when those at the top grow fat. They care nothing for the soldiers on the front lines. You teach a man to shoot, to kill, and then you abandon him. Leave him no food. It turns him into an animal. He has to survive. So what does he do? Plunders his own people. Kills women and children." Veterans had been teaming up with deserting soldiers and local thugs. Unable to take their revenge on the government, some were taking it on the citizens. Abandoned by the army, and with no living allowance whatsoever, a disabled veteran with no family could survive only by begging on the street.

As I listened to Captain Tan talk about corrupt officials, I thought about the well-fed general in Anlong and the two skinny teens he had executed. Rich people and corrupt officials caused so much injustice, so much misery. If only I could change the unfairness of this world. But how?

Captain Tan began describing how the Eighth Route Army, the rebel group in central China, was so much more disciplined and honourable. Unlike Kuomintang troops, those soldiers were brave and honest, he said. This was news to me. I thought the Eighth Route Army, like the Tung Kong Battalion, were Communists. And weren't *they* just native thugs, demanding money from us at checkpoints? His private merely listened and looked away, but the adults in the group who were listening nodded in agreement.

According to Captain Tan, the Eighth Route Army—he never actually used the word "Communists"—was made up of refugees, honest peasants who had lost everything to the invaders. They truly loved our nation and were dedicated to fighting the Japanese. The Kuomintang, on the other hand, was wasting its resources fighting the Communists—its own people—instead of the Japanese. And the corrupt Kuomintang officials were robbing their own men, with-holding salary and rations intended for their troops. Formerly brave and honourable veterans were turning desperate, becoming blood-thirsty bandits.

Captain Tan was a sincere man, a man determined to fight for China. Maybe the Eighth Route Army wasn't so bad. Maybe its soldiers were like Captain Tan.

When we arrived in Chongqing, K.K. and I wanted to learn more about the Communists. We bought the *Xinhua Daily News,* a Communist newspaper. We learned that, on the surface at least, the

Kuomintang seemed to tolerate the Communists since they were also fighting the Japanese. Actually, throughout Chongqing, the alliance pulsated with tension. This was the wartime capital, and Japanese and other foreign spies were everywhere. We could identify Chiang Kai-shek's agents by the pins they wore. These agents, who often acted as his team of personal bodyguards, had the authority to override any police, military, or information bureau agent. We heard about other agents too—from the police, the military, and the Central Investigation Department. The American and Chinese governments had even established a special agency to track Communist activities.

Nobody talked politics, though. Restaurants posted large signs warning patrons, "No discussion of politics; only talk of the weather and other trifles." The sense of secrecy and danger only heightened our curiosity. Every day K.K. and I walked two hours from our home in a suburb into Chongqing to pick up our rations from the Bank of China kitchen. While in the city, we visited Xinhua Books, a Communist bookstore. All sorts of people, many of them secret agents, staked out the bookstore and the *Xinhua Daily* newsstand. Occasionally, we heard shots. We learned that Chiang Kai-shek's agents arrested suspected Communists and executed them on the spot. One girl, I heard, was jailed because she wore red ribbons in her hair. Red was a dangerous colour.

The hawkers near the newsstand didn't wear red, and we guessed that they were Kuomintang spies watching those browsing in the bookstore. But the old man who sold crispy rice looked particularly Communist. His customers huddled about him, sipping hot water with crispy rice and sugar, sometimes joking loudly and sometimes whispering. We were sure they were Communists. K.K. and I always slipped quickly past the old man's stand, not wanting to be executed for being Communists.

Today was no exception. We slid by him with the stealth of experienced secret agents. After looking to our left and then our right, we put down our money at the newsstand. One of us would slip the

Xinhua Daily inside his shirt to ensure that no one could read its name, emblazoned in bold black characters on the front page. In the bookstore, we browsed the two aisles as nonchalantly as possible. We glanced at the classical literature, some Marxist literature, and a magazine with stories from the Communist liberation areas. I thumbed through storybooks. K.K. bought a small booklet entitled "The Chinese Revolution and the Chinese Communist Party" by Mao Zedong, which he folded and tucked into his jacket pocket. At the time, we didn't know who Mao Zedong was, that he was the leader of the Chinese Communist Party. We only knew about the Eighth Route Army. "Watch out for Kuomintang spies," K.K. whispered to me. With a dramatic flourish, we tapped our chests, where we had hidden everything. If we were careful, we wouldn't get shot. As we did when we had stolen the haw cakes, we felt a sense of heady excitement.

Once we were out of the city, heading back home, we talked more freely. Although I had no intention of becoming a Communist, I was curious about what K.K. was reading. Besides, I was thrilled by the adventure stories in the *Xinhua Daily*.

"Would you join the Eighth Route Army?" I asked K.K.

"Sure, if they let me shoot the Japs."

"I would trust them. Remember what Captain Tan said about them issuing promissory notes to peasants for any food they took?"

K.K. nodded and read aloud a *Xinhua* story about how the brave Eighth Route Army guerrillas had defended a village. It was hard to understand why the Kuomintang would execute such brave and patriotic people. I had to believe that Captain Tan had told me the truth. But I couldn't forget Mr. Soong's vivid tales in Kowloon about the Big Sabre troops. K.K. and I discussed it all the way home. In the end, we decided to put our faith in Chiang Kai-shek. He seemed to be the only leader capable of seeing us through the war, and surely most of the Kuomintang soldiers were noble and brave.

And I, too, could be a soldier or, better yet, a pilot. In the summer of 1944, the Kuomintang government announced a pilot-training program for elementary students that was very attractive. The government would provide academic schooling, board, uniform, and food, including eggs, meat, milk, and plenty of rice. Upon graduation, about forty cadets would be chosen to go to the United States for further training. I was thrilled by the news. Finally, I could be a pilot and fight the Japanese. Chongqing had no schools for refugee students like us, so my parents agreed to let K.K. and me apply.

At thirteen, K.K. was over age but was allowed to take the physical and medical exam, which he passed. I passed the academic exam but failed the physical exam, a parachuting test. Ascending the swirling stairs up the parachute tower to a dizzying height made me more anxious than I had expected. At the top were four balconies. Each had an opened parachute attached to an extended iron arm with a large iron ring. Two men attached the parachute straps to my jumper while they explained that, after jumping from the balcony, I would swing in the air for a while. When the swinging stopped, I was to pull the string hanging beside me to release the open parachute from the iron ring.

"Don't look down, just look out into the distance," one of the men warned me.

I nodded numbly.

They finished buckling me up, and I walked to the edge of the balcony. But instead of following their instructions, my curiosity overcame me and I looked down. *The buildings and cars were so small. How high up was I?* I started to shake as I felt the height.

I was still trembling when it was my turn to jump. The jump and the swinging in the air made me gasp for air. I was quaking with so much fear that I didn't have the strength to pull the string. I kept trying, but it was no use. The men lowered the extended arm to the ground while I hung there, humiliated. Nearing the ground, the parachute finally came off the ring. I landed on the ground as the parachute enveloped me, covering my face and concealing my embarrassment. K.K. laughed and teased me for being so afraid. I, too, laughed at my fear, but only much later.

K.K. and I still dreamt of how we would someday help win the war, maybe as soldiers if not as pilots. We plodded and plotted our way down the sloping mountainside highway. Reaching home and hot from the trek, we flopped down in the shade of the vines I had planted on one side of our house. We had even hauled boulders down the mountains to create a little enclosure. K.K. and I enjoyed our cooling breaks here. Since we had no school to attend, our daily routine consisted of fetching our rations from the bank's kitchen, visiting the bookstore, resting under the vines, and playing in the terraced rice fields.

To reach the fields we had to cross the highway and slide down a ten-foot embankment. We had often splashed about during planting season, trying to catch the slimy eels that swam in the flooded fields; this time of year, after the farmers had drained the fields so the rice could grow, we could hunt the ducks that crowded onto the pond. I gripped my slingshot. Our best design ever; fashioned from a strip of inner tube and a sturdy Y-shaped branch, this slingshot fired with deadly force and accuracy. K.K. and I gathered our ammunition carefully: round stones, neither too heavy nor too light, neither too large nor too small. Our prey had no premonition of their fate. Quiet and alert, we crouched among the vegetables at the edge of the rice plots. While we waited for our opportunity, we plucked a few beans to munch on. The bursting pods squirted their sweet, milky liquid in our mouths. A hunter must fuel his strength. We snacked some more. Then we took aim. *Bang.* One duck. *Bang.* Another one. Then another.

What marksmanship. What if Generalissimo Chiang, who lived nearby, saw us one day on his way into the city? He would command his driver to stop. "Go, fetch those young men," he would tell his guard. "We must recruit them immediately into our elite corps." He would give us the finest rifles and send us on desperate missions. We would become heroes.

Our daydreams continued, but I soon became bored. Leaving K.K. to munch on beans, I scrambled up the embankment. *Oomph.*

Climbing up took more muscles than sliding down. Just as I stood up, a broad hand slapped me hard across the face. Tears spurted from my eyes and stars danced above my head. As my vision cleared, I saw a soldier. I hadn't even noticed him standing there.

"Crawl back down into the field and stay there," he barked.

Cheeks burning, I obeyed. *How dare he?* Only the Japanese had ever slapped me before. Chinese people didn't do that, especially to their own people. What did I do wrong? Why did he hit me? I fumed as I hid under the bushes.

On the road above, three cars cruised by, all of them black. Soldiers standing on the side platforms guarded each car. And in each rode someone who looked like Chiang Kai-shek. Three generalissimos, each wearing the same type of uniform. Chiang seemed so powerful, so protected in his car. He even had other men pretending to be him, to protect him from assassins. They would die for him.

I sat down on a patch of grass, mulling over these thoughts. The Japanese soldiers who slapped me in Kowloon had power. They had power because they had guns. The Kuomintang soldier who just slapped me had power. He, too, had a gun. Chiang Kai-shek had power because he had guns and money. Many rich people had power. Money equalled power. In Kowloon, people used to joke that "if you have money, even a ghost will pull your rickshaw." It was all so unfair. I wanted to fight the wealthy, the rotten officials who had so much power. I wanted to charge into a restaurant and smash wine bottles over their heads. Make them march barefoot in the snow for miles and miles. Starve them until the fat melted from their well-fed bellies. I wanted to take their banquet food and feed it to their hungry troops.

All I wanted was justice—justice for our soldiers, and justice for the poor.

K.K. and I were in the rice fields shooting at rats with our slingshots one afternoon when we saw groups of peasants talking excitedly and flapping their arms. Some were running onto the highway. It was August 15, 1945.

"We won! We won!" they yelled. "The Japanese surrendered. We won the war. The Japanese surrendered to Sichuan!" Most of the peasants had never ventured outside Sichuan province, and for them, Sichuan was China. They had no idea how big China was, how big the war was. They thought their Sichuan had defeated Japan.

"How do you know?" we asked, hardly daring to hope that the news was true.

"The newspaper boys are shouting that the Japanese surrendered."

We raced home. Mama had not yet heard anything. How could it be true? After all, these peasants didn't even know who was fighting the Japanese. But when Father came home, he confirmed the news. The war was over.

K.K. roared and whooped. I picked up Mei Mei and danced around the room. Around and around.

That night, the locals celebrated with firecrackers. People poured into the streets, laughing and talking late into the night. The next day, Father brought home news that the Americans had dropped big bombs, a new "atomic" kind, on two Japanese cities. That's why the emperor surrendered. I was relieved to know there would be no more air raids, death, or hunger. I longed more than anything to simply go back to school and resume a normal life.

In October, as we piled into the bank's trucks leaving Chongqing, I thought about all the places we had lived and the people we had met. People like Shih Yee, whom I longed to see again. It would take one week for us to reach Sun Cheong, where the bank had already sent Father. Sun Cheong was close to Taishan, which in turn was only two days' sail to Wuzhou. We could visit Shih Yee, I hoped.

Arriving in Sun Cheong, we joined up with Nanny, who had travelled a long way from her village near Swatow, where she'd stayed during the war. Everything seemed reassuringly the same as before when we finally sat down for dinner. We were just a little older, nothing else.

I was chewing on chicken when Mama mentioned that Kit had written a letter from Wuzhou. After the war, he had gone back to look for Shih Yee. Instantly, I perked up. "How is she? Are they getting married?"

"No." Mama looked at me searchingly in a pause that stretched uneasily. Slowly, Mama added, "He never saw her."

"Why not?"

For an answer, Mama began reading Kit's letter aloud.

I trust this finds you all in good health. I regret to bring you ill news.

Immediately upon arriving in Wuzhou a few weeks ago, I took a train to Shih Yee's village. I found her house with little trouble. A two-storey house with a solid stone fence stands out in the countryside. But it stood vacant. Its well-landscaped garden was overgrown with weeds. Its walls, riddled with bullet holes. A few children whispered nonsense about ghosts.

The whole family was slaughtered, the villagers told me, by robbers. The servants on guard didn't have a chance against the machine gun fire. Veterans, most likely. Everyone, men and women, old and young, died. Everyone except Shih Yee.

The neighbours found her cowering under a table afterward, shrieking like a madwoman. Screaming for her brother and mother. Sobbing uncontrollably. Horrible. The slightest noise or sudden movement threw her into terror.

Even when lucid, Shih Yee agonized over the murders. She described the whole bloody scene to all who would listen. No one could comfort her. It didn't take long for the grief and madness to kill her.

Shih Yee is dead. Killed by those pledged to defend civilians like her. How ironic. And I? I, a man who had come seeking a bride, shall return a monk.

With the letter, Kit sent a photograph of himself. In a dark monk's robe and with a dark cloth over his head, he sat cross-legged and put his hands in front of his chest in the Buddhist meditative style. His lips curved slightly in a bitter-sad smile.

After looking at the photo, my family kept on eating. I wanted to scream at them, to shake them. How could they remain so unmoved? But they didn't know Shih Yee like I did. She hadn't helped K.K. with his homework or taught Mei Mei songs. Shih Yee was *my* friend, *my* big sister. I pushed my bowl away. Tears came to my eyes, but I blinked them back. I refused to cry in front of everyone.

After the unbearably long dinner, I ran outside. I didn't know how she actually died, only that the robbers killed her family, and in so doing, somehow, killed her, too. In a dark corner, I let myself give way to sobs that wracked my body. In the fury of my tears, one phrase repeated itself. *It's not fair. It's not fair.* My fist ploughed into a brick wall, again and again, until blood trickled from my knuckles. *She's dead. I wasn't there to save her. They killed her. They killed my beloved Shih Yee, and I wasn't there to save her.* If only I were pounding one of those robbers to a pulp, beating him senseless, splattering his blood on the street.

Finally, my harsh animal sobs subsided into whimpers, and I stared at the night sky. The silver-grey moonlight couldn't quite reach my corner. Somewhere down the street, a dog howled. Then, in the quiet of the evening, I heard Shih Yee's voice, crooning softly.

She picks a fresh red azalea …
Beloved, when you return from the battlefield, I will place this
    azalea on your chest, no longer to adorn my hair.

In my mind's eye, I saw Shih Yee, a beautiful young village girl, wandering the streets with an azalea in her hair, lost and alone. If only I could talk to her one more time, or see her eyes crinkle as she laughed. If only I could see the sunlight gleaming on her braids and on her pale blue dress. As I trudged back inside the house, I felt my heart contract—small and tight and very, very cold.

5

GOLDEN BOWLS OF RICE

1945–1947 Sun Cheong and Taishan, Guangdong province, China
1947 Guangzhou, Guangdong province, China

K.K. pedalled furiously, as though demons were nipping at his heels. I perched precariously behind him on the bicycle seat while my legs dangled down, my toes dangerously close to every passing rock that studded the pitted dirt road. As the air rushing past us whipped our hair, I squinted at the shops and warehouses flashing by.

"Watch out," I yelled.

K.K. swerved to avoid barrelling into a farmer and his wares. The suitcase roped in a shallow basket on the handlebars nearly slid off onto the deteriorated road, but my brother caught it, then hurtled us out of the city, onto the freedom of the broader open road.

The first thing Mama did when we arrived in Sun Cheong in 1945 was to find a school for K.K. and me. As there were no high schools in Sun Cheong, we had to go to school in the neighbouring town of Taishan, where the Christian boarding school Pui Ying Junior High School took us in. We had two breaks each year: two weeks in January, just before Chinese New Year, and August, our summer break. It was now August 1947, and K.K. had completed grade nine, and I, grade eight. We were glad to be done with school for another year as memorized lessons receded into the past and our month break lay ahead of us.

"Let's take a shortcut," K.K. puffed.

"Are you sure?" I shouted into the wind.

Without answering, he veered onto an abandoned single lane gravel road. Mud splattered our legs as we rode past massive holes the army had dug to stop enemy tanks from passing. We were keeping carefully to the side of the road.

Abruptly, the bicycle tilted and the tires squealed in protest as we skidded in the mud. Instinctively, I leapt onto the road while K.K., along with the bicycle and suitcase, splashed into a pit. I peered down at K.K., struggling to stand in the water. "Why did you jump off?" He glared at me, as wet and muddy as a water buffalo. "You threw the bike off balance."

My only reply was a roar of laughter. Even after he managed to climb out of the ten-foot-deep pit—without any help from me—I was still bent over, guffawing. Anyone but K.K. would have left me laughing on the roadside, but K.K., who had always protected me, simply gave me another smouldering look, then heaved the suitcase onto the bicycle. Smothering another chuckle, I hopped on behind him. In another hour, we would be home with Mama in Sun Cheong.

It felt good to laugh. At school, we had sought out every opportunity to laugh, making up pranks that could sometimes bring tears of laughter to our eyes. Once, we stuck a matchstick between the toes of a sleeping classmate and lit it. Although this student was as round as Xian Lok, the stableboy in Anlong, he leapt out of bed much faster. He yelled louder, too. After swearing at us, he joined us in laughter.

When we weren't playing pranks, we were studying hard. Burying myself in my books or games gave me an excuse not to think. Or feel. Just before the end of the semester, I was chosen to represent the school in the provincial Boy Scout competition. We would go to the outskirts of Guangzhou and learn about camping. I learned how to start a fire from scratch, tie different types of knots, and use flag signals. In this way, keeping busy, I pushed the memories of Shih Yee away, and held back my tears at night. Sometimes I distracted myself with fantasies of torturing the robber veterans who had hurt her, then had to remind myself there was no point. After fighting for our country, the veterans had been discarded. Some had been disabled in the war. They had no food, no money, no family, and no home. They had learned to survive through cruelty.

I blamed the rich officials who, by stealing rations and wasting government funds, had forced the veterans to thievery. Yes, it was the corrupt officials who had killed my beloved Shih Yee. But she was gone. Nothing, not blame, not anger, could bring her back. So I laughed and tried to forget. I tried to pacify myself with what was left of my boyhood faith in the Kuomintang. Surely, corruption among officials could not cancel the successes of the entire Nationalist government.

In the autumn of 1947, I wasn't the only one asking questions. Political tension was again in the air. Although the Japanese had surrendered, the Communists were occupying northern China, fighting the Kuomintang, many of whom were preparing to flee. The Kuomintang government was trying to remedy the economic crisis by printing paper money, money that bought less and less. Prices were soaring as more and more Kuomintang officials fled with the gold bars that were meant to back up the currency. Through bribery and abuse of their power, these officials changed Kuomintang paper money into U.S. money and gold bars. The future of China, and our own future, was dark and uncertain.

I was now fourteen and my family was scattered in three places. Father stayed in Sun Cheong with the Bank of China. The bank was enjoying brisk business, channelling the funds that had begun flowing in from overseas relatives since the end of the war. Mama had returned with Mei Mei to what she hoped would be the relative safety of British-protected Kowloon, where she set up a black-market medical practice among Swatow expatriates. Mama hoped that a specialist in Kowloon could treat Mei Mei's leg, which, except for the swollen knee, had shrunk almost to the bone.

K.K. and I were now enrolled at another boarding school, the Chinese German high school in Guangzhou. I had jumped a grade, as the school had no junior-high class, so we both were entering grade ten. The school had six hundred students from grades ten to twelve, but most of them were older than us. With the war over, many of those who could afford to returned to school, even though they were now eighteen, nineteen, or even in their twenties.

Under the Kuomintang government, all high-school students received military training as part of the curriculum. Wearing our uniforms, we assembled and marched in the morning before breakfast and again in the evening before dinner. I loved to hear the bugle: it sounded three times a day, alerting us to get out of bed, to assemble on the grounds, and to retire to the dormitory in the evenings. A battalion captain and soldiers were assigned by the Kuomintang government to guard the school. Each dormitory had a soldier assigned to it. This guard kept a close eye on us, ensuring that we had made our beds properly and kept our rooms tidy and our uniforms in order.

Boarding costs were high. Each time we sent Father a monthly budget, it proved inadequate by the time the money arrived a few weeks later, even though we tried to allow for rising prices. A pound of rice that had cost ten yuan the year before now sold for one thousand yuan one day, five thousand the next, and ten thousand the day after that. Some upper-middle-class people, I heard, held million-yuan banknotes; only months before, the largest banknote had been five hundred yuan. On the streets, rich people with black-market connections were exchanging money for gold bars. Everyone was panicking amid the frenzy of the skyrocketing inflation. Middle-class men in suits carried sacks of rice, a safer currency for salaries than banknotes. Ordinary people, however, had to accept their wages in banknotes—if they had jobs, that is. Every week, we saw more beggars, and more people without enough clothing. Boys and girls as young as fourteen wore rags.

As the tattered economy worsened in the fever of inflation, our school cafeteria, run by the principal's relatives, raised its prices, even though it always served the cheapest vegetables in season, no matter if this meant the same vegetable every day for an entire month. Each month, K.K. and I could afford only twenty-five days of meals at the school's cafeteria. On the Sunday prior to the last week of the month, with no money left even for the bus, we would walk two hours from our school in the country to hawk belongings in downtown Guangzhou.

Normally, with our meagre profits, we would go to the small restaurant on the edge of our school property, also run by the principal's relatives, that served à la carte Guangzhouese dishes with meat and fish—fancier dishes than served in the cafeteria. But we would only buy a bowl of plain rice noodles, all we could afford for the next few days until the end of the month.

One time, after spending a few hours selling our belongings, we counted our profits: twenty thousand yuan. More than usual.

"Will that last us, do you think?" I asked K.K.

"Probably not," he replied. It still was not enough to pay for meals until our allowance arrived the following week. As we stood there, feeling gloomy, the tantalizing aroma of onions and garlic filled the air. Lured down the street, we found a man selling fragrant dishes. The cheapest was the fried bean sprouts.

"How much?" we asked, longing for a taste.

"Five thousand yuan for a plate." He poured hot sauce into his wok. "A thousand yuan for a bowl of rice."

My brother and I stared at each other. *How could we spend so much on one meal?* Sprouts and soy sauce sizzled in the wok. We could smell the freshly cooked rice in the steamer. "Let's be brave," K.K. exhorted. "We'll eat now and starve the next few days."

We ordered a plate of sprouts and six bowls of rice to share. The hawker craftily stir-fried the sprouts just enough to heat them but not enough for them to become matted and limp. That way, he only had to use half as many sprouts to fill the plate. K.K. and I stared at the plate. *It's so small!* We each picked up a single bean sprout, savouring the tang of ginger and garlic. One bean sprout, one mouthful of rice. We made that plate of sprouts last halfway into our second bowl of rice. Then we doused the rest of our rice with soy sauce and gobbled it. That was the best meal we had tasted for some time. Grinning, we walked back to the school. For the first time in months, we went to bed with our stomachs full.

We paid for our extravagance over the next few days. With only nine thousand yuan to stretch to the end of the month, we were surviving on a bowl of plain rice noodles a day—the canteen's cheapest item—and on the rice friends secreted from the school cafeteria. We never fell to temptation again, spending eleven thousand yuan for a meal and, instead, ate what we could afford.

Like many of our friends, Wong, with his hunched back and balding head, had been surviving on the same sparse diet from the school cafeteria. "Green beans again," he scowled.

Cheung, the eighteen-year-old son of a Kuomintang general, drew glances from a few girls at the next table as he strolled back from the restaurant. I didn't envy him his perfectly pressed, tailored trousers and fine linen shirts, but I did covet the handgun he toted everywhere— and the plate of beef with garlic-and-black-bean sauce on rice he carried today into the cafeteria.

"Du nei lao mo," cursed Wong, whom I suspected was a Communist. "It's not fair that those who have money get healthy meals, while we starve. Those greedy fucking relatives of the principal are just exploiting us. Fucking capitalists." Wong's glasses steamed up, either from his noodles or his indignation; I'm not sure which. Wong, a crude, ill-educated peasant with little reason and much bravado, had a certain clownish appeal. He wore shoes too big for him, the heels slapping the floor like slippers when he walked. Even though swearing enough to make the girls and even some of us boys blush, Wong

managed to grin throughout his frequent tirades. Often his smile did not match his words.

Cheung, who, oddly enough, favoured the Communists, made no apologies. "We've paid for our room and board here," he agreed, deflecting any blame. "They can't just stop feeding us at the end of the month because the fucking Kuomintang yuan is worthless. *Hui sei.*"

A few others chimed in excitedly. We had all made sacrifices during the war. We had gone hungry before to save money for the war effort. Now we wanted full bellies.

"*Tu.* So what's the fucking Kuomintang doing with our money?" Wong spat out the question. "They're wasting it fighting the Communists. What for? Only the Communists care anything about the poor."

"Chiang Kai-shek's useless," added Cheung. "He doesn't even have any reserves for the fucking currency. That's why the *tu* fucking yuan is plummeting." Because his father was a Kuomintang general, we trusted that Cheung knew the truth. Certainly none of us would, without good reason, disagree with a father who was a general.

"But what do we care about the yuan?" someone called out. "I'm just hungry."

With a grand flourish, Cheung responded by treating all of us rice-noodle students to a bowl of rice each. Pouring on the soy sauce, we pledged him our eternal loyalty.

The general's son had a military plan. We would attack the enemy and seize our rightful property by raiding the restaurant. Fierce whispers spread throughout the twenty rooms in the boys' dormitory. Everyone was eager to join the raid against the miserly, thieving principal and his family. We wanted revenge.

Late that night, after the final bugle call and the school officials had made their rounds, some eighty of us crept into the dark halls. The generator had been turned off for the night, and the school grounds were dark except for the light from the moon. The restaurant, an open hut cobbled together with wood and bamboo, stood some distance from the dormitory, on the edge of the school grounds, gleaming in the moonlight. We charged, following Cheung, who brandished his gun, Wong by his side. We smashed shelves, dishes, and furniture. We twisted the wooden legs off the tables and used them to break open the glass cabinet where supplies were stored. We popped cake into our mouths and stuffed candies, cigarettes, and bottled soft drinks into our pockets.

Exhilarated, we raced back to the dormitory, victorious soldiers who had vanquished the principal and his greedy relatives. Our steps echoed in the corridors, but what did the noise matter now? The guards, who had by this time raised the alarm, chased us through the halls, blundering about in the dark, hollering. Shots rang out. We hid behind a low wall at the hall's edge and tried to quiet our thudding hearts.

A half hour passed before the principal found someone to restart the generator. As we heard the engine begin to hum, we stuffed the last bites of cake into our mouths and threw the unopened bottles of soft drinks out our windows into the river below. By the time the guards searched our rooms, the evidence had disappeared. I didn't notice anyone missing from our dormitory room, and assumed that we had all made it back safely.

The next day, however, there were reports that the guards had caught some of the students. We heard that two of our classmates had gunshot wounds. *"Tu na sing,"* muttered Wong. "They didn't have to do that."

Because so many students had been involved, we could not be singled out for punishment, and so we went to classes the next day as usual. Yet we simmered, longing for retaliation for the shootings. But what could we do? Among us, only Cheung owned a gun. One pistol was no match for the guards' rifles. After our classes, we took our frustration to the river behind the dormitory and dove in, hunting for the unopened soft drink bottles.

Shortly before the end of the school year, Cheung and Wong pulled K.K. and me aside to tell us about an upcoming demonstration in Sha Mian, a British pocket of Guangzhou. It was an anti-foreign protest. Some students wanted to also protest that the Kuomintang had betrayed China by catering to foreign powers. "Why don't you come with us?" Cheung invited me. "It's the least you can do for your country."

I believed that the students were right to take a stand against the foreign presence in our country, but Father had cautioned us to focus on our studies rather than get entangled in politics. K.K. and I did not attend the demonstration, but those who did returned pale-faced. Some angry, some frightened, the students spilled out their stories about what they had witnessed.

"It was awful. I wish I hadn't gone."

"Horrible. Blood everywhere."

"Hooks as big as my fucking fist. We could've died. *Du nei lao mo.* They fucking killed a guy, right in front of me." Cheung shook his head at the memory of the hooks. Coolies lifted two-hundred-pound sacks of grain using the very same hooks. Now, they were used to yank out the collarbones of unarmed students. *Had it really been the Kuomintang's henchmen who killed students?* Cheung said it had been gangsters hired by the Kuomintang.

I started to believe that Chiang Kai-shek's Nationalists persecuted and killed Chinese students. They had done other things: their generals had abused and neglected Chinese soldiers; their lack of economic planning had sent the yuan spiralling out of control, condemning millions of Chinese to starvation. They wouldn't let students get in their way. It was dawning on me who was ruining my country. My hope that the Kuomintang could usher in a free and strong China was disintegrating.

I felt terribly lost as K.K. and I boarded a train for Kowloon, where we would join Mama and Mei Mei, classes having ended for the year. In the third-class world of cattle-car-turned-circus, bodies pressed against me and a raucous clamour cut me off from even the solace of my own thoughts. The hawkers' shouts of "Soft drinks! Candy! Barbecued pork buns!" rose above the din of bellowing babies and fussing mothers. "It's noisy," I mouthed to K.K. beside me, but he only shrugged, unable to make out my words. He hoisted our meagre luggage onto the rack, and I turned my attention to guarding our window seat against encroachers.

The hawkers disembarked at the next station, and the train chugged its way through the countryside, lulling passengers to sleep with the steady clackety-clack of its wheels. Gazing out the window, I saw farmers in their bamboo hats tending chickens and cows; I saw leafy green vegetable patches and golden rice fields. These sleepy villages seemed to have been untouched by the ravages of inflation, so rampant in the city. I turned to K.K. "Do you think it's true? Cheung said that the Communists and the People's Liberation Army are closing in on Guangzhou. But everything looks so normal out here."

K.K. shrugged.

"Remember those soldiers and government officials we passed on the way to the station? Do you think they're sneaking weapons and top-secret documents out of the city?"

"Maybe."

"Cheung said they're evacuating the troops and smuggling crates of stuff out. Gold bars and everything. I wonder where they're shipping it. Taiwan?"

"Doesn't matter where they're taking it. We'll never get it back. The Kuomintang is ruining China."

"What if they strip the country of everything? Just like the Qing Dynasty." I remembered from my history studies how the Qing Dynasty had been forced to pay Japan compensation equal to three years of Japan's gross national revenue. Thousands of thousands of gold and silver bars, as well as priceless antiques, were paid to Japan and other foreign powers when China lost the Opium Wars. Now the country was again being stripped of its treasures. Rumours abounded about how the Kuomintang and its four ruling clans—the Soongs, the

Hung, the Chan, and Generalissimo Chiang's own family—were smuggling gold, silver, and other valuables out of China.

"How can we stop them?" I asked.

As answer, K.K. rammed his fist into the train car's wood panelling. In the taut silence that ensued, I stared out the window. Miles and miles of fields, train stations, and bun-selling window hawkers slipped by before Kowloon's skyline loomed into view.

Just a month before school ended in August, Mama had come to visit. She thought the tension between the Kuomintang government and the Communists made Guangzhou's situation dangerous. She decided K.K. and I should join her in Kowloon when we had finished the semester. We longed to return to the city that filled our childhood memories, and to be with Mama again, and so naturally were thrilled with the idea.

The first stop in Kowloon was Mong Kok Station, within walking distance of our old flat on Fa Yuen Street. It looked the same, with its Garden Confectionery, a famous bread and biscuit store, plastered with posters. I remembered walking through the neighbourhood with Mama, shopping for sticky buns, dried shrimp, and sweet preserved dates. We would walk home to Fa Yuen Street, where I would sleep in my own familiar bed. Now, Kowloon looked so normal. Perhaps the war had been nothing but a hideous dream.

After the train arrived at its final stop, Tsim Sha Tsui Station, K.K. and I headed for one of the waiting taxis to take us the short distance to Mama's. The driver grunted when we handed him the address of our new home on Temple Street in the Yau Ma Tei district, where Mama was waiting for us. The driver stubbed out his cigarette and merged into the traffic on Canton Road. As we passed Kowloon Wharf, I poked K.K. in the ribs, "Hey! Uncle's flat. That's where I saw the two coolies hanging."

My brother elbowed me back, "Remember selling cigarettes over there?"

"Yeah, that stupid Jap slapped me."

"You're lucky he didn't shoot you."

The taxi drove past rickshaws, coolies, street vendors, and shoppers, then turned onto Austin Road. After turning onto Temple Street not far from our old flat, we found the address we were seeking. Over the door hung a sign boasting the Quan Do Tailor Shop.

"Mama's a tailor?" I asked K.K.

"She didn't say anything," he muttered as he unloaded our bags.

I picked up my half-empty suitcase and left my brother to settle the taxi fare. *Could Mama have given us the wrong address?* I walked up to the storefront. The silk cheongsams in the showcase gleamed in the hazy afternoon sunlight. I pushed open the door and saw, to my right, a candy counter. A middle-aged woman stood behind it selling Coca-Cola, ice cream, cigarettes, notions—all the small but necessary trinkets of life. The woman, plumper than most Hong Kong women in the postwar era, glanced at me, then at my suitcase. Her eyes strayed to the doorway where K.K. now loomed. Then she smiled. "Kee Ngai? K.K.? Wel … come … home."

Each syllable oozed out of her mouth with great effort, as though her tongue had stuck to her cheek and had trouble turning itself over. She reached up and stroked my hair, the way older women do when they're fussing over how much you've grown and what a handsome young man you've become. I found it awkward being touched by a stranger. Noticing my perplexed expression, she said, "I'm Miss Chan, your mother's … business … part … ner. Your mother … out … visiting … pa … tients."

At the back of the room, two men—the tailors I assumed—straightened up to peer at us. Their curiosity satisfied, they bent over their worktable again. That table, announced Miss Chan, would be our bunk bed. Then she called out, "Ah Sim! Ah Sim!"

A thin ghostlike woman appeared out of nowhere. Her melancholy eyes, like pools of ink, dominated her young features. Ah Sim's whisper floated in the air, a light and silky ribbon. "Yes, Ma'am?"

Ah Sim bowed awkwardly as Miss Chan introduced us, and agreed to settle us in.

"Who's this? Are these the boys?" a shrill voice pierced the air. "Welcome, welcome, welcome, K.K. and Kee Ngai. Why, Auntie didn't tell us her boys were so good looking."

I turned around to spy a wiry older woman marching through the door toward me. She reached up to pinch my cheek. "My, my, you're so tall and strong." No, I'm not, protested a muddled voice in my mind. *Why were all these women patting us this way?*

"I'm Pao Tse," the woman said. "I just got back from helping your mother deliver Mrs. Tai's baby. That child is lucky to be alive. Twelve hours. We've been at their house since before dawn. I'm exhausted. Had to walk all the way there. Your mother, bless the woman, walks *everywhere*. Won't waste a penny on bus fare. Works day and night. She's still out giving injections. Won't be home until late tonight. Half the Swatow community must be sick. I would still be with her, but she insisted I come home to rest. And good thing I did or else you would've been here without a clue as to what's going on. I'll bet that cursed black widow Ah Sim hasn't explained a thing to you. And Miss Chan …"

Abruptly, Pao Tse paused for a rare breath, turned over a thought, then continued. "Miss Chan, of course, has probably told you everything. Ah Sim, you go heat up soup for the boys. I'll take care of them. These are the tailors, Mr. Ng and Mr. Choi. This here is Miss Chan's bedroom."

Arms waving this way and that, Pao Tse beckoned us to follow her behind the counter and down a narrow hallway. Although the coarse cotton smock she wore indicated she was a servant like Ah Sim, Pao Tse acted as though she ran the household. Miss Chan seemed accustomed to this state of affairs and deferred to our self-appointed hostess, who proceeded with her running commentary. "The kitchen has been moved out to the courtyard so that your mother can run a clinic in this backroom. Ah Sim and I sleep in the waiting area at night. This bedroom your mother and sister share."

"Where *is* Mei Mei?" I interrupted.

Pao Tse, a bit annoyed, pointed at Mama's bedroom. "In there. She's always in there. Never comes out. Just lies in bed all day. You two should go in to see her. Maybe you can coax her to eat something. That girl is as skinny as a stick. Won't touch her food." She dropped her voice to a conspiratorial whisper. "It's costing your mother everything to keep the child alive: fresh milk, eggs, chicken. Chicken! Can you believe that, every day? You know how much chicken costs? Fresh milk and eggs, who can afford it these days? But the child won't touch any of it. Her lunch is probably still there, cold as stone."

The curtains in Mei Mei's room were tightly drawn. As my eyes adjusted to the dim light, I made out the frail form of my sister lying on her bed, facing the wall. Only her tangled mass of hair was visible above the covers. *What had happened to my squirmy little sister?*

"Hey there," I mumbled, prodding her.

She turned, glanced at us, and grunted.

I looked helplessly at K.K., who shrugged.

During our years on the road, the disease of bone tuberculosis had spread throughout my sister's body. Not even Mama had heard of the disease until a specialist diagnosed it. Tuberculosis in the lungs, yes, but in the bone? The swelling in Mei Mei's knee was from the tuberculosis, not malnutrition. The surgeon who had operated on her shin just before the Japanese invasion had likely inadvertently planted the infection.

"I'm going to die." Mei Mei whispered, trying the words out on her tongue. I reached out awkwardly to pat her leg, but drew back.

"No, you're not." My words rang hollow. I had only to look at her to be convinced of the truth of her words.

Her narrow shoulders shrugged. She looked so young, but sounded like a grandmother. "What does it matter?" she muttered.

I cast about for a joke or story to tell, but could think of nothing that might bring my little sister back to me. Mutely I handed her a piece of chocolate. She took a bite and let the rest drop to the side. Ah

Sim came in to clear away the lunch dishes, and Mei Mei, who had not touched her meal, turned again to face the wall.

As soon as we had eaten dinner that night, K.K. and I fell asleep, exhausted from our journey. Around midnight, I woke to hear the front door open and see Mama walk quietly past us. K.K., curled up under the tailors' table, was snoring.

Pao Tse greeted Mama from the kitchen. "Have some soup, Auntie. You need your strength. You can't keep working so hard."

Scrambling off the tabletop, I went toward the kitchen, but stopped in the hallway and watched my mother as she drank the soup. The angles of her face seemed sharper than before, her lips thinner, with more lines around them. She was worried about Mei Mei, and Father, and us. I could see that, with all these burdens, Mama was tired and depressed.

"You're home," she said, noticing me standing in the hallway. Her weary eyes and smile held a warm welcome. "Did you eat something? Any problems on the train? Was it very crowded?"

"Yes, Mama, we ate already. We arrived in the afternoon. The train was crowded with refugees, but K.K. found us seats, so we were fine. There were no problems."

She nodded, relieved that we had made it back without trouble, and returned to her meal. I returned to bed, content at having seen her. A few hours later I was awakened by a banging on the door. Another baby to deliver. Could the good doctor please come quickly?

When I awoke the next morning, Mama was giving Mei Mei an injection before heading out to see patients. "It's a new medication for tuberculosis," she told me. "Streptomycin. Maybe this will help." At two injections per day, the daily dose cost 140 Hong Kong dollars, almost enough to pay both Pao Tse and Ah Sim for the month.

Two or three times a day, Mama poked Mei Mei with needles. Liver concentrate, calcium glucose, vitamins—my sister endured all the injections without complaining. Back in Wuzhou, she had hollered and screamed when we forced her medicine down. At least then she put up a fight. At least she became crabby and irritable. Now, she didn't care.

And the injections weren't helping. As I watched Mei Mei's body continue to shrink and her complexion fade, I was convinced that, even with the special food and injections, it was hopeless. But Mama refused to give up. As time passed, I began to notice how my mother too was fading and shrinking, how after a long night her eyes looked hollow and her hands shook. I noticed, but did little to ease her burdens.

6

TRUST THE PARTY

1948–1949 Hong Kong, British colony

As K.K. and I settled in Kowloon with Mama, she insisted that K.K. and I not work. Our job, she said, was to study hard. At most, she would let us run errands. We liked delivering orders of cheongsams from the tailors and treats from the snack counter to glamorous aspiring starlets who lived in the neighbourhood. Certainly, some of our classmates at Oriental Senior High School would have enjoyed running these errands for us, no doubt bragging afterward about imaginary conquests. These boys spent their days playing soccer and basketball, flirting with girls, and provoking teachers. They talked constantly in class and swore more than Cheung and Wong in Guangzhou had. I had no respect for them.

Nor did I respect the two pro-Kuomintang students who always seemed to be smoking in the schoolyard. Their low marks showed that they didn't study much. All they did was debate with a left-wing student in our class. Each day, the leftist read aloud from a newspaper Communist teachings and stories that spurred the Kuomintang students to argue with him. The leftist always lost, conceding to us that Communism had no rational foundation.

"He's not a real Communist," muttered Leung Ming, another classmate. "He's only pretending. That's their strategy for spreading Kuomintang propaganda."

Leung I did respect. He was not impressive in any obvious way, being neither athletic, good looking, nor brilliant but, rather, dark and skinny, and barely taller than me. He was in my grade—grade ten, which, after skipping grade nine, I had to repeat—even though he was already twenty-two years old. Leung carried himself in a way that somehow made him seem both humble and confident. He didn't swagger, but nor did he shuffle or hang his head. And he shared my love for folk songs. He even approved of classical music, an interest that had been growing in K.K. and me since we had returned to Kowloon.

Every night, K.K. and I listened to Hong Kong Radio. Radios were expensive; instead, we rented a Rediffusion unit, which broadcast via cable directly to the loudspeaker hanging from our ceiling. There were two channels: one Cantonese, the other English. I turned to the Cantonese channel. In unhurried, cultured tones, Madam Low Mo Yin introduced us to the passion and drama of classical music. She described the themes of Mozart's *A Little Night Music,* J.S. Bach's *Air on G String,* and Beethoven's *Fate,* the first movement of his *Symphony No. 5.* She talked about the lives of the composers. My favourite piece was the *Humoresque,* a violin solo by Dvořák.

Inspired, I found myself a second-hand violin and tried to teach myself to play. Violin lessons cost too much, but the school choir was free to join. I joined. So did Leung Ming, and that's how I came to know him.

At the end of our third rehearsal, this rumpled figure came up to chat with me. Leung dressed modestly, seldom bothering to iron his shirt or slacks, even though he came from a rich family. In a voice that sounded like the third string of my violin—strikingly soft, yet with firm and distinct notes—he asked, "You like singing?"

"Yes." The word stretched itself on my tongue, arched momentarily into a question, then landed tentatively as an observation. A qualifier followed swiftly. "I like the war resistance songs about the Japanese, and folk songs. But I don't like popular songs."

Leung eyed me for a moment. His eyes narrowed, but his tone remained nonchalant. "Why?"

"Popular songs have no meaning, except to describe love."

"What folk songs have you sung?"

I drew in my breath sharply at the unexpected reminder of Shih Yee. "A good friend taught me 'Lugouqiao Bridge,' 'On the Shung Far River,' and 'Song of the Azalea.'"

"Which one do you like the most?"

"'Lugouqiao Bridge.'"

Leung's tone grew warmer, more casual. "Some classmates and I will be having a picnic later this semester. Would you like to come?"

I accepted eagerly; finally, I had found someone who appreciated Shih Yee's songs. Twice a week, Leung and I walked home after choir practice. I confided in him my grief over Shih Yee's death, and how I could not rid myself of the image of the two coolies hanging beneath my uncle's flat, nor of the two soldiers executed in Anlong.

Leung shared openly his desire to help the poor and make China a strong country. He also told me about his love for music, for Chinese ethnic songs, and for oil painting. He would take me to his sister's restaurant on Temple Street and treat me to lunch. Leung lived upstairs on the third floor in a partitioned room. There, he showed me his oil paintings; he even painted a portrait of me.

Leung told me tales about the People's Liberation Army and its predecessor, the Eighth Route Army. I learned about the Communists in China and Russia, and about left-wing activities in Hong Kong. "Would you like to read it for yourself?" Leung asked me one day, offering me a copy of the left-wing *Wah Shang News*. Hong Kong under British rule enjoyed freedom of the press and one usually had no trouble finding left-wing newspapers at newsstands, in among the *South China Morning Post, Hong Kong Standard,* and Kuomintang's *Hong Kong Times*.

I declined. I didn't want any more propaganda. I wasn't interested in politics. Father had warned me to focus on my studies. Still, Leung's stories intrigued me. Ever since we had lived in Chongqing, K.K. had been exploring Marxist philosophy. But surely, I thought, it wouldn't hurt to listen to stories of Communist bravery. After all, I had to agree that the Kuomintang was corrupt and the Japanese were cruel. And so, I listened as Leung spun out story after story about how the Eighth Route Army's "Little Devil Troop" had fought the Japanese.

"Xian Ur was only nine," began one such story. "He was a farmer boy watching his family's cow on a mountainside. The Japanese troop found him playing a bamboo flute and demanded he reveal the Little Devil Troop's whereabouts." Young Xian Ur's courage in diverting the enemy moved me deeply. When Leung described with dramatic flourish how the soldiers hurled his small body over a cliff, I wept openly, then cheered when the Little Devil Troop killed the young martyr's murderers. The tale reminded me of those Captain Tan had told us during the truck ride to Chongqing. *They must be true.*

Leung told these stories for weeks whenever the two of us were together. When I asked him for more stories, Leung offered me the *Wah Shang News* again. This time, I seized the newspaper from him. Just for the stories, I told myself. *I'm not going to get involved in politics.*

On our long walks home, Leung placated my doubts about Communism.

"I heard that the Communist troops seized peasants' crops and livestock in the countryside. That's what I hated about the Kuomintang. They stole from our own people."

"Those soldiers could not have been true Communists. They weren't following the rules. Remember the Three Rules of Discipline set out in *Wah Shang News*?"

Yes, I remembered the rules: always obey orders, don't take anything from anyone, and hand in all property that was captured. And I had remembered the Eight Points of Attention, too. I respected the principles these Communists followed, including simple ones such as "Do not hit or swear at people" and "Pay for anything you damage."

These were noble objectives that included paying fairly for items bought, returning borrowed items, and not taking advantage of women.

If the Communists truly lived by these principles, there was hope for China's future. Nevertheless, one memory continued to haunt me. A bloodied skull lying in a field near Anlong spoke to me of betrayal and corruption.

"What if you're wrongfully accused by your comrades?" I asked. "What if you're killed by your own people?"

My deepest fear was that the revolutionary troops would murder their own people. Leung soothed my fears with promises of a moral government. Only the Communists loved the Chinese people. Only Mao Zedong could save the country. The Communists would never kill their comrades, my friend assured me.

It was a clear spring Sunday in 1949. Thirty of us from the school had taken the bus to Tung Tau Village, near Kowloon's Kai Tak Airport, and then hiked up Lion Rock, so named because the shape of the summit resembles a lion. Sandwiches and fruit weighed down my backpack, but I resolved not to complain. Leung had stayed up all night making sandwiches for everyone. Although his backpack held the heaviest items, he cheerfully urged everyone on, leading them in rousing, patriotic songs.

In a few months, I had come to respect and trust Leung completely. His tirades against the Kuomintang rang true for me, given the corruption I had witnessed. I admired the Communist principles he cited. *He's honest and has integrity.* He always had time to talk to his classmates. He lent them money and helped them with homework. *He really cares about people.* I had helped him organize rowing parties, picnics, singalongs, and all sorts of other activities. He always handled the toughest jobs. He stayed up late preparing for events and stayed behind cleaning up afterward. *He never complains.*

As we climbed, I watched Leung lift items from another student's backpack and add them to his own load. Beads of sweat dripped off his eyebrows. He puffed along good-naturedly until we reached the top of Lion Rock. A hush fell over us as we gazed down at Red

Blossom Valley. At our feet, a lush green field lay resplendent with petunias, salish, daisies, azaleas, roses, and other wildflowers in bloom. I inhaled deeply, letting the earthy fragrance clear my lungs of stale city air. I could see Kowloon and Hong Kong Island in the distance, but at this moment, they only served as a backdrop for this idyllic garden.

Invigorated, we set up our picnic on the grass. Leung passed out song sheets. He had painstakingly etched lyrics in wax to print them for us. Today, he wanted us to learn "The Yellow River" ballad. The melody was fierce and fervent at times, yet melancholy and poignant. The first part of the song reveals the power of the river and that there were many miles of fertile land where healthy crops grew and families lived happily together.

For generations, our people had lived in peace along the Yellow River, but then the Japanese came and our countrymen suffered much hardship.

Pillaged! Killed! People ... scattered seeking refuge, no home and village to return to,
Like the unceasing waters of the Yellow River rushing to the East, families scattered, wives and children lost, everywhere.

In my mind's eye, I again saw images of refugees, young and old, clothed in rags and clawing for stale buns, as I had witnessed many times during the war. Gripping the song sheet, I wandered over to a corner of the field to be alone. A brook nearby percolated its way through the spring grass; its chortling soothed my heart.

A light tap on my shoulder startled me out of my reverie. Leung held out a sandwich and soft drink. I shook my head. My appetite had deserted me. Easing himself onto the grass next to me, Leung hummed "The Yellow River" to himself.

"Beijing fell in January," he said. His voice, though soft, was insistent. His words masqueraded as small talk, but each held a note of urgency. "Very soon, the People's Liberation Army will liberate all of China. Our dear comrades' lives will change significantly. There will be no more suffering." He cradled an azalea in his fingers, stroking the blossom gently. "The Communists will build a new China. A strong, wealthy, free, new China. Thousands upon thousands of martyrs laid down their lives for our people." The azalea's stem snapped. "They died as heroes. The Communist Party members and the soldiers of the People's Liberation Army sacrificed their lives for a single goal."

The stories of Xian Ur and other martyrs remained fresh in my mind. Yes, many people had died for China. The People's Liberation Army, said *Wah Shang News,* was closing in on Guangdong province. Chiang Kai-shek was preparing to flee to Taiwan. The saying on the street was "Defeated troops collapse like a landslide down a mountain." The Kuomintang no longer held any hope for China. Chinese sentiment was that the country's future depended on the Communists alone.

Leung squeezed my shoulder. "You care about people. You have a passion for the poor. I've noticed many times how you give your pocket money to beggars. But how much will your pennies really help them?"

It was true. Beggars clogged the streets of Kowloon. I couldn't bear the sight of their tiny cardboard huts. Ragamuffins and gaunt old men huddled over street stoves to warm up someone's garbage for their dinners. I gave them what I could. My pocket money was better than nothing, but when I had nothing to give, I felt helpless.

My friend scanned my face while these images played out in my mind. He continued to press his point. "Imagine a world without deprivation or oppression, a society equal and free. Everyone would have a job. Everyone would have what he or she needs. There would be no more beggars. No one would have to sleep on the street."

"I'm seeking a way to help the poor." My voice whispered my thoughts. "If only there were a system that let all people have enough to live on, a system that distributed wealth equally."

"You can't possibly change society on your own," Leung said. His sentences, with their Communist slogans, gained momentum, building pressure like a river of thought breaking through my dam of doubt. "To successfully overturn a system, the right political party, the right vision is needed. The Communist Party is working toward this goal. Mao Zedong's vision directs us toward success."

With quiet intensity, Leung probed me further. "Would you like to dedicate your life to the poor and to the people of China?"

"Yes."

"Would you like to carry out your hope and see for yourself a China that is strong, free, equal, and wealthy?"

"Yes."

"Would you like to relieve our fellow countrymen from deep distress?"

"Yes."

"Would you like to join the Communist Youth League?"

There. The question was out.

Leung explained that the Youth League was an organization led by the Communist Party in Hong Kong that operated underground. "That means no one knows you are a member, not even your parents, not even your closest friends," he said. "It might be dangerous. You must make sacrifices or even risk your life." He allowed the words to lodge firmly in my consciousness. Then, crisply, he asked again, "Do you want to join?"

As if taking a marriage vow, I answered solemnly, "Yes."

That afternoon, the thirty of us lost ourselves in folk dances. We whirled and spun about, laughing and cheering each other on and singing "The Graduation Song," which Leung had taught us. Its rousing chorus exhorted us to devote our strength and energy to saving our people, regardless of personal danger:

Fellow students! Rise up! Together we strive to shoulder the burden of our nation!...

Today, we, like the morning fragrance, are students of China,
    tomorrow, we will be the pillars of our society!

Our voices rang out lustily as we trekked back along the Lion Rock
trail. Hand in hand, we marched, comrades to the end.

I was sworn in the following Sunday.

⁜

It was dangerous to be openly Communist in Hong Kong. The British
Hong Kong government unofficially endorsed the right-wing movements, and only six thousand people in Hong Kong—one percent
of the population—considered themselves left wing. Nervous chills
chased up my spine as I stood on a street corner waiting for Leung.
I had taken a ferry across the harbour to Hong Kong Island and
then a tram to a residential area in North Point. *Why was he late?*
Anything might happen to a secret agent. Before my mind could
explore all the dangerous scenarios, Leung arrived.

He guided me through unfamiliar streets to an old building. We
arrived at precisely 10 A.M. I followed Leung up five flights of stairs.
He turned a key and we stepped into a modest, two-bedroom flat. The
sitting room was bare except for six chairs and a desk. "This place is
only used for Party meetings," Leung explained. "Don't ever come
near here again. We're not supposed to meet other comrades. Meet
only with your official contacts."

With an ease born of practice, he moved the desk and three chairs
away from the wall and pulled out from now-revealed drawers a poster
of Chairman Mao, which he carefully tacked on the wall. Unfurling
two Communist flags, he tacked these too on the wall so they flanked
the poster at forty-five-degree angles. The room was now adequately
adorned for the ceremony.

At exactly 10:30 A.M., a well-built man in a Hawaiian shirt strode
into the flat. He looked like a fat businessman, though he held himself
tall, his back straight like a soldier. Leung introduced him only as

"Comrade." This portly man was our superior and would represent the Party for my swearing-in.

"If you see him on the street," hissed Leung, "ignore him. We are all strangers, understood?"

I nodded mutely. That wouldn't be hard. I could barely make out his features in the dim lighting. Comrade, on the other hand, already knew me by name. "Comrade Ore Kee Ngai, welcome," he exclaimed, seizing my hand. His manly shakes infused me with a sense of mission. I squared my shoulders and sat down with my back straight and legs apart. Leung rose to take the role of host.

"Stand up."

I snapped to attention.

"Bow to the Party flag and to Mao."

Deeply, reverently, I bowed.

"Three minutes' silence in memory of the martyrs who sacrificed their lives fighting the Japanese and Chiang Kai-shek."

Silence.

"Sing 'The International.'"

We each had a song sheet. Leung led off quietly with his off-key notes but was quickly drowned out by Comrade's rumbling bass and my clear tenor. The song called all people to rise up and struggle for the truth and not to depend on any higher being but to create our own destiny. I sang loudly and clearly,

Force red the flame in the stove; strike the iron when it is hot!
This is the last exertion, united to tomorrow, international
    Communism must succeed!

How my heart pounded. Finally, I was pledging myself to a cause that would save China.

Leung looked in my eyes and ordered, "Please raise your right hand and repeat after me: "I, Ore Kee Ngai, swear that I will abide by the rules and regulations of the Communist Youth League. I will obey the leadership of the organization. I will devote myself to the world Communist movement. I will dedicate my life to the people of China and for the cause of the revolution here in Hong Kong. I will not expose our comrades or the organization under any circumstances, even at risk of losing my life."

My voice shook at first but soon steadied. By the last sentence, my words shot out, confident and proud. The words of the oath sank into my soul in the leaden silence that followed. Then came Leung's formal charge: "Do you, Ore Kee Ngai, swear on your life to uphold these principles?"

"I do."

Comrade nodded approvingly and welcomed me with stern injunctions: "I represent the Party as a witness to this ceremony, and welcome Comrade Ore in joining the Communist Youth League. Comrade Ore, you bring fresh strength to the Communist Youth League, and I hope you will devote all of it to the revolution here in Hong Kong. You must respect the laws of working underground. You must be completely devoted to the Party. The Party will take care of you when needed. Trust the Party. Remember, the Party is always great, glorious, and correct."

His final words booming—"great, glorious, and correct"—echoed in my ears as Leung launched into a speech of his own.

"Comrade Ore, you have always been a supportive activist. You are concerned with the welfare of the people, and you love our country. I welcome you and congratulate you on joining the Communist Youth League. You are a member of the glorious Communist Youth League. You must make strict demands of yourself. You must serve the Chinese people with all your heart and soul. You must dare to fight and overcome all obstacles. Be resolute. Fear no sacrifice. And surmount every difficulty to win the victory."

Comrade briskly shook my hand again and departed. On this day, I was reborn. The song, the speeches, my solemn vow—all these buzzed in my mind. The sixteen-year-old Ore Kee Ngai who had mounted these stairs a little over an hour earlier was not the same patriotic young man who marched down.

Before leaving, Comrade had cautioned me, "You must appear politically neutral. We don't want you to expose yourself. Stay a student as long as possible. Don't worry. The Party won't use you as a soldier right away." At that moment, had they asked, I would have gladly marched four hundred miles to fight alongside my comrades at the Guangdong-Hunan border. I was ready to eliminate the Kuomintang. I was ready to die for my country.

7

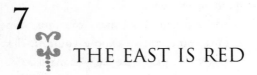

THE EAST IS RED

1949–1951 Hong Kong, British colony

As a newly baptized Communist Youth League member, I scoured *Wah Shang News* to track our victories in China. It was 1949 and the Communists had taken control of Nanjing, the capital of Jiangsu province, on April 23, and Hangzhou, the capital of Zhejiang province, on May 13. Could Shanghai, or even Hong Kong, be far behind? True to its name, the People's Liberation Army freed city after city from the Kuomintang's grasp.

All of Hong Kong knew Chiang Kai-shek's government was doomed. "Like the splitting of a bamboo stalk," the old men in teahouses nodded sagely. Even the sturdiest bamboo, once split, cracks all the way to its base. The splinters are good for picking one's teeth, perhaps, or torturing an enemy, but not much else. The Kuomintang was cracking from top to bottom and I cheered its splintering.

While I was absorbing every detail of the battle for Hangzhou, southwest of Shanghai, K.K. burst into our flat waving a fresh copy of *Wah Shang News*. "Ka-ka-ka kum-kum," he spluttered. His face grew scarlet as his heaving chest choked off each syllable. With great effort he spread out the newspaper, pointed to a narrow column of text, and cried, "Look!"

100

"The Communist Party and the Southern Region People's Liberation Army are calling the students and youth in Hong Kong to support our country by joining the People's Liberation Army cadres training class." K.K. stared at me without saying anything, letting the news sink in. "Ka-ka-Kee Ngai, duh-do-don't you see?"

I looked at the newspaper, then at my brother's flushed face. Crushing the paper in his hands, K.K. knocked me over the head with it. "They need cadres to work in all the liberated areas. China is such a huge country. There aren't enough cadres. They need me."

So that's what this was about. K.K. had always wanted to join the army. I could be a cadre, too, but something held me back. My contact in the Youth League hadn't given me permission; I was to finish my studies in Hong Kong. How I envied K.K. at that moment. "That's great," I injected enthusiasm into my voice. Of course it was great. K.K. would help liberate our country on the mainland. I would fight imperialism in Hong Kong. Each soldier had his own battlefield.

The next morning, K.K. filled his schoolbag with clothes instead of books and left a goodbye note on Mama's desk. As we walked toward Mong Kok Station, my heart swelled with pride. My brother would be a real soldier in the Liberation Army. He would protect and minister to our people. I didn't know when I would see K.K. again. Already I missed his bulky frame and stuttering speech, and the way he rushed through dinner. I smiled at the memory of K.K. popping shrimp into his mouth. He never bothered peeling them—it was faster to eat them with the shells still on. Yes, I would miss him. As we walked past our old flat on Fa Yuen Street, the shrieks of bombs and flower girls rang out from another lifetime. We had faced so much together, my brother and I. Now, I would be alone.

At first, K.K. chattered about how excited he was to be joining an army in which soldiers and officers lived equally. He was sure there would be no corruption in the People's Liberation Army. He longed to shoulder his rifle and march on the front lines. My glum face, however, stemmed his flow of words. We trudged in silence up the hill to the station. K.K. purchased his ticket and we pushed through the gate to the platform, ignoring the hawkers and coolies milling about.

As the train approached, I reached up to touch K.K. on the shoulder. "Take care of yourself."

He nodded and cuffed me on the ear. "Take care of Mama and Mei Mei. You're the man of the house now."

I blinked back a tear.

A handshake, and he was gone.

⚜

"What does he think he's doing?" Mama bellowed when she read K.K.'s note. "He's going to get himself killed."

She paced across the room, crimson creeping up her neck and staining her cheeks.

"I've hauled him home before," she fumed. "I can't guard him all his life."

K.K.'s note shrivelled in Mama's fist. She paced, she fretted, she ranted, and she paced some more. Finally, the pacing ceased. "That boy is going to worry me to death. I give up," she capitulated, her shoulders sagging.

I tried to reassure her. "K.K.'s safe. He's only going for training to help run the country after they win." Something in my voice must have alerted my mother. She wheeled sharply on me, eyes narrowing, "You're not going to join the People's Liberation Army too, are you?"

"No, no, of course not," I reassured her.

To my relief, Mama dropped the subject. But her lips tightened into a thin line. Her downward glance as she turned away was not quick enough to hide a look somewhere between exhaustion and desperation. She straightened her bony shoulders and stalked down the hall. At the doorway to her bedroom, she paused to stare at Mei Mei, who in turn stared into empty space. Despite the needles and nutritious meals, my sister continued to waste away. We knew she was dying. Only Mama refused to admit it.

As she slumped against that doorway, though, I didn't see a fighter. For the first time, I saw my mother as an old woman. I felt an urge to stroke her bent head, but just then, a patient entered the flat and called out for Mama. Lifting her head, the always-in-control doctor who was my mother returned.

"Want to hear a story?" I turned to the lump under the blanket.

Mei Mei shrugged. Taking that as a "yes," I plunged into my favourite tale of Xian Ur and the Little Devil Troop.

"... Enraged, they hurled his tiny body over the steep cliff ..." My voice trailed off when the impassioned account failed to draw any response.

"Weren't you moved by his courage?"

No reaction.

"Do you want to hear any more?"

No comment.

"Well, I have to go now. I'm helping Leung print song sheets for tomorrow's singalong. I'll teach you some of the songs?" With still no reaction from Mei Mei, I headed out of the flat. "I won't be home for dinner," I called over my shoulder to no one in particular.

As I jogged down the street, a voice in my head told me I shouldn't abandon Mama and Mei Mei. *I do my part,* I argued back. Every day after school I tried to cheer up Mei Mei with my stories so that she wouldn't think so much about dying. Mama didn't need my help. We're not starving, I told myself. My country needed me more than my mother did right now. To worry about making money was selfish and bourgeois. Besides, in an ideal Communist world, Mei Mei would receive the food and medicine she needed for free.

All the way to Leung's house, I beat my inner voice into submission. Once there, my comrade strengthened my resolve. "Look at all the youths involved in gangs," Leung reminded me. "They have no hope in this corrupt society. You can't just focus on your own family."

As we painstakingly etched lyrics into wax and printed by hand dozens of song sheets, I became convinced that I had a role to play in this revolution. The rowing parties and picnics we organized recruited youth to our cause. Together, we could overthrow Chiang Kai-shek and rid China of imperialism. By the time I dragged myself into the flat, long past midnight, missing dinner seemed an insignificant sacrifice for my country. Fasting helped me identify better with my starving comrades.

"Eat something," Mama urged. "Where were you?" she asked as she made preparations to respond to another medical emergency.

"I went to Leung's to help print song sheets."

Mama did not ask too many questions; she didn't have time to talk. She was probably comforted to know I wasn't hanging out with a local gang.

I ate as she suggested, and then I slept.

✣

My life was full. As a Communist Youth League member and also the executive director for the Mong Kok district of the Literature Youth Fellowship Association, one of thirty-eight left-wing societies in Hong Kong at the time, I was busy recruiting students, attending meetings, and handing out newsletters. There was always plenty more to do.

I soon fell into a routine: go to school, cheer up Mei Mei, organize Youth League and Youth Fellowship events, tiptoe home in the early morning, eat dinner, drop into bed. During summer vacation, I brought students to tour Heung To, a left-wing school in Kowloon, to show them a better way of living and learning. Every student I could possibly contact through my network visited the school. After one of these tours, I returned home to check on Mei Mei.

"Poor child, poor child!" Pao Tse's wailing greeted me at the door. The storefront was empty, but I caught a glimpse of Ah Sim. "What happened?" I asked.

She nodded without a word toward Mama and Mei Mei's bedroom. There, I found Mama sitting on the bed stroking my sister's bare leg.

Miss Chan appeared to be offering condolences, but couldn't get the words out of her mouth.

"What's wrong?"

Mama looked up at me. "The specialist says your sister needs an amputation. Without it, she'll die," she said. Her voice was tight but matter-of-fact. For once, my mother had to concede defeat. Disappointment carved the lines deeper into her face. I studied my sister's lower left leg, which had turned the purplish-grey of mashed taro root. The diseased leg was six inches shorter than the other. Mei Mei's face was blank. Her eyes refused to meet my gaze.

"I don't care if I die," she muttered.

"Don't say that," Mama scolded.

Mei Mei shrugged without looking at us. With the slightest sneer, she whispered, "Why? Because it would be your fault?"

I sucked in a sharp breath as Mama winced. Without a word, she left the room.

"Do-don't say … that to … your … mother," Miss Chan remonstrated before following Mama out the door.

Mei Mei clenched her jaw until it hardened into sharp angles like Mama's. That look in her dark eyes, was it bitterness or despair? It wasn't repentance. I suppose, as her older brother, I should have lectured her on respecting her elders, but who was I to scold? Father had often hinted that Mama had failed to take proper care of Mei Mei. I knew it wasn't true, but I didn't know what to say. Only one thought dominated my mind. *What if she dies before the amputation?*

The question hissed at me until I feared Mei Mei could hear it. To distract both of us, I told her more stories about the Little Devil Troop. No response. Striking a Charlie Chaplin pose, I performed a sloppy jazz dance to tease a smile from her. It worked. She giggled for the first time in months. Gratified by my success, I urged her to sip some chicken broth. No luck. *Oh well, at least I made her laugh.*

On the day we went to the hospital, however, I had no comic routines ready. Joviality seemed disrespectful, even crass, considering my sister was about to lose her leg. Mama, Ah Sim, Mei Mei, and I boarded the crowded ferry from Kowloon to Hong Kong Island with all the levity of a funeral procession. Without expression or comment, we slid into our first-class seats. But not even first-class tickets procured air conditioning on a Hong Kong ferry in 1949. Our sweat thickened to glue and its odour ripened in the August heat until a sea breeze swept away the stickiness and stench as the ferry began chugging its way across Victoria Harbour.

I leaned past Mei Mei to peer out the window at the vessels around us. Junks, pleasure boats, sailboats, and sampans bustled about like farmers' wives at a market—they puttered, manifestly busy with their own business, deftly skirting any obstacles, and occasionally hollering greetings or warnings. A handful of freighters had dropped anchor in the harbour. Crews rushed to unload wooden crates of cargo onto the barges clustering around the ships. The coolies' muscles bulged. The fierce summer sun had roasted these men to the toughness of beef jerky and yet they stomped, they grunted, and they lifted the cargo. They were *alive*.

And my sister was dying. At only thirteen years of age, she should be full of life. How could the harbour thrive with so much energy while my heart withered? I glanced at Mei Mei. She had shuttered her soul. I could read nothing in her vacant eyes, and she seemed to see nothing of the vibrant scene before us.

Mama pointed things out to Mei Mei. "Look at the birds—seagulls! They're following us!" She sounded like an overeager matchmaker. Mei Mei remained unimpressed. For once, I pitied my mother. All her efforts to save the leg had failed. Now her attempts to ease Mei Mei's despair were failing. We sat the rest of the ferry trip in silence, worry furrowing our brows.

From the terminal, a taxi deposited us in front of a hulking concrete building set high on a hill. The view from Queen Mary's Hospital was impressive and panoramic. As Ah Sim piggybacked Mei Mei up the driveway, I paused by a flower stand to survey the scenery. The hospital overlooked a vast valley flanked by two small hills. A few villages, clusters of bungalows and farmyards, dotted the landscape. Beyond them lay the blue-upon-blue of the South China Sea. *Mei Mei will rest peacefully here.*

"She's too weak to survive an operation," the doctor pronounced bluntly after poking and prodding Mei Mei. He gripped her wrist with his thumb and forefinger. Lifting it up, he frowned at Mama, "Don't you feed her?"

"We try," I answered. "She won't eat."

"She's dehydrated. We'll have to keep her here until she can withstand the operation."

"How long will that be?" asked Mama.

"A few days, maybe a week. It depends ..." the doctor paused to fix Mei Mei with a solemn look, "... it depends on how cooperative she is. You, young lady, must eat everything we feed you. Understood?"

Intimidated by his gaze and no-nonsense voice, Mei Mei stared at the bedsheets for a few minutes before nodding. As it turned out, she liked the Western-style meals served at the hospital and by the fifth day had improved enough for the amputation to go ahead.

That summer, I was taking a course to advance my English. On the day of Mei Mei's operation, the English lesson made no impression on me. My eyes followed the flight of the sparrows on the other side of the window. The clock ticked unbearably slowly. If only I could wait at the hospital with Mama.

Finally, I was free to go. I raced down the street to the ferry terminal. The fifteen-minute wait seemed like an hour. Finally, foot passengers were allowed to surge onto the gangplank. A half-hour bus ride from the terminal on the Hong Kong side, and I had arrived at the hospital. I bounded up the steps three at a time, crashing through the front doors. The woman at the admitting desk smiled a welcome, but I sprinted past her to the elevator. Push, push, push. The elevator doors slid open, only to reveal a mass of passengers of every size and description. *Forget this.* I yanked open the door to the stairwell and raced to the fifth floor.

The soapy, mild-antiseptic scent of Lysol greeted me in the ward. My chest heaving, I slowed my pace. The floors, the corridors, the nurses—they looked so neat and clean. Their tidiness reassured me.

In Mei Mei's room I found Mama leaning against the window, looking out meditatively at the ocean view. At the sound of my steps, she turned, raised a finger to her lips, and pointed to the slender form on the bed. Her skin the green-grey colour of a corpse, Mei Mei was sleeping.

I put my hand on Mama's shoulder, "How is she?"

"Tired. She could barely say a word. Mostly slept today."

"But she'll be all right?"

Mama nodded and turned back to the window. I stared at the empty space where Mei Mei's leg should have been.

※

Mei Mei was sitting up when Mama and I came to visit the next day. She even smiled. I couldn't believe it. My sister had smiled. "Hey there," I punched her arm. "How does it feel?"

"You know, I can feel my toes itching. Help me hoist my leg up so I can scratch my toes."

"But it's not there," I blurted out. Her leg from above the knee was clearly gone. "How can you scratch what isn't there?"

Mei Mei's smile stretched into a grin. Was she playing a joke on me or did she feel silly for her mistake? I couldn't tell.

The tension on my mother's face relaxed a little. Mama pulled out an orange and began peeling it for Mei Mei.

"Did you enjoy your breakfast?" I asked.

"Yes. I had scrambled eggs and toast for breakfast. I preferred that to plain old congee."

Mei Mei's mood had changed. Her disease was gone. By the time Mei Mei returned home ten days later, her cheeks glowed with the softest tinge of pink. I was surprised—we all were—at how quickly my sister recovered. It didn't take long for her to regain weight.

"Thank goodness," Mama confided to Miss Chan. "It's like a millstone has been lifted from my neck." For the first time since returning to Kowloon, I heard my mother laugh.

A month later, Mei Mei tried out crutches for the first time. It was my turn to laugh. "You look like a stork or a flamingo walking like that," I teased. She swung one of her crutches at me, but I ducked easily. Unsure whether she was really mad at me, I apologized: "Sorry. Here, I'll help you get into bed and treat you to a show."

Mei Mei grimaced. "Oh, no! Don't tell me you're going to perform another one of your silly dances."

"And why not? How often do you get to see the cha-cha?"

We both knew my contortions resembled nothing close to a cha-cha or samba, but my funny faces did make her giggle. When I emerged from the bedroom-cum-theatre, face flushed, she called after me, "Hey, isn't it time for the news report?"

Sure enough, it was almost 9 P.M. I switched on the Rediffusion unit to Hong Kong Radio. The familiar notes of Haydn's *Trumpet Concerto in E Flat Major* filled the flat. I didn't mind the tune when it introduced the Chinese-language news. The same notes heralded the British BBC's seven o'clock news on the English channel. *Nothing but enemy propaganda.* Still, I listened to that news also, as it was the best way to practise English.

At the tailors' table, I spread out my books and began scribbling. Someone knocked on the door. Only my mother's patients visited us this late. I swung open the door and my jaw dropped. It was K.K. He looked like the raggedy beggars who sleep on Nathan Road. He smelled like one, too. The grime caked on his torn shirt could have been anything from mud to manure to soy sauce. For a minute, I gaped, stunned that my brother would be wearing anything that filthy.

He smiled weakly, "Hello, Kee Ngai."

"K.K.? K.K. Hey, everybody, it's K.K.!"

I whooped and hollered until Mama and Miss Chan rushed into the room, Pao Tse following close behind. Even Mei Mei hobbled out to join us and Ah Sim peered at us from the hallway.

"What happened? Where have you been? How come your pants are torn? Did you get injured in a glorious battle?" My questions tumbled out in one breath and without any order.

Mama was more pragmatic. "Here, sit down, K.K. Ah Sim, why don't you cook some dinner for him? Pao Tse, we could all use a cup of tea."

When she returned with the tea, Pao Tse couldn't help clucking, "Look at you. Nothing but bones. Poor boy, poor boy. What did they do to you? Did you get caught by enemy soldiers? Poor child."

K.K. untied his canvas Liberation Brand shoes and eased them off his feet. I noticed the rubber soles were almost worn through. He drained several cups of tea before speaking.

"I quit. Deserted. Had to walk home."

His terse statements only encouraged more questions. Mama finally intervened. "Let the boy rest, all of you. Go take a bath, K.K., and then eat your dinner. You must be exhausted. We can talk in the morning."

After Mama and the others went to bed, K.K. joined me at the tailors' table. I couldn't believe that after these five months, my brother would again be sleeping under the table, just as he used to. We hadn't heard from him the whole time he had been away. It was so good to have him home. Still, I was reluctant to prepare our bedding. There were too many questions, too many stories to share.

K.K. pulled his chair closer to mine and fixed me with a serious-talk-with-big-brother gaze. "Kee Ngai, you need to learn from my experiences with the revolution," he said slowly and carefully. "Don't trust the Communists."

The sharp statement shocked me.

After a week in the city of Siu Kwan, in Guangdong province, K.K. and the rest of his company had set out for an unknown destination. They marched from dawn to dusk for a dozen days. Eventually, the young recruits arrived at an army base near Kunming, a city three provinces away.

"They lied to us, Kee Ngai, they lied. You know what I believed about the Communists before; well, many things were different. They have class distinction in the army. The higher the rank, the more food rations and servants they have. High-ranking officers eat four-dish meals every day. They have chicken, beef, vegetables, and soup. We ordinary soldiers ate only one dish and a bowl of soup. We saw only a thin slice of pork once a week."

It couldn't be true and yet, he had lost so much weight. Besides, my brother didn't lie. I trusted him. But I didn't want to believe what he was telling me. I didn't want to give up on the only hope for China.

"There was no equality between soldiers and officers. They used us as servants and bodyguards for the high-ranking officers. The officers scolded us. They even slapped us. They didn't train us to be cadres. We were just free labour for them. Those officers are as corrupt as the ones I saw in Guilin. Many, many of the recruits deserted. I wasn't the only one."

Disillusioned by the abuses, K.K. had simply walked away from the base. It took him months to walk the nine hundred miles back home. He told me about the kind strangers who gave him food and clothes. I shuddered at the thought of dogs chasing him and all the nights he had slept in ditches and fields. The stark, intense pleas he lobbed at me threatened to explode my world. K.K. made up in earnestness what he lacked in debating skill. He wanted to save his little brother.

"Kee Ngai, the Communists deceived us with their propaganda. All those ideas and stories in *Xinhua News* and *Wah Shang News*—they were just good propaganda. The reality is totally different from what they told us."

We talked until four o'clock in the morning. His stories confused and frightened me. I tried to explain them away as isolated incidents and misunderstandings. Never one to argue, my brother finally stopped talking altogether. In the days that followed, he spent hours sitting by himself, saying nothing to anyone, paying rapt attention only to his fingertips. He listened to Western classical music on the Rediffusion unit. Sometimes, he grew agitated and anxious, even angry with me. Other times, he tried patient persuasion. We couldn't agree. He wanted me to see his truth about the Communists and I wanted him to see mine.

By this time, the Communist Youth League through Leung had transferred me to study in a new right-wing school, Kwong Tai Senior High School. I had told Mama that Kwong Tai had a better academic reputation than Oriental, and she was too busy with her practice and Mei Mei to investigate. At Kwong Tai, I had a new contact, Foo, an honest-looking fellow with a warm face. He always carried an umbrella, rain or shine—because of his weak constitution, I assumed. He was all right, but he wasn't Leung. I felt a sense of loyalty to Leung.

When I questioned Foo about K.K.'s experiences in China, he mumbled something about not listening to right-wing traitors. His response did nothing to dispel my doubts. I pressed him for answers. "What if someone is killed by his own people? Would the Party kill its own comrades?" I asked. My old fears from Anlong resurfaced.

"Trust the Party. This won't happen inside the Party," Foo smiled blandly.

I wasn't convinced. K.K. had never lied to me. Yet, I fervently believed only the Communist Party could save China and its poor. *Was it possible that Communist officers could execute their own men as the Kuomintang had? Would a corrupt Communist government betray its people too?* Confused and troubled, I now moped nearly as often as K.K. did.

One day, the phone rang. It was Leung, asking whether he could visit. *Could he?* My heart leapt. Leung would make everything clear again. He had to. I trusted him more than anyone else I knew in the Party. Once or twice we had passed each other on the street, but true to our oaths as part of the Communist underground, we pretended not to recognize each other. It had been so hard not to greet him, to ask him for answers. Though I still considered Leung a friend, we could meet only under Party orders. *How did he know I needed to talk?* Superiors, I began to realize, knew everything about their charges.

After listening patiently as I described K.K.'s gruelling months in China, Leung remained unimpressed. "Your brother was weak. He couldn't tolerate hardship," he concluded.

I couldn't accept that. K.K. worked harder and endured pain better than anyone I knew. During the war, while we retreated from one town to another, K.K. lifted our luggage and carried the water—the heaviest jobs. He needed only a few bowls of rice to fill his stomach, nothing else.

Sensing my disbelief, Leung continued, "But I'm not surprised inequality exists. Anything can happen in such a huge troop of cadres. This proves we should work harder to correct our mistakes."

Now, that made more sense. I went home relieved. I loved my brother and wanted to save him from his false ideas. He was also my fellow countryman. As a member of the Communist Youth League, I was responsible for the welfare of my comrades. Pulling K.K. to one side, I tried to reason with him: "You know, it's not surprising you encountered these incidents in the People's Liberation Army. Just think. All the members of the troop came from different places. They had different life experiences and education. Some of them had no education at all."

My brother agreed that some of the officers were poorly educated. One fellow had tried to light his cigarette on a light bulb. *"Ta ma da!"* the man cursed. "Fire is light, light is fire. Why can't I light my cigarette?"

"Maybe you came across a few crooked individuals," I suggested. "That doesn't mean Communism is bad. Our duty is to fight these corrupt officials. After all, the revolution is against all evil, even within our own troops."

Bit by bit, I laid a foundation for renewed faith in our cause. With daily news of victories—the Communists had by this time taken

Shanghai and Chongqing—the political mood in Hong Kong began to swing more to the left. On the streets, the newspaper boys shouted the latest headlines: "Special edition! People's Liberation Army takes Guangzhou!" "Guangzhou is free!"

All over the city, people talked excitedly. Even at the market, shoppers and vendors had heated discussions. Some said the Chinese army wouldn't stop at the Shenzhen River border: it would march straight into the colony. As proof, some pointed out the fact that a few right-wing schools in Hong Kong had hoisted the Communists' flag.

Even in our little store on Temple Street, Mama, the tailors, the servants, and K.K. and I were having fervent debates about the future. Would the People's Liberation Army come and liberate Hong Kong? On the street, neighbours holding that day's special edition of the newspaper stopped K.K. and me to talk. Everybody was enthused.

K.K. began to hope again.

Then came the announcement from their capital in Beijing: the Communists proclaimed themselves the People's Central Government. October 1, 1949, would be the first National Day of the People's Republic of China. The Kuomintang Nationalists had been defeated.

Hong Kong's left-wing groups celebrated the historic event in Kowloon's Astor Theatre. It was a momentous thing for left-leaning citizens to celebrate such a day openly in British-ruled Hong Kong. Such left-wing celebrations had never taken place there before. I took K.K. with me.

The theatre's one thousand seats were filled. We were surrounded by other impassioned young people. Dozens of red flags, emblazoned with the republic's five-star emblem, created a dramatic backdrop. A massive red banner hung on the walls, encircling us in a sea of red. About two dozen representatives of trade unions and workers' societies sat on the stage, ready to host the celebration.

A band playing traditional Chinese instruments struck the first notes to "The East Is Red." We stood up and began to sing. China's new national anthem, "March of Volunteers," followed. This was a

Sino-Japanese war resistance song, a passionate melody that every Chinese person knew. A tear rolled down my brother's cheek; stirred to the depths of my heart, I wept too.

One speaker shared his vision for China. K.K. nodded his approval for the new direction of our country. Another speaker exhorted the left-wing masses in Hong Kong to fulfill their duty. My brother's flushed face revealed his excitement.

We cheered and clapped for the dances, skits, and songs about the revolution. Then, clasping each other's hand, we joined in a rousing chorus of "Sing, Beloved Country."

The next day, K.K. bought a copy of *Wah Shang News*. He even began planning for his future. "I don't want to finish high school," he confided to me. "I like fixing things. Maybe I'll take vocational training."

Six months later, when K.K. had finished his courses in auto repair and electronics, I encouraged him to teach at the left-wing Mongkok Workers' Children School. It was, Leung had assured me, the perfect job for K.K. "You'll be teaching electronics," I pointed out, then added, "Of course, it doesn't pay much." Whereas a public school teacher earned two hundred Hong Kong dollars a month, the Workers' Children School paid a monthly salary of only eighty dollars.

"I don't care about pay," K.K. said.

"I know you don't. That's why I suggested it. You'll be teaching the children of struggling, underpaid workers. That's just like fighting for our country."

K.K. agreed. Leung made the arrangements. My brother was safe—safe again under Communist philosophy.

We were not the only people in Hong Kong swept up by the left-wing fervour. The unions were gaining strength, too. The Tramway Workers' Union, in particular, grew bolder in its demands for fair wages and better working hours. The tram operators claimed they did not have enough time off to eat a meal. Many ate while driving and developed stomach ulcers. They also had to stand the entire shift and were not allowed washroom breaks.

The British-owned Hong Kong Tram Company, however, refused to give in, as it saw the union as a threat to its stability and power. The company had full support from the British Hong Kong government, which provided policing. A right-wing worker's union, representing only twenty percent of the tram workers, tried to negotiate a contract on behalf of all the workers. By January 1950, the dispute had exploded into a full-scale strike.

The tram company occupied the whole south block of Russell Street. Its building on the south side of the road was used as the administration office and streetcar loop. On the north side stood a four-storey privately owned residential building, the flats rented mostly by the tram workers and their families. The Tramway Workers' Union was headquartered in a flat on the fourth floor. On the ground floor were grocery and hardware shops, and in front of these, vegetable, meat, and fish stalls, as well as food stands selling wonton soup and fried noodles. The streetcar rails lay in the middle of this busy street. Even though no vehicles except the tramcars going through the loop were allowed on the street, it was always hectic.

To mark the strike, the Tramway Workers' Union hung banners from its balconies. Strikers and workers from supporting unions clogged the street and prevented trams from entering or leaving the station. It had always been illegal in Hong Kong to strike, and the local police, a mix of Chinese, Indian, and British, soon converged on Russell Street to arrest the strikers and those blocking the trams' movement. The strikers fought back, injuring a British officer and a few Chinese policemen. British troops, based in the New Territories, were called in to assist. They sealed off the street and cleared it of vendors and pedestrians. Using clubs and tear gas, the troops fought the striking union workers, who retreated into the buildings. With only the police and troops on the street, the residents threw pans, cutting boards, flowerpots, and chairs onto the heads below.

The executive committee of Hong Kong's thirty-eight left-wing youth societies called an emergency meeting to discuss the situation. The Communists had created these societies covertly after World War II. They organized the youth, young workers, and students of Hong Kong, creating many groups with different interests: choir, band, drama, reading, writing, folk dancing, and hiking. Each youth society rented space for offices and gatherings. By 1949, we had thousands of participants. The societies often held joint social events and performances. As I represented the Mong Kok district in the Literature Youth Fellowship Association, I was asked to attend the meeting. I had, of course, never disclosed my Communist Youth League membership to the other youths and young workers.

"By suppressing the tram workers, the police are showing force to all left-wing groups," said one of the executives.

"They're just testing us. They want to see what the new Communist government will do," replied another.

We concluded that we needed not only to show solidarity but to stand up to this harassment by imperialistic Britain. On January 31, two hundred youth society representatives assembled at the Hung Hom ferry terminal in Kowloon. We were on our way to a "comfort meeting" to offer support to the striking union members. We ferried across to the Hong Kong side and began the thirty-minute walk to Russell Street. In our white short-sleeved shirts and grey cotton slacks and skirts, we looked like a school choir.

A barbed-wire barricade greeted us at the edge of the strike zone. The small opening the police had left for local residents to pass through reminded me of the narrow gate in the Japanese barricades that day Mama and I visited Uncle. Although the union had obtained a permit to hold the meeting, the British troops and Hong Kong police wouldn't let us through. Thousands of people from other unions, youth associations, and left-wing groups milled about. Even local residents joined the crowd. Corruption on the force and its mistreatment of the poor had led to widespread resentment of the police, and it was not uncommon for ordinary citizens to join in skirmishes with them. Indeed, there were weekly brawls, which were always reported in the newspapers. A brawl was what the police feared amid this swelling crowd, and so they kept us outside the fenced-off area.

The Tramway Workers' Union was holding its mass meeting on the rooftop. Union representatives emerged to negotiate with the police to let us through the barricade. As the union members led us toward a stairway, a fight broke out on the street. The police beat back the strikers with clubs. The demonstrators responded by breaking tables and chairs from a nearby restaurant and defending themselves with the splintered furniture. From their upper-floor flats, residents threw flowerpots and other heavy objects to hamper the police. The scene terrified me. I had no weapon, not even a table leg. *How can I fight with my bare hands?* I was saved by a group of burly men who appeared beside us and escorted us to the rooftop.

Including us, there were about two thousand people at the meeting. We did our best to encourage the strikers. The fighting had been going on sporadically all day, a union representative explained. "We fought them back to their miserable barricades and we seized the main gate of the tram station," he said smugly.

A stage was set up and a youth group had prepared a presentation. There were encouraging speeches and a choir sang. I could see the workers were excited to have so much support, that they were not forgotten. As I was watching the performers, I heard screams and shots.

"They're coming," someone shouted.

"Let them up. We'll teach them a lesson," another worker cried belligerently.

Something hissed and exploded at the back of the crowd.

"Tear gas. Trench mortars," muttered a man near me.

"Get the young people out of here. Clear them out—*now*," a union leader ordered. He wanted to protect the representatives of the youth societies, as well as those from the other unions. After long negotiations, the British troops and police agreed to a thirty-minute truce that would allow us to leave. And so, the youth association delegates escaped before the real fighting began.

Aboard the ferry home, we slapped each other on the back. I felt so brave. More than two hundred of us youths rushed onto the third-class deck. There were few seats there, but we didn't care. We performed folk dances, including the northern Chinese Yeung Kor,* as we circled the engine room and sang revolutionary songs with gusto. The other passengers had heard about the riot and they applauded us and expressed their support. By comforting the strikers, we had stood up to the foreign devils and their local running dogs, the corruption-riddled police force.

I arrived at Temple Street a few minutes past one o'clock in the morning. Ah Sim opened the door when I knocked. Mama was waiting. "Did you get a good taste of tear gas?" she asked dryly. But I saw the faintest of twinkles in her eye. "I was worried about you. Have something to eat."

Relieved that she wasn't furious, I drank the soup Ah Sim had made. "The vegetable soup will clear the tear gas poison out of your system," Mama said. She listened with interest when I told her what had happened—how we arrived at the barricade, the meeting on the rooftop, the fight, and how we sang and danced on the ferry coming home.

---

* Yeung Kor is a northern China folk dance that was popular in the liberated areas before 1949. In Hong Kong this type of dance was recognized as representative of the leftists, the Eighth Route Army, and the Communists. It was performed only at left-wing gatherings and not on the street or in any public areas. In 1949, as the victory of the People's Liberation Army swept across China and then later the area bordering Hong Kong was liberated, many Chinese became supportive of the Communists, hoping they would build a strong China. After this time, Yeung Kor was often performed openly, and we did, on the ferry back from Macau.

"Just be careful," she said.

As I sat on my bed and gulped down my dinner, I mused about how I had passed a crucial test. "With a bit more training, I'll have enough confidence to fight for my country," I declared out loud to the empty room. K.K. was not with me that night; he had already moved to the Workers' Children School.

The riot lasted thirty hours. When it was over, two British policemen, many local officers, and many workers were injured. The government responded by cracking down on the left-wing societies. Although they sensed our powerful influence, they hadn't realized how quickly we could mobilize our people. Perhaps we had made a mistake by showing our strength.

The police raided the offices of the youth societies and arrested left-wing leaders, including a school principal. They issued an order to each of the thirty-eight societies, cancelling their operating licences. They suggested that the societies reregister under the newly passed Societies Law. But no one trusted reregistration: that was just a right-wing ploy to monitor our activities. The government, we were convinced, was secretly supporting the Kuomintang. Instead, the societies chose to close down altogether.

The British thought it was time to suppress the leftists before we became too strong. The government believed in balancing the Nationalists and Communists. Of the two Chinese police chiefs, one was left-wing and the other right-wing. The superior chief was British, of course, and was presumed to be neutral. As the British looked for Communist spies, the situation in Hong Kong grew tense.

"Be careful, the situation is getting worse," Foo warned me. "If anything happens, run away. Do not get arrested. Don't sleep too deeply at night. Be alert for any noise and prepare to run." He told me to clear out my left-wing papers. I became keenly aware of the cardinal rule: do not betray the Party or your comrades.

That evening I went through my books, magazines, and newspaper clippings. I burned many of my photographs. Early the next morning,

I hauled several full boxes to the nearest garbage collection spot where I knew the pick-up would be that morning.

Then one day, Foo had nothing more to tell me. It was the summer of 1951, and we were supposed to meet at the monument in front of the Diocesan Girls' School on Jordan Road at precisely 4:30 P.M. When I joined the Youth League, Leung had given several instructions: meet contacts in a public place, wait no more than ten minutes, watch out for spies who might follow, don't greet any comrade who has no direct contact with you, and when making appointments over the phone, subtract one unit of measure from the day and hour. I was told not to ask unrelated questions at the meetings: if the Party wanted me to know something, it would let me know.

I waited fifteen minutes for Foo, despite Party instructions. *Anything could have happened. He may have been shot. This could be a trap. I should leave.* Yet, I reasoned, perhaps Foo had only been delayed by traffic. But he never showed.

Every Thursday, at the same time, at the same spot, I waited. I came to memorize every detail of the granite obelisk in the centre of that rectangular enclosure. I toyed with the thick iron chains strung between the concrete pillars marking the boundaries. The pillars matched the grey of the granite stonework. The girls in their neatly pressed uniforms would glance at me as they passed by. Half curious, half wary, they edged past me. Who knew why this young man with the melancholy, fretful expression showed up week after week? Perhaps his lover had abandoned him.

After three months of waiting for word from my beloved Party, I had to accept that I had lost contact and was now alone.

8

WHERE ARE THE COMMUNISTS?

1952–1957   Hong Kong, British colony

On a Saturday afternoon in March 1952, a wiry man dressed in a rumpled Chinese tunic, as was post-liberation style, stepped into the tailor shop. The hunch of his shoulders made him appear elderly but his skin—though sagging and etched with worry—did not yet crinkle with age. Each of his arms dragged a large suitcase, and a long black umbrella hung from one wrist. Miss Chan looked up.

"May I help you?" she asked.

The tailors at their table paused in their labour. All eyes rested on the stranger.

Then I spoke up. "Father."

Yes, yes, this was my father. Had it really been seven years since we had seen each other? After the war in 1945, Father had continued to work for the Bank of China in Sun Cheong. The rest of us had coped well enough without him, and I was now nineteen years old.

"Have you eaten?" we asked.

He looked relieved as he sat down at the kitchen table and Ah Sim poured him tea before going off to heat up congee and preserved vegetables.

"What is the situation like here?" he asked. He hadn't been in Hong Kong for twelve years. He wanted to know if he should expect any problems in the area.

"There's no trouble in this district. No gangs and not much crime," I answered.

Why was he here? Had he left his job in Sun Cheong? He had to escape, he said. No one expected the Chinese-British border near Kowloon to remain open for much longer. As it turned out, he crossed over just in time—the border closed two months later.

"Leave while you can," a friend had warned him. "Those Communists will destroy anyone who is not a local or who has overseas relations. You'll be labelled a traitor."

"So what are you going to do now?" I asked.

"Work for my old friend Mr. Seto. He is the sole proprietor of a Sino-British gasoline company. I start on Monday."

He stretched out his legs, leaned back in his chair, and reflected on an eventful past. "I was lucky. Before Swatow fell to the Japanese, I came to Hong Kong. Before Hong Kong fell to the Japanese, I went to Taishan. Before Taishan fell, I went to Wuzhou, and before Wuzhou fell, I went to Chongqing. Now, before the Communists ruin Sun Cheong, I've escaped back here to Hong Kong."

There was no point arguing with him about Communism.

Mei Mei showed him her new school uniforms: a dark blue woolen pinafore for winter, a white linen sailor-style dress, complete with stripes, for summer.

"Good girl! St. Mary's has a good reputation," Father enthused. "Study hard while you have the chance to go to school. I finished Form Three with Honours, second in my class, and was offered a scholarship to St. Paul's Co-Educational School. But your grandfather didn't allow me to continue. He ordered me to learn business at his company instead.

"I could've worked for your grandfather's import-and-export business and inherited my portion of shares in the company. It would've been worth a handsome amount. But even in the early years, when I worked for the Supreme Court, I decided not to work for my father nor take my share of the inheritance. I didn't want to quarrel with the concubines' families and siblings over money.

"No, I had no need for that," Father reflected. "I found work on my own."

Father seemed genuinely pleased with Mei Mei. "You'll have no trouble finding work when you graduate. So, how's that leg doing?" We were quiet as Father gently examined the scarred stump. "If only your mother had had enough sense to take better care of you, you would still have both legs. If only I could've been here. Maybe if I hadn't moved to Taishan ..."

I knew it was not Mama's fault, but it was not my place to talk back to Father. I kept silent.

"Where is your mother?" Father asked.

"Out," said Mei Mei.

"She's seeing patients," I added.

My father nodded.

Mama worked long hours to pay for Mei Mei's expenses. She had even hired a tutor to ensure my sister would be accepted into St. Mary's, a prominent Catholic school. Without Mama's earnings, Mei Mei wouldn't have such opportunities. "She's a cripple now," Mama had said. "She'll need the best education to survive in Hong Kong."

In the days that followed, I realized that, having lived apart for so much of their marriage, my parents no longer knew each other. All the same, when Father returned, they shared the bedroom and Mei Mei turned the patient examination room into her bedroom. Mama created another space for the exam room.

When I told Father about my studies at Wellingdon English College, he was pleased. "Good, good. You must perfect your English. You did the right thing," he said. It was comforting to hear his approval. At least someone approved. Ever since the Youth League had cut off contact with me so abruptly last year, I had felt like a riderless horse wandering far from any known path. I was willing to serve, but lacked direction and leadership. My last instructions from the Youth League were to remain a student as long as possible, to recruit other students, and to stay in Hong Kong. Wellingdon College allowed me to do all that while I patiently awaited further instructions.

Father was less pleased, however, with K.K. working and living at a left-wing school. "Don't be foolish," he warned my brother when he came for a visit. "In 1924, I was there in Swatow and I saw what the Communist troops did under Zhou Enlai. They beat the locals and burned down buildings. The Chinese Communists and Kuomintang were the same gang but with different brand names. They just lie to young people."

K.K. reacted swiftly and angrily. A familiar red stain crept up his throat and across his face as he swallowed hard. "H-h-how ca-ca-can you ... How can you say that? The Kuomintang murder their own men. Their officers are corrupt."

"And you really think the Communists are any different? You'll see."

"Those are just a few individuals. The Eighth Route Army saved our people."

"The successful becomes king, the failed becomes a bandit."

They argued until their voices went hoarse. Mama tried to defend K.K., who was never good at winning an argument.

"'On Nanjing Road in Shanghai, a company of Communist soldiers sleep on the street, rather than break into people's houses. They abide by the Eighth Route Army rules,'" she quoted from a newspaper article I had shown her.

"Don't parrot what you don't understand," Father dismissed her with a snort.

I kept my own counsel. Joining the debate would still not convince my father and only expose my position. *Father was seriously against the Communists. I'd better not reveal anything to him.* I agreed with him that corruption was a terrible thing and that we should do all we could to save the people. Afterward, I soothed K.K. with assurances that the only true hope for China rested with the Communists. Father, we decided, was a counter-revolutionary and not to be trusted. From that day on, we hid our left-wing materials from him.

"Don't be like your brother," Father warned me. "Don't believe the Communists. Just concentrate on your studies. You've always wanted to be a doctor. Why don't you study medicine?"

"I'm not sure if my marks are good enough for Hong Kong University."

"Well, I can't afford HKU anyway. That would cost my entire salary. How about Taiwan? I could send you to study medicine in Taiwan."

How I longed to be a doctor. It was my dream ever since I could remember. Things had come so naturally to me when I helped Mama take care of her patients during the war. If I became a doctor, I could help people's suffering in practical ways. But as a Communist Youth League member, I reminded myself, I was also helping with the revolution. The strength of an organization, I was taught, depends on the unity of the members. A member must be an obedient tool for the Party, allowing the leader to freely direct. I wanted to be obedient.

I knew the Communist Youth League would not allow me to go to Taiwan. It had already ordered me to stay in Hong Kong. Besides, I might be arrested as a Communist spy in Kuomintang Taiwan. A loyal soldier must sacrifice his own desires for the good of his country. The Party needed me to continue my efforts here. I had to stay.

Disappointment clogged my throat, but I kept my tone nonchalant. "No, Chung Chi College will be fine."

"Are you sure you want to go there?"

My unadorned "yes" did not please him. He was proud of my academic achievements. They seemed to compensate for K.K.'s choices. Yet, my decision to stay in Hong Kong made no sense to him. A full scholarship from Chung Chi, however, eased his displeasure.

Chung Chi, meaning "Worshipping Christ," was a private Protestant college that in academic standards ranked second only to Hong Kong University. Being practical, I decided to major in economics and business administration in the hopes of getting a good government job. Without any Youth League contacts to caution me, and with extra change in my pocket, I indulged in my college life, and my love for sports and classical music. I participated in weightlifting, fencing, sail boating, and rowing. Working at a temporary job at the college, I earned a few dollars to buy myself a camera and film-developing equipment. At home, between the front window showcase and the tailors' table, I set up a little darkroom for my hobby. I attended classical music concerts. I bought a phonograph and classical records.

In my second year at college, the school's Christian fellowship invited students to teach in the evenings at its free elementary school, the Chung Chi College Free Primary Evening School, which was for children whose families were unable to pay school fees. *What a great opportunity to help the poor*. I joined thirty schoolmates to teach from 6:30 P.M. to 9 P.M. during the week. It was rewarding to help these children in some small way. After teaching, we teachers would go to Canton Road squatter market, near my grandfather's old flat in Kowloon, to buy dinner from the food stalls—noodle soup, fried rice, steamed hot buns. I taught at the free elementary school until I graduated from college.

Without tuition fees to pay, Mama bought me a second-hand British Sunbeam-Talbot car. My friends and I toured the New Territories, dined at late-night restaurants, and saw movies. No one told me these were bourgeois activities. Besides, Kuomintang and various religious groups were at the college trying to convert students. While I enjoyed my activities, I saw them as a means to develop potential recruits, too.

Mei Mei's friends from St. Mary's were also a good source of contacts. Who knew? These giggly high school girls could one day hold important government positions. They often walked Mei Mei home from school; with my sister leaning on her crutch, it took them forty-five minutes to navigate six blocks. Once they reached our flat, they squeezed into Mei Mei's room, where I sometimes joined them for a cola.

Shirley, a Portuguese girl, waved gracefully when I poked my head into the room to say hello. She was a ballet student and it showed. Gliding a step or two toward me, she asked, "Kenneth, have you seen the movie about Charlie Chaplin and the ballerina?"

"The one with Claire Bloom? *Limelight*?"

Shirley nodded.

"Seen it? He's watched it ten times," Mei Mei piped up.

I tried to justify my interest: "Bloom does a beautiful ballet solo in it, at the end, when Chaplin dies. There's something about how the dance communicated her love for the old comedian."

"That's so romantic," sighed Shirley. "I liked the earlier part, when Chaplin gave her up so she could marry that young soldier. I cried at the end."

"Yeah, it was pretty noble," I nodded. After the old artist passed away, the young artist continued dancing. Life goes on. Especially under the glamorous limelight, the old must give way to the young.

In the void left by the Youth League, the movies had become a refuge. Perhaps, like Chaplin's character, the Party had disappeared from my life for my benefit. It was protecting me from government persecution. Even though I felt as abandoned as Terry, Bloom's character, I knew someone would contact me as soon as it was safe to do so.

"Anyone see that other ballet movie, *The Red Shoes*?" I asked.

"Oh yes, I loved it," exclaimed Shirley.

"I saw it with Mei Mei," said Myra, another classmate. Her baby face broke into a grin. "That one was a romantic story, too."

"That poor ballerina," Mei Mei said, "condemned to dance until she died from exhaustion. Just for putting on those red shoes."

"I thought she was beautiful," said Myra. "Especially in that evening gown. You know, in the scene where Lermontov, the ballet company master, summons her."

"That's a great scene," I agreed. "Lermontov asks her, 'Why do you want to dance?' She answers, 'Why do you want to live?' Now that's an artist. I thought the dancing was wonderful, too."

Shirley looked at me thoughtfully for a moment, then said, "So, you liked the ballet?" When I answered yes, she asked, "Would you like to learn, Kenneth? My teacher, Azalea Reynolds—we call her Babs—doesn't charge boys anything, although we girls have to pay thirty dollars a month."

Mei Mei edged forward. "Why don't you take a few lessons and see if you really like it?"

"Hey, Kenneth, it'll be good for you," added Myra. "You love classical music and there's a lot of classical music in ballet."

I didn't need much persuading. Every Tuesday and Thursday evening thereafter, I eagerly showed up at the Azalea Reynolds School of Ballet in my white T-shirt and black tights. There were many girls but only three boys other than me in the class. We, along with two boys at another school, became the first generation of male ballet dancers in Hong Kong.

I made many mistakes in the first months. In particular, I had difficulty with tempo. Because Babs could not afford a pianist, we used a gramophone. Babs counted the beats, "and one, and two, and three, and four."

"One and, two and," I counted, incorrectly emphasizing the full beats as the heavy beats. In ballet jumps, I was to jump up on the heavy beat and land on the light beat. My timing was off whenever I did jeté, battement tendu, grand battement, and échappé.

I greatly admired Babs. She had not only beauty and skill but also an indefinable artistic quality to her dancing. Nevertheless, she was strict and harsh in class. When I fell during a jump and hurt my ankle, she ordered me, without a hint of mercy, to stand up: "What if you fall on stage during a performance; you're just going to lie there? Even if you're hurt and cannot continue, you do your utmost to improvise a few steps. Dance back through the wing to the backstage."

So I learned.

I loved ballet class, enjoying both barre and centre practice, though it was hard work. It was tiring to go to class after a day of studying. But as soon as I stepped into the studio, my fatigue disappeared. Placing my right hand on the barre, chin up, back straight, all I felt was pride. I was proud to be a male dancer. As my spirit rose, I found I had all the strength and energy needed for the two-hour class.

Within a couple of years, I had moved into the advanced class. To me, ballet was sacred and inviolable. The girls in the class were beautiful and I liked them. But I didn't know if any of them were Youth League members, so I did not pursue any as a girlfriend.

I was studying for final exams one afternoon when I heard Mei Mei and her friends come home. Snatches of their conversation drifted to me long before their faces appeared.

"My favourite is still *Three Coins in the Fountain*."

"What about *The Last Waltz*?"

"Not bad."

"Is it ever hot today. This cola is perfect."

We had converted the waiting room into an examination room, where I did my homework when Mama wasn't receiving patients. The girls had to pass through my temporary study to reach Mei Mei's bedroom. Myra and Shirley greeted me as they traipsed through.

"Tired from yesterday's rehearsal?" I asked Shirley. "Babs wasn't pleased."

"Exhausted, but today's better. How about you?"

"Very tired. Grand jeté, cabrioles, and those développé at the barre ... My muscles ache, but I enjoyed it."

"Yeah, my toes hurt from standing on pointe so much. There's a lot of pirouettes and arabesques in *Arabian Nights*."

"Is *Arabian Nights* your next performance?" Myra asked.

Shirley nodded. "The newspapers have announced it already. We're performing next month at the Lock Kung Theatre in Tsim Sha Tsui."

Myra was impressed. "Wow, the Lock Kung? That's the biggest theatre in Kowloon. How much for a ticket?"

"Can we see the dress rehearsal?" asked Mei Mei. "That'll save us paying for tickets."

We promised to check. Myra turned to me. "Say, Kenneth, if you like ballet so much, why don't you join a dance club?"

"What dance club? I don't like ballroom dancing." To me, only ballet offered purity of line and could be deemed true art. I had no interest in pursuing other kinds of dancing, even if only to socialize.

"It's not ballroom dancing," Myra assured me. "Have you heard of the Hok Yau Dance Club?"

"No," I lied. I knew a lot about the Hok Yau Chinese and Western Dance Study Club. "Hok Yau" meant "student fellowship." Serious dance study was not done at this club. Instead, it was a recruiting tool of the Communists to attract students from right-wing schools. The leaders, I had guessed, were Communists. Perhaps Myra was also secretly a leftist. Mei Mei might have told her I was sympathetic to left-wing views. Had I found a comrade? To be safe, I pretended to know nothing about the club.

"It isn't a left-wing club, is it?" asked Mei Mei, ever suspicious of my leftist leanings. She agreed with Father that Communists could not be trusted.

"Nope," said Myra. "They don't discuss politics. It's just a place for students to spend their free time."

"Don't get my brother mixed up with any gangs."

"Don't worry, it isn't what you think. Most of the members are top students from the best schools. They sing and learn folk dances, that's all." Turning back to me, Myra said, "They'll have a picnic next Sunday at Castle Peak. It costs only a dollar for bus fare and food. Why don't you go and see for yourself?"

"Sounds great."

"I'll go to the picnic too and introduce you. Everyone there is so friendly and helpful."

Even while accepting her invitation, I tried to disguise my excitement. This would be a good chance to stay involved with a left-wing group. *Yes, I can do something for my country.*

As promised, no one discussed politics at the picnic. We played games, performed folk dances, and sang Chinese and Western folksongs. Many of the club members invited me to their Saturday evening get-together. The following Saturday, hoping to meet some comrades, I arrived at 129 Yen Chow Street in Kowloon at the appointed time. I climbed to the fourth floor and knocked on the door. It opened into a spacious room where a few dozen young people were gathered. Many of them I had already met at the picnic. Again, we did not talk about how to ease the pain of the world's poor or about the growing corruption within the Hong Kong police department. Instead, we sang folksongs and then moved to the rooftop to practise Chinese folk dances. The discussion as we wound down for the evening revolved around plans for the following weekend. *Where are the Communists?* Even here, I concluded, left-wing activities remained secretive. *My comrades cannot risk exposing their true identities.*

Even though Communism itself could not be made illegal in Hong Kong, Communist activities could be, and were. People could buy left-wing newspapers and books from China Emporium, a Chinese-owned department store, or from Triad Books, or Student Book Store, but it was rumoured that these stores were under constant surveillance by plainclothes policemen. Many people avoided even walking in front of these stores. Besides, there was a general dislike by the public of those who were openly left wing. So it made sense that Hok Yau maintained a neutral front.

I was certain I had comrades at the club. Someday, I thought, the Youth League would call me into service again. But since I still had had no contact with it, I was unable to do any recruiting other than, perhaps, by way of making friends. And staying involved with Hok Yau would make it easier for my contact to locate me. So I settled into life at school, my ballet classes, Hok Yau, and waited. And waited.

It had been almost six years and I still had not been contacted.

I graduated from Chung Chi College in 1956. That summer, I took a job with the Church World Service to help the poor in areas like Hong Kong's Shek Kip Mei village—situated on the hillside adjacent to the public housing of Shep Kip Mei Estate—where the city's poorest squatters lived. My role was to investigate applicants, people who had applied for aid. Did they truly need assistance? The answer broke my heart.

On a wickedly hot day, I approached a tiny shack cobbled together from cardboard and plastic sheets. *Six people live here? It's smaller than Mama's bedroom.* Yards from the door, a stench sent me reeling. I held my breath and fought off waves of nausea as I picked my way through the mud left by the rains the day before. Sidestepping piles of manure, I peered inside, only to be greeted by two hogs. That explained the manure and some of the stench. Walking carefully among the scraps of tattered cardboard scattered across the churned-mud floor, I approached the elderly woman curled up on a bamboo mat. A bed for four, she told me. Above the pigpen was a smaller bed for two.

A six-year-old boy dodged past me, baby sister in tow. They were going to fetch water from the tap down the hill. "If anyone hits you, run," his grandmother called after him. She shook her head, "When it gets hot and there's no water, people fight."

The children's parents had found casual work this day. The old woman quoted a proverb: "Hand stop, mouth stop." No work, no food.

Keeping my breaths shallow to avoid inhaling the putrid odours, I nodded sympathetically. I left as quickly as I could without appearing rude. This family was only one of thousands clamouring for survival in this shantytown. Most were immigrants from China. Depending on the location, they paid as much as one or two hundred Hong Kong dollars—almost as much as a junior clerk's monthly salary—in protection money to local gangs for the right to squat on an eight-by-ten-foot patch of land. The police did nothing to protect them.

Even in the high-density social housing nearby, built a few years earlier after a fire had wiped out most of the makeshift huts, people lived a hellish existence. With only one communal bathroom on each floor, the dimly lit high-rises provided the perfect setting for rapes and grisly gang-related executions. The newspapers reported such crimes daily.

In those days, the late 1950s and early 1960s, the people of Hong Kong had no civil rights to speak of. The police could do whatever they saw fit. Firefighters would wait for bribes before attempting rescues: no money, no water. Government officials treated the public as worthless, despicable people. Corruption was rampant throughout the city.

There was also a high unemployment rate; even for someone possessing skills, jobs were scarce. Many of the poor resorted to street vending—selling noodles, clothes, or vegetables from a wooden cart. They obtained the merchandise on credit and then sold it, earning the difference. The government strictly enforced its law against street vending, and the police frequently beat or arrested vendors. This, of course, resulted in deep resentment from the poor. Street vending was the only way most of them could earn a living, as humble as it was.

If a street vendor did not run quickly enough at the first warning cry of *Jau kwai!—Run! Cops!*—he faced jail and fines. The police beat, kicked, scolded, and slapped at their discretion. A vendor might beg for mercy; inside, he nursed a death wish for his persecutors. And once he was captured, his property was confiscated. He was left with nothing. Again, the newspapers reported the all too common suicides and devastation of vendors' families.

People unable to pay for private medical care, meanwhile, lined up for hours at the free clinics. For vaccinations, men, women, and children queued and bared their bottoms in public. Nurses rudely injected needles and then shoved patients away before they could pull up their pants.

People blamed their misery on the British imperialists and their lackeys, the police, whether Chinese, Indian, or British. Life for the poor was apparently no better under British rule than it was under Kuomintang rule. People merely had the freedom to starve and rot as they wished.

The humiliation of decades of foreign rule made it easy to galvanize mobs to attack the police. Nothing seemed to have changed since the Tramway Workers' Union strike six years earlier, and this continued bitterness fuelled public support for the Kowloon riot.

On October 10, 1956, right-wing supporters in Hong Kong celebrated Taiwan Kuomintang Republic of China's National Day—the Double Ten festival. The British turned a blind eye to the festivities, as they had no diplomatic relations with Taiwan as an independent nation. That day, the Kuomintang activists draped four-storey-high Nationalist flags on the seven-storey high-rises in Kowloon's Li Cheng UK Estate, another public housing development, in a show of support. The city's left-wing newspaper reported that Kuomintang supporters ripped a few of their own flags and then accused left-wing groups of vandalism. They then attacked left-wing schools and the offices of workers' unions.

At about 10 o'clock that morning, I was walking along Nathan Road, five blocks or so from Li Cheng UK Estate, when I saw a group of people shouting and throwing stones at the Mong Kok police station. It soon turned into a full-scale riot that lasted a week. According to a Hong Kong Radio news release, an estate official removed a Nationalist flag, which led to rioting by pro-Kuomintang groups.

Under pressure from Beijing, Britain two days later sent in troops and armoured vehicles from its army base in the New Territories. Once again in our city barbed-wire barricades sprang up and soldiers enforced a curfew. Beijing voiced its concern about the rioting and said it would send in China's People's Liberation Army if the British were unable to protect the Chinese people. In response to Beijing and to protect the left-wing institutes, British troops and the police cordoned off riot areas and left-wing institutions, including Heung To middle school, Kowloon Bus Workers' Union, Hong Kong Government Clerk's Association, and Mongkok Workers' Children School. The left-wing press, however, reported that several institutes— the labour unions in Kowloon, the trade union clinics in Tsuen Wan district—and parts of Kowloon were left unprotected. Many union staff were reported killed, and there were further reports of clinic nurses being raped and killed.

"They've blocked off access to the school," K.K. told me over the phone. "No one can come or go."

Mongkok Workers' Children School, like other institutions, had asked staff members to stay and guard the premises against rioters. The school, however, did not have enough food for the teachers and students behind the barricades.

"We need rice, Kee Ngai. We don't know how long this riot will last."

"How much?"

"The more the better."

I told Mama I was going to buy and deliver rice to K.K.'s school. "They've been surrounded for two days and don't know how long this riot will last. Many students and teachers are preparing to fight off vandals, but they're running out of food."

"Don't go; it'll be dangerous. What if a rioter beats you up?" said Mama. Still, Mama was worried about K.K. too. Finally, she relented. "I'll go with you. They might hurt a man, but they won't attack a woman. Since the British soldiers are surrounding the school, Mei Mei can come along to translate. Her English is better than yours."

Although Mei Mei didn't approve of leftists, she agreed to come along.

"We want to buy a two-hundred-pound sack of rice and drop it off at the Mongkok Workers' Children School," I informed the taxi driver. I wanted to be sure of his cooperation before we set out. The last thing we needed was for him to abandon us somewhere.

A block from the school, British soldiers stopped us in front of a barricade. One aimed a machine gun at us. "Where are you going?" he barked.

"Good afternoon, sir," Mei Mei greeted him politely, explaining our mission in fluent English. He checked the rice in the trunk and waved us on. When we came to the police barricade, it was Mama's turn. With a smile, my mother told the officer about the rice. Having observed the British soldier inspect our trunk, he waved us through.

The taxi driver helped me unload the rice outside the school's front gate. K.K. and others waved their thanks from a distance as we sped away. There was no time to talk to K.K.—it was too dangerous to linger in front of a left-wing institute.

The British press and Hong Kong's Chinese press told the same story, that common gangsters had seized the chance to take revenge on underworld enemies. Left-wing papers, on the other hand, accused the government of using Kuomintang supporters to suppress the Communists. I was totally inclined toward the Communists and my stomach churned at the injustice. *What could I do?* I was alone and without resources. Someday, the Party would contact me again and make everything right.

Then that someday came. There was nothing remarkable about the day. The sun did not blaze hotter or brighter, nor did I have any premonition. I was on my way to teach ballet at Hok Yau that evening. Mei Mei stepped through the door, home from her classes at Hong Kong Technical College.

"People are so rude," she fumed. "Ignorant. 'Look, look at the cripple,' they point and smirk. I'm missing a leg, not my ears. I can hear."

It happened often. Housewives at the market, old men at a bus stop, children in the park—every day, people gawked at the girl with the missing leg. Mei Mei usually bore with it, but today bitterness crept into her voice. Ah Sim made sympathetic noises as she brought out Mei Mei's meal. I stretched out a hand to pat my sister on the shoulder just as the phone rang.

"Hello?"

It was Leung! "Thursday at 10 A.M., Honolulu Café." He hung up.

I wasn't expecting my contact to be him, of all people. Besides, I had already been transferred to another superior—Foo. I felt excited and a sense of anticipation.

Just before 9 A.M. that Wednesday—one unit of measure earlier, hour and day, than what we had agreed to over the phone—I stood outside Honolulu Café. When he arrived, Leung issued terse instructions for meeting my new contact, a woman named Chan. Then he was gone. He didn't explain why the Party had not contacted me for so many years. Nor did I ask.

On the appointed day, I made my way to a dim sum house—Mayflower Restaurant on Nathan Road. Dressed in a white shirt and brown slacks as instructed, I watched for a woman in a blue poplin cheongsam. She would wear a white flower in her hair, like a widow. Ten minutes after I sat down, a young woman in her twenties who fit the description walked in. I signalled her. She responded with a smile and joined me.

"Are you looking for *Ha Kau June*?" she asked.

That was my cue. *Ha Kau June* was a book about a young boy's struggles. Popular among students, it contained left-wing sentiments but was not truly Communist. It was a safe subject for a code phrase.

"Yes, I have found the book," was my prearranged response.

Finally, the Communist Youth League reconnected with me. It had been six years. The day was July 15, 1957, and I was twenty-four.

Chan launched into a series of questions. She wanted to know about my activities since 1951: Chung Chi College, learning and teaching ballet, working with the Church World Service, teaching at a Christian free primary school, and joining Hok Yau. She wanted to know whom I had met, what I had done. I told her everything.

"So, what do you think about Hok Yau?" Chan asked.

"I thought it was left wing. I just wanted to help, so I joined its activities."

"Good. Stay there. We will give you further instructions when the time comes."

After two hours of questioning, Chan stood up to leave. She gave me the meeting time and place for the following week and departed.

I sat there with my never-to-be-answered query. There was no further discussion, no explanation for the loss of contact. I comforted myself with the thought that the Party would tell me anything they needed me to know.

My mother, Wai Chi, in Hong Kong, 1953.
(collection of Kenneth Ore)

With my father and older brother, K.K.,
in Swatow, 1936. *(collection of Kenneth Ore)*

My application photo for the Kuomintang young pilot training program in Chongqing, 1944. *(collection of Kenneth Ore)*

In student uniform at the Chinese German High School in Guangzhou, 1947. *(collection of Kenneth Ore)*

Making a speech at a Chung Chi
College society meeting, 1955.
(collection of Kenneth Ore)

Students of the Azalea Reynolds School of Ballet in the opening of
Les Sylphides. The performance was staged at a local theatre
in Kowloon, 1955. I am in the centre. *(collection of Kenneth Ore)*

Dancing as Prince Siegfried in the ballet *Swan Lake*, 1959.
(collection of Kenneth Ore)

Performing a pas de deux with Alice Lee, 1959.
(collection of Kenneth Ore)

My wedding tea party photo with all the Hok Yau young women, 1963.
(collection of Kenneth Ore)

My wedding tea party photo with all the Hok Yau young men, 1963.
(collection of Kenneth Ore)

Jeany Chong and I in a Chinese ballet with music composed by Alfred Lee, 1965. *(collection of Kenneth Ore)*

Jianggashan, 1970. I led a group of Hok Yau activists to China for "study and sightseeing." We were not allowed to take group photos, only individual ones. *(collection of Kenneth Ore)*

9

THREE HANDS OF LEADERSHIP

1958–1965 Hong Kong, British colony

With an empty chair for company, I slouched in my seat and stretched out my legs. A kitchen god peered at me from his perch high in a corner of the diner. Through a cloud of incense and cigarette smoke, the red-and-gold figurine glared his disapproval. No, I did not look dignified, but I was tired of waiting. My tea had grown as tepid as my waiter's welcome. The waiter-cum-bouncer cocked an eyebrow at the lid of the teapot, delicately balancing itself along the handle, a signal that the customer wanted more tea. "Yes," said the eyebrow, "I know you want more tea, but do you really expect to take up a table all day without ordering? This is a restaurant."

Before the waiter could open his mouth, I straightened my spine and hurriedly ordered one of the daily specials scrawled on posters around the room. A plate of something I couldn't afford and didn't care to ingest soon appeared on my table. Another restaurant, another contact, another wasted meal.

Chan had been a lousy superior, often keeping me waiting, forcing me to squander my savings in countless restaurants. Now, my new contact was proving equally unreliable. Big Yung, the favoured son of

148

a wealthy family, lacked dedication and discipline. Like Leung, he had inherited his family's business, a restaurant. Unlike Leung, he did not renounce his capitalistic interests. Yung compromised. And a man who compromises himself cannot expect others to comply with him. This is why he always prefaced Party directives with "I suggest …" After all, who was he to impose Party policies and tactics when he himself did not comply with all the directives? His methods were similar to Confucian principles, not agreeing or disagreeing, never saying yes or no, but instead keeping a balanced middle ground. Behind his back, the members of Hok Yau's secret leadership called Big Yung "Confucius the Second."

I, on the other hand, dedicated myself fully to the Communist cause. I patiently accepted the shortcomings of my superiors while doing exactly as I was told. "It doesn't matter how incompetent they are," I consoled myself, "I'm serving the people. I'm serving the Party."

Many Party and Youth League members had their own agendas for joining. Students from the left-wing schools and trade unionists depended on the Party to provide them with jobs. I did not. Ironically, this was probably why my superiors did not wholly trust me, since I neither wanted nor needed anything from them. Why would a well-educated young man who had so much to gain in the business world join the underground left-wing movement? Meanwhile, few people outside my intimate circle would suspect me of being a Communist. As a college graduate who loved Western classical music and ballet, I had an excellent cover. The Party could use me.

"Good, you're here already," Confucius wheezed. He eased his Buddha-like frame into the seat and gave me a generous smile. After exchanging pleasantries, he asked, as he did at every appointment, "So, any girlfriends?"

"No."

At our first meeting, Confucius had found it hard to believe I could dance so intimately with scantily clad women without being attracted to them. As the months wore on, he accepted my explanation: ballet was my religion. Ballet was like a haven, an escape from my burdens and my memories. The music flooded my being and drove all other thoughts from my mind. In the music and in the dance, I lived.

With a shake of his head, Confucius accepted my customary reply but added, "Well, if you ever consider finding a girlfriend, remember that it is always best to find one of our own, from the Youth League. You cannot work underground otherwise." This meant I would have to try to guess who was and wasn't a member of the Youth League, and then ask my superior for approval.

After helping himself to my untouched meal, Confucius launched into his message. "You know Szeto Wah, of course." I nodded. Szeto lectured on Chinese literature at Hok Yau. That was his cover. His underground assignment was heading up the Shadow Core, the leaders who secretly controlled the club. They reported directly to Leung. Although I was never explicitly told this, it was easy enough for me to guess.

"There have been, how shall I say, differences of opinion between Szeto and the Party ..." Confucius paused. "He has not been following orders for more than a year now."

I drew in a sharp breath. Szeto was a hard worker and seemed trustworthy. *Could it be true?* An operative must never disobey a direct order. Confucius had my full attention.

Szeto, explained Confucius, had wanted to limit Hok Yau's growth. The Party considered 150 members too few. "'If the water is muddy, it is easier to hide more fish,'" said Confucius, quoting a Chinese saying.

Confucius pointed out that, of the 150 members, only 40 or 50 regularly joined the club's activities. As there weren't that many activities, those members bonded as friends and the circle quickly became a closed one. The small number of members was a small pond, unable to hide all the fish from the watchful eyes of the British Hong Kong government. The Party wanted to tap into the club's full potential, using it to infiltrate and network within the right-wing schools to recruit new members. Szeto had disagreed with the Party's directive, instead wanting to work with a small number of potential recruits whom he could devote time to and train well. He demanded a meeting with Leung's superior. I was told he even wanted to plead his case all the way to the Party Central Committee in Beijing.

"The Party has no choice. It has decided to remove him and his followers."

"Remove the Shadow Core?" This information was coming from Confucius, my single contact. I could not verify its authenticity.

Confucius nodded. "And also Szeto's supporters in the open leadership." By "open leadership" he meant the executive committee, the people who publicly led Hok Yau. Every left-wing institution followed this two-handed operational principle. By having both public and secret leaders, the Party maintained control of its organization. Communist Youth League and Party members shared executive positions with sympathetic activists who held no Party affiliation. To outsiders, the executive committee controlled the organization: if anyone asked, the committee always made decisions together and voted on issues—a democratic system. However, since all Shadow Core members were also on the public executive committee, true power rested within the Shadow Core.

To ensure a successful transition of leadership and that their people remained in positions of power, the Party issued an "iron voucher." Before the general elections, the Party would send six hundred or so students from left-wing schools to join the club, just in time to vote. These members would be the "iron voucher" voters who would vote as the Party dictated.

We practised this common Communist tactic at Hok Yau.* Among newcomers to the club was a slender girl wearing horn-rimmed spectacles. Their angular frame gave her a perpetual frown. Tam Wei Yee,

---

* Even after 1997, when the Hong Kong legislative members were "elected" from their local constituencies, the Communists called all left-wing supporters in each district to vote for the "selected" member. Since eligible voters would vote for various candidates or not vote at all, left-wing supporters all voting for the same person in a district could ensure the success of electing the desired candidate.

with her pronounced overbite and twiglike limbs, was not the most glamorous or beautiful young woman at the club, but she was undoubtedly the most driven. All iron-voucher voters soon knew that this enthusiastic leftist would chair the new executive committee. A few of us also knew, through our respective superiors, that she would soon replace Szeto as leader of the Hok Yau Club.

Election day held no surprises. As instructed, our new left-wing members dutifully put Wei Yee and her team in power.

"Their first task," Confucius informed me, "will be to appoint you as secretary of the club."

Soon after their defeat, Szeto and his supporters one by one quietly left the club. In the months that followed, most of the left-wing iron-voucher students also left. They had served their purpose.

Although I was at that time a willing participant of the process, I had for the first time witnessed the Communists' distortion of the electoral process. But I didn't feel it was wrong. I believed the Party was right and knew what was best for Hok Yau and for China.

The Party transferred responsibility for the Shadow Core from Leung to Confucius. Later, I learned that this was because Leung was passing too much information to his underling. He was transferred from the students' movement to the workers' movement, and given the responsibility of running a Young Workers' magazine, a superficially neutral magazine geared toward young people who had graduated and were working but didn't belong to the left-wing workers' unions. Its aim was to draw them to the readers' club that Leung organized.

Although the reshaping of its leadership was now complete, the changes at Hok Yau had only begun. To raise the club's profile and increase membership, the new Shadow Core leaders—me among them—implemented a strategy known as the "united front." We began to cultivate relationships with the press, businesses, and well-known artists in the community. We mounted charity performances in local theatres and encouraged our members to ask their friends to help out. Our willingness to work with a wide range of groups and individuals made us appear politically neutral. Hok Yau, the public believed, was a place where the youth could devote their energy to improving society instead of joining gangs. Our membership exploded in one year from 150 to 800.

As club secretary, I was responsible for building and maintaining this united front. More accurately, my job was to implement whatever the Communist Youth League wanted. Like all appointed secretaries and advisers in Communist-controlled institutions, I reported directly to my superior—Confucius—rather than to the club's official head. Although my powers paralleled those of Wei Yee, the chairperson, she didn't know about all my Youth League activities.*

The Party authorized me to summon any leftists in the club, including those assigned to other leaders. Although Confucius was never at the club, and club members did not know about his role as leader of the Shadow Core or even about the Shadow Core itself, my role as secretary essentially gave him direct access to and control of the club's members. The "two hands" of leadership were in fact three—the public executive committee, the Shadow Core, and me.

Through regular meetings with Hok Yau's secret core, individual contact with core members, and meetings with me, Confucius obtained and verified information about each of the students connected with us, both inside and outside the club. I, the club's secretary, was Confucius's separate hand, and this hand was free to discuss anything with anyone without calling a formal meeting. I discussed things with these other contacts without making it sound as though

---

* "On the mainland [China], every organ of government, every factory and every company—including foreign joint ventures—has a party unit, whose head outranks all other leaders. Politically, party secretaries outrank provincial governors or city mayors. The Chinese organizations in Hong Kong operate the same way, but because the party is technically illegal here, they go by different names." "Hong Kong Facing Communist Secret" by Maggie Farley, *The Vancouver Sun*, March 15, 1997.

I was checking on them—asking in general conversation about their work, health, family, and thoughts on various subjects.

One had to marvel at the details contained in these reports: the person's health, financial situation, academic record, connections with classmates, love affairs, and parents' and siblings' identities and affiliations. Almost everything about everyone connected to the person had been memorized, reported, and recorded. Reports on potential recruits contained even more in-depth information, including what the contact talked about and how he or she reacted to certain things, which was updated at every meeting with Confucius. This system of reporting applied not only to each of the contacts but to the contact's contacts as well, in a spider's web–like network. For every useful person the Communists encountered, whether left or right wing, there was a dossier filed in Guangzhou, where the leader responsible for Party work in Hong Kong and Macau was stationed. Our policies and tactics came from there, with particularly important problems or information being passed on to Beijing. Based on the information he received, Confucius would order me to carry out his instructions to assist members of the executive committee. Typically, this involved rectifying any wrongdoing; repairing relationships if someone was seriously or wrongly reprimanded; discussing plans or Mao's teachings; and watching to see how certain Party or Youth League members carried out the Party's policies.

In the meantime, Wei Yee had divided the rapidly growing club membership into thirteen groups, including folk dancing, literature, electronics, and ballet. Each group was headed by Youth League members. I arranged to meet with Lee, a leader of the drama group. Although he didn't officially report to me, he responded to my request for a meeting without question. My mission was to promote the Party's policies within Hok Yau, as well as at many of the prestigious schools at which our members had contacts.

What activities did his group promote? How were the students responding? How many of them were potential recruits? What was their success rate? I quizzed Lee about his drama group for an hour before suggesting new strategies. Together, we planned to put on an anti-Japanese skit featuring singalong war songs, and also decided to invite a World War II veteran to share his stories with the group. Such activities were designed to sow seeds of patriotism among the club members. As these seeds germinated and took root, the youth would believe the Party's ideas to be their own and therefore would pursue the Party's goals more wholeheartedly.

Without disclosing my involvement, Lee implemented our strategy. Ting, another leader of the drama group, grew suspicious at the shift in activities and questioned Lee about it. His superior had not told him anything about the plan.

"I suggest Lee give him no answers," Confucius instructed. "Ting will forget his suspicions in time. Otherwise, it might expose your involvement."

As he gathered his things to leave, Confucius asked, almost as an afterthought, "Girlfriend?" For a moment, he seemed almost caring.

"Well …" I hesitated, then confessed, "there's one girl from the Heung To left-wing school. She came to vote Wei Yee into office." He listened to me ramble about Manny. She loved Chinese classical dance and seemed honest. I had watched her study and admired how hard she worked. Her gentle spirit attracted me.

"No." The answer was simple. She wasn't a Youth League or Party member.

Like a flick of a switch, I erased Manny from my thoughts. She was a potential recruit, but not a potential girlfriend. I did not waste time dwelling on what might have been.

⁜

In the summer of 1959, the Azalea Reynolds School of Ballet scheduled a performance of *Swan Lake* at the Lock Kung Theatre. At the same time, Hok Yau was organizing its tenth anniversary celebration by presenting a variety show at Hong Kong's Grand Theatre.

A few weeks before the ballet performance, several of us gathered at Hok Yau to put up the posters advertising the variety show around the city. I was paired with Ling Ling and assigned the area of Nathan and Jordan Roads to the Star Ferry station in Tsim Sha Tsui. I'd met Ling Ling at Hok Yau many times before. I knew she went to a well-known Christian girls' school. That night, she wore her blue cheongsam school uniform.

"Are you nervous?" she breathed shyly, pointing at the posters in my hand.

In my mind I was dancing the *Swan Lake* pas de deux. I imagined the first strains from the orchestra quivering in the air, teasing at first, now lilting, now floating, then building steadily. I heard nothing, saw nothing, felt, tasted, and smelled nothing except the music. A delicate swan queen leaned on my curved arm, her neck a graceful arc. My fingertips brushed her taut waist. A magical pirouette, and I braced for the lift. Timing was critical. Babs, my partner and teacher, on pointe stood three inches taller than I did. I had to evince power and strength. I was the warrior charged with protecting all that was fragile and precious. My muscles flexed and a ballerina floated effortlessly skyward, light as the feathers and tulle of her costume. Our bodies aligned perfectly. The audience exploded in applause.

Ling Ling knew nothing of the dance in my mind. Head tilted to one side, a bit of a swan queen herself, she waited for my reply.

"Maybe a little bit," I confessed. "Babs and I need to work on the pas de deux for *Swan Lake*."

"I love the music in *Swan Lake*—me la ti do re me do me, do la fa do la …" Her arm cut gracefully across the cool evening air in fluid strokes. When I chuckled at her girlish gesture, she drew back. "Classical music is so elegant," she said, slightly flustered.

"Like you." The words spilled out before I realized I had uttered them. Ling Ling glanced away. Had I dared move closer, I'm sure the heat glowing from her face would have matched mine. Well, she *was* elegant. There was something about the curve of her neck and the way she walked, a graceful swaying, like a willow being kissed by the wind. But she was a bashful willow, and any explanations on my part would only have embarrassed her more.

We glued up posters for several blocks without another word, each lost in our own thoughts. *Odd, I didn't notice her shoulders at first. Such a soft roundness to them. Soft. That's it. Everything's so soft about her. Her voice, her curves, her spirit. Why hadn't I noticed before?* My hands instinctively reached for hers, but I pulled them back. It wouldn't do. Even in our modern world, holding a girl's hand in public was akin to proposing marriage. Instead, I engaged her in small talk. "Do you have any siblings?"

"No, I'm an only child. How about you?"

"An older brother and a baby sister." We chatted about her family, and she told me about her school and classmates. Ling Ling lived on the Hong Kong side and, as it was midnight, I escorted her home. On the ferry, we launched into a full-scale discussion of society and politics.

"I wish we could do more for them," she sighed, referring to the city's large gang problem. "They don't care about their future or about studying. All they do is talk tough and swagger. Even some of the boys at the club are like that."

My ears perked up. *What does she notice in a boy?*

As though she had heard me, she said, "They can be so arrogant. I can't stand that. A man should be confident and masculine, not conceited. Just as a woman should be gentle and feminine, a man must be a man."

As I listened to Ling Ling's silken voice, so soft and melodic, I longed to hold her. I felt an exhilarating warmth surge through my body. I desired nothing more than to protect this gentle, elegant woman sitting next to me. As the ferry chugged its way across Hong Kong's harbour, I fell in love.

Eventually, Ling Ling invited me to meet her parents. Her father was an executive at a foreign company, and her mother, educated and intelligent, was a homemaker. They led me into the living room and served tea. After greetings, they retreated to their room. Later, Ling Ling showed me her room. Her parents didn't object to our unchaperoned conversations in her bedroom. Nor did it feel strange that, when we went out on dates, we held hands. Then came the dreaded appointment with Confucius.

I reported how well I was doing in my day job with the East Asiatic Company—a Danish trading company. My English, coupled with having such a job in the first place, was proving useful, and no one suspected me of being a Communist because I made too much money, even though in reality I saw little of it. Most of my salary went to my comrades or the Party. My subordinates in the Youth League had devoted themselves as activists and had little money for their monthly expenses, so I gave each what I could from my paycheque. I kept some money for my own expenses, which were few since I was still living with Mama and not paying rent, and the rest went to the Party treasury. Mama was not in any real need, I thought, so I left nothing for her. That night, after I summarized for Confucius the plans we had at Hok Yau and handed over what was left of my month's earnings, Confucius looked directly at me and asked, "Girlfriend?"

Should I lie? No other girl had ever made me feel the way Ling Ling did, and I was loath to let her go. Eventually, though, my oath of loyalty to the Party compelled me to confess.

Again, his answer was simple: "No."

For one insane moment, I toyed with the idea of recruiting Ling Ling. That would make our relationship legitimate in the eyes of the Party, wouldn't it? We could be together. I could marry her. My nobler instincts made me decide against it. If I recruited her for my own selfish reasons, my motives would be wrong. Besides, even if she joined the Youth League, the Party might transfer her elsewhere. We could still be separated.

"You must find someone in the Youth League," Confucius emphasized.

How can I marry within the Party when I don't know who is and who isn't a member? Despite my inner struggle, I did not argue aloud with my superior. The Party's verdict could not be appealed, and my job was to carry out the sentence. As eagerly as I had pursued Ling Ling, I now, heart aching, avoided her. No phone calls, no explanations. When we passed each other at the club, her eyes searched mine for answers, but they received none. I tossed a casual, too-bright "hello" to her, then marched briskly by. The same guilt that kept me awake night after night had stiffened my greeting and posture. In time, Ling Ling and I came to treat each other as brother and sister. She never asked what had happened. It wasn't in her nature to pry, and I couldn't tell her of the Party's objection to our relationship. I could not ease her pain without betraying the Party, so I betrayed her instead.

I've often felt guilty because I couldn't tell her the truth. Ling Ling never did become a Communist Youth League member—which probably saved her from many disappointments and betrayals. The sacrifices she would have had to make as a Youth League member would have made her life miserable. Knowing this helped ease my guilt. Even so, for weeks after I stopped seeing Ling Ling I carried on imaginary conversations with her. In my mind, her gentle voice whispered, "It's all right, I understand. Our country must come first."

⚜

After the performance of *Swan Lake* that summer, I stopped dancing on stage, though I did continue taking lessons at the school. By this time, Hok Yau had begun to put on one or two variety shows a year. With those performances to prepare for and rehearse, my day job at the East Asiatic Company, ballet lessons in the evenings, as well as contact meetings and keeping up connections with the press, businesses, and artists for the united front, it was an exhausting eighteen-hour day, with always more to do.

Many of my Party comrades did not share my feelings about ballet and performances. Even though they understood that the ballet lessons I was teaching at the club were attracting many students, especially girls, a few of my comrades ridiculed ballet as bourgeois art. Then I choreographed *The Little Match Girl,* set to the story by Hans Christian Andersen, which Hok Yau performed at the prestigious King's Theatre. The performance was enthusiastically received by audiences of all political leanings. When the Party praised, within the membership, my choice of *The Little Match Girl* as being "very proletariat," I felt a sense of satisfaction—that Western ballet *could* be a revolutionary tool. Perhaps the Party would send me to Shanghai or England for further ballet training? After all, Hok Yau's ethnic dance leader had been sent to Guangzhou many times for training. Confucius flatly refused, giving no explanation. And my comrades continued to criticize me behind my back, jealous, perhaps, at my achievement.

Instead, in September of 1960, the Party asked me to quit my job at East Asiatic to devote more time to Hok Yau as a full-time secretary. With the Party's influence, the Hok Yau executive committee passed a resolution to hire me for a monthly salary of 120 Hong Kong dollars. I welcomed the change, as I was burdened with so much Hok Yau business that had to be done during office hours, including arranging performance venues and obtaining permits from City Hall. Even though I always completed my work at East Asiatic, I felt guilty sneaking out of the office to do Hok Yau business. I thought I wouldn't need much money, so the small salary did not worry me, although it hardly covered transportation and food expenses. *The Party will take care of you,* a voice in my head reminded me. The revolution must come first.

The change in my life had just begun. I avoided my old friends, co-workers, and relatives. I had quit my job with a reputable foreign company. What could I say when I was asked, how is work? What do you do now? I couldn't say my main occupation was Hok Yau's secretary—it had no status in Hong Kong because I made practically no money. And so, I was forced to cut many people out of my life. If I saw anyone I knew walking toward me, I turned down a side street.

To survive on such a low salary, I ate at the cheapest places I could find: back-lane kitchens where beggars and coolies had their meals. Ling Ling would have been shocked to see me now. From my friends in the arts community and former colleagues in the air-conditioned downtown office I now traced an obscure path, weaving in and out of shops to avoid detection. Gone was my neatly pressed suit. In its place I wore only my undershirt and a pair of coolie pants, which I changed into before heading to the back-lane kitchens. The outfit helped me blend in, and I could squat amid the alley sludge without worrying about keeping clean.

One advantage of eating at the kitchens was the queer brand of privacy it provided. When you are reduced to eating other people's garbage, no one asks questions. Regardless, I felt proud to be eating with the lower class. I wanted to experience a part of their lives. I didn't feel bad because, compared with the poorest, this was not suffering. I was strong; my body could fight off any germs.

I stared at my plate of slop—scraps of fish heads, pickled mustard greens, chicken feet, and other leftovers boiled in a cast-iron pot and ladled over steaming rice—a specialty known as "A hundred birds returning to nest." The vendor, who boasted burly forearms and a coarse, distinctly un-Asian beard, had collected the scraps from local restaurants the night before. Under a crude plastic awning, he sold slop for fifty cents a man-sized bowl. The potent olfactory cocktail of urine, vomit, and body odour made the daily special even harder to stomach, but at least the meal was hot. And I never ate the same dish twice.

Other than a few comrades, no one suspected I dined with beggars and vagrants in the alley behind the Wan Chai Public Market. But I had miscalculated. I soon discovered that 120 Hong Kong dollars was not enough to cover three meals a day as well as the travel expenses incurred in carrying out Hok Yau business. Some days, K.K. paid for me to eat at his school canteen. Without beef to eat, and with increasingly low energy, I gave up my ballet lessons. And although I didn't lose any more weight—I had previously lost many pounds because of my heavy workload and ballet classes—I struggled daily to fill my empty stomach. Nevertheless, I was happy to devote still more to the revolution.

We had food at home, of course, but eating there was too shameful. Mama and the others thought I still worked for a powerful foreign company, where my salary exceeded all of theirs combined. Yet I brought nothing home. Not a penny. They didn't know I now had a pitiful allowance. After finishing my responsibilities at Hok Yau, I would come home late at night and rummage through the refrigerator. Ah Sim stared at me reproachfully, pointing at each dish saying, "This is for your mother. This is for Mei Mei."

Ah Sim was right. I had no right to eat their food. It was customary to live with one's parents until you married. It was also customary to give your parents your salary. My parents never asked me where my money went, nor did they ask for support. Somehow, Mama managed to upgrade our living quarters, paying for the new flat on her own. We moved to the sixteenth floor of the Nation Building, at Nathan and Jordan Roads. It was a larger flat with views of the harbour, mountains, and ocean. In the distance we could see Hong Kong's Central district, commercial high-rises, and Victoria Peak.

Mama constantly bragged about the flat, which aggravated her relationship with Father. "You see this flat?" Mama often said, with a grand wave of her hand. "It's mine. My own hard work. You think that husband of mine could have bought a place like this? He only makes three hundred dollars a month at that gasoline company." She told friends, patients, everyone the same story. And I suppose Mama needed to brag. My father's relatives had always criticized, made sarcastic remarks, and disrespected Mama, and Father had never defended her.

Meanwhile, Father pointed out to Mei Mei and me, "If it weren't for me putting her through medical school, she wouldn't be making four times my salary today. Who knows if it was a real medical school?

Maybe she's only a midwife or a nurse. And I sacrificed so much of myself for her."

I knew Father was wrong. Nurses and midwives trained through apprenticeship. Mama had trained to be a doctor for three years at the Guangdong Gynecology, Pediatrics and Obstetrics Medical School. I remember Mama trying to describe her anatomy course in which she had dissected a corpse, and although I was fascinated, Pao Tse didn't want to hear about it. In Hong Kong, Mama had been too busy working in order to pay for Mei Mei's treatments—expensive injections, amputation, nutritious food—to take the test she needed to get her licence to practise medicine here. So instead, Mama worked under my aunt's licence, looking after Swatow expatriates. People from the same village were like family.

But it didn't matter. Father continued to blame Mama for the loss of Mei Mei's leg. The expensive artificial leg Mama bought for my sister could not make up for her carelessness, which caused the infection in the first place. My sister's misfortunes, according to Father, were because of Mama's negligence. And I had no choice but to keep my silence; I couldn't correct my own father or his relatives.

Tensions had been mounting for years. Mama had seen Father at a theatre with a girl to whom he was giving private English lessons, and although he protested his innocence, it made no difference. He moved out to a rental and, after a year, he left Hong Kong altogether, moving in the summer of 1961 to work as an accountant at a friend's Chinese restaurant in Addis Ababa, Ethiopia. By this time, Mei Mei was working for the Finling Supreme Court in Finling, New Territories, and had moved into staff quarters. Had Father stayed in Hong Kong, perhaps he would have pitied Mama.

My mother's black-market medical practice was successful until another doctor heard about it through a mutual patient and reported Mama to the authorities. Fortunately, someone tipped Mama off before the police raided our flat. They arrived only to find an ordinary flat, with no pharmaceuticals or medical equipment in sight.

Mama, deeply hurt that a friend had disclosed her practice, fell into a depression. Luckily, Pao Tse, her faithful servant, was there to sympathize, comfort her, and support her. And although she told me that Mama had lost her appetite and wasn't sleeping at night, I, as usual, was running off to meetings and so never spoke to Mama about her health.

Frightened by the raid, Mama gave up her practice. After a few weeks of depression, her ingenuity and survival instincts bounced back. She recalled her loans from her friends, but no one was able to repay her. So instead, she paid the bills by opening our flat to mah-jong players, providing tea, snacks, and mah-jong tables and tiles. If a group needed another player to make up a foursome, she filled in. For these services, the players paid her a small fee, enough to cover our monthly expenses. I didn't approve of this gambling. The paunchy, middle-aged shop owners and housewives rendered the flat more like an opium den than the home of a doctor. But what right did I have to complain? I could have helped with the bills when I had a good salary. But the people in China and beggars in Kowloon needed my help much more than my mother did.

⚜

Around 1960, the Party had called for a "patriotic education movement." Educating club members and students about patriotism became an ongoing policy.

"I suggest," Confucius intoned, "that you encourage the students at Hok Yau to be more patriotic; educate them on the history of the Japanese invasion of China."

This was to foster extreme nationalism as part of the "thought transformation" we recruiters practised on our students at Hok Yau. The first stage was simple. We encouraged our youths not to join gangs, not to smoke, use drugs, gamble, or go ballroom or disco dancing. They were encouraged to respect others, including their parents. The second stage was to create a deeper sense of purpose and mission in their lives. We taught them to sympathize with the poor, to love the people, and to love China. The third stage was to recruit them to become members of the Communist Youth League. Once they were members, they would be transferred outside of Hok Yau, as the Party did not want these new recruits to risk exposure by continuing with the club's activities. Some of them even worked at right-wing institutions until the Party called on them to go public.

Lang, for example, was a member of Hok Yau until he left to teach at a right-wing Christian high school. He taught there diligently for twenty years—until the day the left-wing Xinhua News Agency announced that Lang had been appointed its senior officer. His colleagues were shocked at first; gradually, they realized that he must have been an underground Communist for many years—surely any senior official at a China-controlled institution had to be a Party member.

Not everyone in the Youth League practised transformation methods. Some members responded to patriotic directives simply by telling their contacts to be more patriotic. They then reported to their superiors that their contacts now knew what to do—that is, to be more patriotic. Those shortcuts weren't good enough for me. How could I change these students' lives, their thoughts? I kept asking myself. How could I make them more patriotic instead of simply telling them to love their country?

⚜

Hon was seventeen and in grade eleven at a private English school when a club member invited him to a barbecue. Even though it was his first time joining a club activity, I noticed his willingness to help carry heavy pots and pans. He was quiet, polite, and a thinker. Wearing a short-sleeved white shirt, brown trousers, and glasses, he looked like a scholar—and a potential recruit.

I began visiting him at his home to find out more about him. Hon lived with his lower-middle-class family in a low-rent but spacious flat in the Kowloon's Sham Shui Pao district. His father worked for an import-export company, his mother in a garment factory. He had an older sister and a younger brother. I made mental notes about his family life. In our discussions about school curriculum and moral matters, Hon seemed honest and full of integrity. My visits became weekly. Sometimes I met him at his home, but more often we walked while I preached to him. I told him about the Opium War with the British and about World War II, and how the Japanese had tortured the Chinese. Hon eagerly listened as I recounted the injustices done to our people, and the bravery and kindness of the Eighth Route Army. He even studied the books I suggested he read.

Hon began to help out at Hok Yau. Even though the economy was good, many poor families were just getting by. In order to serve them, Hok Yau operated a co-op grocery store from the club, selling non-perishables such as rice, dry noodles, sausage, and canned meat. As head of this department, I purchased bulk and retailed at a lower price to the club members and their families. Hon began by helping at the store, collecting orders and diligently packing them for delivery. Later, I promoted him to lead and organize a group of students for grocery delivery. It was Hon's last year in high school but, overwhelmed by this work, he was not able to get his grades above average.

Two years after I had first met Hon, I felt he was ready for the next step. As we were walking along Prince Edward Road one day, I told him about a secret Communist organization—the Chinese Communist Youth League—operating in Hong Kong. I invited him to join us. As usual, his reaction was muted, but I saw a glint of excitement in his eyes.

He held my hands and looked me straight in the eyes. "I always thought you were a leftist or a Communist by your attitude toward work at Hok Yau. I didn't know about the Chinese Communist Youth League, but I did guess there must be a secret organization in Hong Kong."

I kept quiet, letting him continue. Calmly, he said, "I am willing to join and work for the liberation of our people."

Hon was sworn in as a Communist Youth League member and then placed by the Party at a state bank; his average academic level made

him unsuitable for the British Hong Kong government departments—
he wouldn't be promoted to a useful position.

The Party chose their candidates carefully. Another of my recruits
who graduated with top honours from King's College, a public high
school, was fluent in English but because he was too chatty, he was
deemed unsuitable for the government departments. He was sent to
work at a bank.

Once my recruits went to work, they were considered transferred
and I usually did not keep in touch with them. Parting was not always
easy. We had built a friendship over the months or years. I wished they
could always be under my guidance and protection, but the Party did
not share this sentiment. As for Hon, I didn't have contact with him
again, but from his brother I learned that he had soon been promoted
to bank manager.

In 1962, the Party transferred a slim man in his mid-twenties from a
left-wing school to Hok Yau. He became the new Shadow Core leader
and my superior, replacing Confucius. A bookworm and math teacher,
Lo had been secluded in left-wing circles and didn't know much about
life in Hong Kong.

Through Lo, the Party instructed me to find a job, staying on as
Hok Yau's secretary part-time. In 1963, at the age of twenty-nine, I
joined an American company, Associated Timber Industries, as assistant office manager. I received an excellent salary, three times more
than other foreign companies were paying. It felt good to once again
be earning money to contribute to the revolution. After a few years of
eating at back-lane kitchens, my stomach was happy, too. And so, my
salary once again flowed into the Party's treasury. Of course, neither
Mama nor Ah Sim knew that. All they knew was that, although I had
gotten a new job, my life revolved around Hok Yau. I led a double life,
juggling secret and public duties, all the while carving out time for
meeting after meeting.

Wei Yee called on a Sunday afternoon. "I'm calling a meeting of the Hok Yau executive committee," she said. "Come to the club tomorrow night at seven o'clock."

"Have you called the others yet?"

"No, you're the club secretary. I decided to call you first."

"I think the singing group leaders are meeting tomorrow night. Isn't Cheung one of the leaders?"

Cheung was a member of the Communist Youth League, and of the "public" Hok Yau executive committee. I had bumped into him on the stairs before the last meeting. He was grumbling about having to reschedule his other meetings because Wei Yee had again summoned us at the last minute, as was her habit.

"They'll have to reschedule," was her pat response.

"Of course, we will reschedule our meetings. The executive is more important. But perhaps next time, you could give us a little more notice?"

I sensed that Wei Yee was annoyed, even though she didn't comment. Instead, she briefed me on the meeting's agenda. It came as no surprise. Long before, Confucius had told me of the Party's anti-Japanese directive.

The orders issued through our superior contacts originated from the Hong Kong and Macau Work Committee. The committee members included Hong Kong citizens, such as a businessman, a math teacher, and a left-wing school principal, who were all underground Communist Party members. It also included people, such as the deputy and chief reporter, who worked at Xinhua News Agency. Instead of having an embassy in Hong Kong, China had set up this news agency like a diplomatic organization to distribute official press releases. Although it was not ever officially stated, the director of Xinhua was a representative of the Chinese Communist Party. Thus, he passed down Party directives. He also led the Work Committee. The committee covertly guided Hong Kong's underground Communist movement. They were our "bosses."

Wei Yee, I, and each executive committee member who belonged to the Communist Youth League received our orders behind closed doors. Once we received our directive, we had to implement it at Hok Yau. Wei Yee and I first talked to the two non-Communist members, suggesting to them what might be best for Hok Yau. We listened to their opinions so that they, in turn, would listen to ours. Soon after we got their agreement to support our ideas, an executive committee meeting was called, where we discussed our ideas. Should we have a picnic, a concert, a variety show? Where, how, and when? What fees should we charge? We would plan all the details and, at important decision points, take a vote. Once we decided on our method of implementation, we informed the Hok Yau activity leaders, such as the Chinese musical instrument group leaders, the choir leaders, and the drama leaders. Sometimes, one would ask, "Who decided all this?" We were able to show our "democracy" by saying that it had been Hok Yau's elected executive members who had decided.

At that Monday night meeting, four hours of planning and debating drained us all. Wei Yee, in particular, looked pale and exhausted by the end of the meeting. "You'll faint unless you eat something," I warned her. She shrugged but did not protest when I treated her to noodles from a street vendor. Even after Wei Yee had emptied her bowl, I half-expected her to faint. Carrying her would have been easy—she weighed less than a hundred-pound sack of rice.

"You work too hard," I mused aloud as I walked her home, a tiny servant's room she rented.

She shrugged. "It's for the good of our people, our country."

I admired her dedication. After her morning teaching session at a primary school, she worked day and night at the club. Her salary from the school was only 180 Hong Kong dollars a month. At the time, a junior clerk in a government or commercial office earned around 370 Hong Kong dollars a month. Wei Yee did not seem to mind sacrificing her health or finances for the sake of the Party. No one, of course, had explicitly told me she was a member of the Communist Youth League, but she had to be. Why else would the Party instruct us to vote her into power?

Well, if she's a Youth League or Party member, then she can be my girlfriend. Not that I had fallen in love. This comrade did not arouse the same passion in me as Ling Ling had, but I respected her. Yes, she managed her time poorly, but I could live with that. She was such a smart, enthusiastic operative otherwise. The idea of Wei Yee being my girlfriend grew more attractive by the week. Every evening after our weekly executive committee meeting, I bought her dinner and walked her home. These could hardly be described as dates: our conversations never strayed from the affairs of the club.

"Don't you think it's time for another performance?" Wei Yee tossed out the suggestion casually, but I could tell the idea had been brewing for a while. "The variety show last year was a great success."

"Remember the cops?" I chuckled. Hok Yau had been under suspicion ever since its inception. In one of our variety shows the previous year, we presented a dance drama consisting of Chinese classical dances accompanied by a Western orchestra. The police demanded to see our scripts beforehand, but because there was no dialogue and therefore no script, two plainclothes officers came to monitor our rehearsals to try to find out the meaning of the dance drama.

"Why do you use an accordion?" one of them asked. "Only Russians and Chinese Communists use accordions," he said naively.

"It's easy to carry and sounds better than a harmonica," I had explained patiently. Accordions were used around the world: they didn't carry a proletariat trademark.

Wei Yee smiled at the memory. "Well, they didn't stop us. After that performance, we gained hundreds of new members. This time, I want to target right-wing schools." Her plan was to stage a show that appealed to the students and teachers from the music and dance departments of Hong Kong's secondary right-wing schools. "It has to be unique. Spectacular."

I thought about her idea for a minute, then said, "Why not combine Chinese classical dance with ballet?"

"You're joking."

"It'll be an experiment. That'll pique their interest."

Our thoughts and words spilled out faster and faster. Before we knew it, we had the skeleton of a Chinese ballet. We would tell the story of a beleaguered town, valiantly resisting a brutal invader. The setting would be ancient times, but the sequence of events would unmistakably parallel the Japanese invasion. A colossal performance, with one hundred dancers and three hundred crew members. Wary of sabotage—someone had stolen our speakers before one performance—we even assigned Hok Yau club members to guard the set.

Trading ideas with Wei Yee exhilarated me. She too wanted to motivate club members and their friends to believe what the Party believed. We did not tell our people to stop using Japanese goods. Rice cookers and air conditioners had become necessities for most families. Instead, we stirred up resentment against the enemy by staging debates and discussions. Impassioned by our skits and patriotic songs, they would themselves choose to boycott foreign goods. This, we both believed, was the best strategy for winning them over.

Then came Wei Yee's mysterious three-day trip to Guangzhou. She wouldn't tell me why she was going, though she seemed pleased I was seeing her off at the club. She walked down a few steps, then glanced back over her shoulder at me. Her passionate look caught me off guard. *Perhaps she is fond of me?*

When she returned, Wei Yee opened up to me. By now, we knew each other to be Youth League members. The Party, she confided, had summoned her to Guangzhou for re-education—a method of correcting thoughts, purification, and making one more obedient to Party orders. This was a common strategy for dealing with problem individuals. Her superiors had criticized her liberal approach. Since she was the chairperson of Hok Yau, the Party wanted to ensure it had control of her and of Hok Yau. In Guangzhou, it had initiated her to study Chairman Mao's teachings and criticize her own shortcomings.

They must have made a mistake. She works so hard. A sudden impulse to protect Wei Yee rushed through me. She had sacrificed so much for the Party that I felt obligated to take care of her. That's when I noticed her blouse. It didn't look like the blouses other girls wore. Neither did her peasant skirt. Some boys would have sneered and called her a country bumpkin. Her outfit bore the unmistakable stamp of the China Emporium, a decidedly unfashionable place to shop in the 1960s. In fact, only leftists shopped there.

A week later I happened to pass the China Emporium and was reminded of Wei Yee. I stopped at the next trendy boutique I came to and bought a practical wool cardigan and skirt. Nothing extravagant, just a simple suit. I didn't think much of my purchase since I had done the same for many other left-wing students who couldn't afford a proper wardrobe. For the sake of the Party, I wanted my comrades to be less conspicuous.

Wei Yee wore the outfit often. When the other Youth League members found out where she had gotten it, one reported to her superior that I bought expensive clothes for Wei Yee and was corrupting the girls at the club with my bourgeois tastes. The accusations filtered their way back to Confucius, even though my superior was now Lo. "I suggest," Confucius hinted when I saw him, "that you be, ahh, a bit more discreet." He did not press his point further, but his eyes narrowed. "Are you interested in her?"

I did not answer at first. Was I interested? Well, yes, I suppose. I was turning thirty and needed to find a wife. Our society was still traditional. My relatives and even Mama's patients would often ask, "Do you have a girlfriend?" K.K. had married two years ago. Life was hard for him, working at a left-wing school and living in social housing in Tung Tau Village, near the airport, but he seemed satisfied with his wife. But since I was to follow the Party's directive to marry someone within the Communist Youth League, I became passive and did not pursue anyone. I was willing to consider marrying anyone who was a Communist member and fond of me.

Wei Yee would do. Who knew when I would find another female Youth League or Party member suitable for marriage? Besides, I admired her hard work for the revolution. She was a dedicated activist. Her weaknesses and lack of finances created a sense of responsibility within me as a comrade, and as a man. I believed love could be culti-vated between two people, as in an arranged marriage.

"Yes. She must be a Youth League member. I would be allowed to marry her, wouldn't I?"

To my surprise, the answer was again "no."

The Party had assigned Wei Yee to marry a superior. *It's like being blind. Why doesn't the Party just assign someone to marry me?*

⁂

"I didn't know that," Wei Yee gasped when I told her of the Party's plan for her marriage. Her shock matched mine. Neither of us knew whom she was to marry. We were torn. We chose to continue our romance, but because of our commitment to the revolution, we would marry only with the Party's approval.

Yet Wei Yee's weak health continued to worry me. She often complained of stomach aches and nausea after meals. On our walks home, she frequently felt dizzy and cold. Her shabby coat didn't help. I bought her a new one. Her father and other family members had tuberculosis; perhaps they had infected her when she lived with them. The doctor even suspected leukemia, but the tests came back negative.

All I could do was ensure she ate properly. I brought her breakfast on my way to work in Hong Kong's Central district—otherwise, she would sleep until noon. At lunchtime, I raced back to Kowloon to bring her another meal. The Party had provided her with a job teach-ing primary school in the afternoon. Without the meals I delivered, she would go through the day without eating. For Wei Yee, sleep was more important than food. Her budget didn't include groceries. Her meagre salary as a primary teacher barely paid the rent.

"Do you think it would be better for you to live with your family?" I suggested. "Then your mother could cook for you."

"No, it's too inconvenient. She already shares a room with my brothers and sisters. I come home so late from Hok Yau, I would wake them up every night." Her mind was made up. "I only go home if I'm really sick."

"If you continue living like this, you'll grow weaker and weaker."

"I'll be all right."

I switched tactics. "Your body is a tool. If your tool is in such poor condition, how can you work effectively for the revolution?"

"I've done it for years."

"You're only contributing with half your strength."

"I'm lucky the school transferred me to an afternoon class. Teaching at 8 A.M. nearly killed me."

"Why don't you get some exercise?"

"I don't even have enough time to run all these meetings and manage the Hok Yau workload as it is. Where would I find time to exercise?"

"If I support you, you won't have to teach. Why don't we get married? Then I can take better care of you." It made sense to me. No one would criticize me for taking care of my wife.

"I don't know …"

I didn't expect an answer right away. We could do nothing without the Party's permission. That permission came months later, with a reprimand. The Party, through Lo, accused us of "murdering first, asking questions later." We had acted without authority. I should have ended the relationship when Confucius told me she was assigned to someone else.

"I suggest," added Confucius, "that you don't have children." Lo repeated the sentiment. They wanted us to be totally devoted to the Party: if we had children, we would have no time for the revolution. Wei Yee and I agreed. Given our youth work, it would be inconvenient if she became pregnant.

Once we had the Party's approval, I approached both our mothers. Mama at first objected to my marrying Wei Yee: "I am worried about her health. She is so weak and ill all the time. You are marrying an herbal medicine pot! Think again, Kee Ngai."

"Her health will improve. After our marriage, she will have a proper place to live and proper care," I said in a determined voice.

"Well, if you've made up your mind to marry her, then I have nothing more to say," Mama said, "but I can help improve her health." Mama immediately arranged with Wei Yee to come for treatments. She prepared chicken and beef soups, chicken essence, and ginseng tea for Wei Yee, as well as a plan for injections of calcium, glucose, liver extract, and vitamin B12.

Wei Yee's mother was not so easily convinced. "Will you register?" she asked.

"No," I said. Neither Wei Yee nor I respected the imperialist government's authority. The marriage certificate was a symbol of British oppression. "We want a traditional wedding."

Wei Yee nodded. Her mother muttered something about a girl's honour and respectability. Then she asked, "How many bridal cakes and banquet tables are you offering?"

There were many Chinese wedding customs and traditions. We could invite our relatives and friends to a banquet. The greater number of tables at the banquet, the more expensive the dishes, and the better the show. Of course, luxurious plates of food were expected. We could order bridal cakes—lotus seed paste cakes, walnut sweet cakes, and pineapple cakes—to be sent to the bride's home to give to relatives. It was also customary for the groom to send a roast pig decorated with flowers. Wei Yee would need a satin wedding cheongsam and new shoes. Wei Yee's mother would provide jewellery and linens.

"Well, we're not following the usual traditions. We want to keep our wedding modest. Many people in the world are starving; it's wasteful to spend such a great amount on food. And we don't need all these new things," I replied.

And so we decided to dispense with most of the wedding customs—the banquet, bridal cakes, roast pig, new furniture, marriage licence, and even the tea ceremony. My prospective mother-in-law was taken aback by the disrespect I was showing her family. How could she "sell" her daughter so cheaply? Because of Wei Yee's mother's disapproval, Wei Yee and I began to think we would have to simply live together, without even a celebratory dinner. Probably fearing that we thought as much, her mother finally gave in.

On our wedding day in September 1963, I drove a borrowed car—the Sunbeam-Talbot having been long since sold—to Wei Yee's family home. Armed with a bouquet of blood-red gladiolas, I fetched my bride. That evening, we hosted a dinner for both families. Only our mothers and siblings were present. My father was still in Ethiopia, and Wei Yee's father lived in Guangzhou with his second wife. The next day, Hok Yau members hosted a party for us, not a lavish banquet but a simple tea party. Wei Yee and I appreciated the warmth of this gesture.

We found a family who had a room to sublet with a shared kitchen and bathroom. It was on the fifth floor of an elevator-less apartment building. Hok Yau was only three blocks away. We happily decorated our six-by-ten-square-foot room with a second-hand bed, second-hand wardrobe, and a new rice cooker. Then, with a touch of smugness, we reflected on how we had managed to celebrate a truly proletariat-style wedding.

⚜

On Friday, January 22, 1965, Father returned from Ethiopia, his contract with the restaurant finished. K.K. and I met him at the airport. When I saw Father, he seemed thin and had more white hairs on his head. There were no hugs, just a quick "Are you hungry? We'll take you to lunch."

We were quiet on the way to the restaurant. There wasn't much to say, and Father seemed tired.

"How are you?" K.K. asked as we settled at our table and he poured Father a cup of tea.

"Let's order something first," I suggested.

"I am not hungry; please don't order too much." Father was frugal as always. He hadn't changed, and I realized how much I had missed him these last three years.

"How was life in Ethiopia?" K.K. asked after ordering.

"Ethiopia is not as busy as Hong Kong. But people were good to us Chinese. I worked as accountant and cashier in the restaurant and lived in the staff quarters. You know the restaurant business—I worked seven days a week, twelve hours a day. No one had official holidays but we took turns taking a day off. How are all of you?"

K.K. didn't have much to say. I told Father Mei Mei had moved to the New Territories, and that I had married and my wife and I had lived in a rented room. More recently, we had moved in with Mama and Ah Sim in Nation Building, as our landlord needed the room for his own family. I also told Father about someone reporting Mama's black-market medical practice to the authorities.

"That's a shame about your mother," Father nodded sympathetically. "I would be interested in asking Mei Mei if I can move in with her. Maybe I can help her in some way." Father was over sixty by now, and he knew he would have difficulty finding work. And I was so preoccupied with my work that I had forgotten Mei Mei had plans to emigrate to Canada. "Canada is much better than Hong Kong. The people there are polite. They won't point and stare at me," she had told me. Apparently, some of her former classmates had already emigrated.

So for a short while, Father did live with Mei Mei, until, in December 1965, she packed up and left for Vancouver, aboard a cargo ship departing from Kowloon. The trip by sea would take six days, but booking one of the ship's passenger compartments was much cheaper than flying. There were no hugs then either. I said a quick "take care of yourself" and headed back to Hok Yau, leaving my parents and her friends to see Mei Mei off.

That same day, Father cleaned up Mei Mei's unit in Finling and moved into Nation Building with Mama. The situation was difficult for Father and Mama, for they had spent many years living separate lives. But with nowhere else to go now, they stayed together.

10

THE MAY RIOT

1966–1968 Hong Kong, British colony

In November of 1966, after applying twenty-four times for a building permit—the government was apparently unwillingly to issue a permit for a left-wing workers' union to build an elementary school—the residents of Taipa, a suburb of Macau, decided to go ahead and build the school anyway. Police were ordered to stop the work.

On December 3, inspired by the patriotic zeal of the Cultural Revolution in Mainland China, residents, teachers, and students protested at the Macau governor's palace. Police and armed troops were sent in, and martial law imposed. The police fired shots into the crowd, killing and injuring citizens. In the official news release, "Reply of the Government of Macau to the Protest Presented by the Representatives of the Chinese Residents of Macau," 8 people were reported killed and 212 people injured. The Macau Portuguese government apologized and announced it would pay compensation, and reimburse medical and funeral costs to the injured and to families of the dead. After the incident, left-wing organizations gained influence over the Macau government. These organizations had political support from the Chinese government, with the power to halt the export of produce and meat to Macau, and to cut off the water supply, among other things. The Macau government began to consult many of these left-wing organizations before making important decisions.

The Party hailed the December 3 Incident—also known as the 1 2 3 Incident because it took place on the third day of the twelfth month—as a victory and ordered us to learn from our comrades in Macau. This would be a good opportunity for our students to deepen their sympathy for the poor and devote themselves to overthrowing the oppressive upper classes—the factory owners and imperialists. Some leftists who came from bourgeois backgrounds would have the opportunity to experience and see this class struggle first-hand.

Wei Yee and I had discussed until late into the night the Party's orders to take select students on a day trip to Macau. Only those chosen for the trip were to know about it. "Bring only contacts who are mature enough," Lo, our superior, had warned me. "They should already be activists." We picked two dozen from Hok Yau's dancing group, students who were patriotic, loved to help people, and displayed left-wing sentiments.

Wing Mui flashed a smile as she walked down the gangplank of the vehicular ferry and joined the rest of the group, which was meeting by the Vehicular Ferry Pier on the Hong Kong side of the harbour before making its way the short distance to the Hong Kong–Macau Ferry Terminal. With heavy-rimmed glasses shielding half her face, Wing Mui reminded me of a much younger Wei Yee. The occasional street hawker wheeled his cart along the road, empty at such an early hour. In an alley, a mother and her son shifted about in their cardboard box that did little to shield them from the chill of the January morning. Even the street people were still sleeping. I yawned. Wing Mui shivered and drew her sweater closer.

I glanced at her as we walked to the Hong Kong–Macau Ferry Terminal. Who could have guessed she would be a mature contact, a potential Youth League candidate? Lo, and most of Hok Yau, had disliked her from the first day she stepped into the club; that was two years ago. Her family, staunch Nationalists, owned a Kuomintang bookstore. She attended True Light Senior High, a prestigious right-wing Protestant high school. Our members were amused by her attachment to Western pop music and lifestyle. They continually mocked her movie-star mannerisms. Although left-wing students disguised their political views when mingling with club members, they pointed out that Wing Mui's exaggerated gestures and affected speech did not fit in with the simple, honest, unadorned style of Hok Yau.

When she first started to attend the club's activities, during her second year at senior high, I began visiting Wing Mui at home. Her father had died years earlier and, as the eldest daughter in the family, she dutifully helped her mother out at home. She often brought her two younger brothers to Hok Yau events. Over time, her mother came to trust the club, and me.

After graduating from True Light, Wing Mui had failed the Hong Kong Certificate of Education Examination, which would have allowed her to advance in her schooling. Her mother had called me for help, frantic: her daughter had left a suicide note. I found Wing Mui walking by the water, not far from where she lived. We walked for a while in silence before she confided that the shock of not passing the exam had made her despair that she had no future. She thought she was hurting her mother by not passing; being the eldest in the family, she could not set an example for her two younger brothers. She didn't know what to do. Should she sit the exam again or look for work instead?

Because the Hong Kong Certificate of Education Examination was a British standards exam, it was optional. However, there was great parental and societal pressure to pass it; indeed, it was shameful to fail. Special suicide hotlines were set up each year after exam results were released to counter the many student suicide attempts. If Wing Mui wished to go to college or university, or even to get a better-paying job, she had to pass the exam.

I persuaded her not to give up so quickly and patiently answered her questions. She could choose to study hard one more year on her own, or repeat her senior year to prepare for the exam, or look for work. To encourage her, I told her there were many job opportunities in left-wing organizations.

Wing Mui decided to look for work and at the same time, with renewed energy, she attended more activities at Hok Yau. She joined the Chinese classical and folk dance group, as well as a secret study group—Hok Yau had many secret study groups for potential recruits, meeting at the homes of leftists, with their parents' approval—to learn Chinese history. This past year, with her involvement at Hok Yau, she had taken her first steps in developing into a Communist activist, and she seemed eager to learn more.

"Why do we need to go to the fireworks factory?" Wing Mui asked as we walked toward the Hong Kong–Macau Ferry Terminal.

We had carefully prepared the answer for students chosen for this trip. I voiced the sentiments I had already sown in her heart: "We need to know how much poverty there is in the world and learn what we can do."

She drifted into a contemplative mood, and I remained silent, letting the idea incubate.

"Let's buy breakfast for the others," I suggested as we passed a small bakery. The barbecued-pork buns and cocktail buns were tempting. The owner grinned broadly at us, his first customers. A hefty sale boded well for the day.

"Better to get the plain buns," Wing Mui mused aloud. "Let's not be self-indulgent." I smiled at how she had grown more mature and frugal under my care. She was more like the other club members now, and less isolated.

Wang and Yeung Yuk Lin, two of my Shadow Core comrades, were waiting for us at the terminal. Wang frowned at our extravagance, but that did not prevent him from gulping down a steaming, fragrant roll. Yuk Lin swallowed hers without comment.

As the other club members arrived, Wing Mui dispensed breakfast. The teenagers gobbled their buns and then chased each other along the pier, their squeals and giggles slicing through the morning air. Wing Mui laughed exuberantly and couldn't resist joining in. At Hok Yau I often played games with the younger students so they would get to know and accept me. This time, carrying the bags of buns, I couldn't join in. Besides, I was twice their age, and such spontaneous behaviour would not have been appropriate for a Communist Party member.

Lo had invited me to join the Party the year before. The freeze on Party membership had finally been lifted, he explained. Since, at thirty-three, I really was far too old to be a Youth League member, did I want to be a full-fledged Party member? I answered "yes" without hesitation. Now both Wei Yee and I were Communist Party members. Ten Youth League and Party members and one hundred activists reported to her. I was responsible for eight members and sixty activists.

Today, I only had to worry about Wang, Yuk Lin, and two dozen students. Two dozen boisterous students, brimming with enthusiasm. It would take three hours to reach Macau. Aboard the ferry, we burst into loud song. The words and tune of "Shenandoah" rang through the third-class deck while I ordered soft drinks for us. As the last strains trailed off, Wing Mui called out, "How about 'Do-Re-Mi'?" Wing Mui loved the film *The Sound of Music*. Soon the boys and girls were singing. But Wang and Yuk Lin didn't know the foreign song. "Western corruption," Wang muttered.

"Not really," I said. "There's a song in the movie, 'Edelweiss.' It's quite patriotic." I went on to tell him the story about the naval captain and his family's resistance against the Nazis, our Fascist enemies. "The song," I explained, "tells of the captain's love for his country." Wang remained unconvinced, but I left him to his opinions. It was almost time to split into discussion groups. Wang, Yuk Lin, and I each briefed our groups on the day's agenda.

A bus met us in Macau, with a union representative as our tour guide. Twenty minutes later, having driven south over a bridge to the underdeveloped island of Taipa, we came to our first stop, the fireworks factory union headquarters. Our tour guide read out a report on the fireworks industry. The statistics stunned me. The owners made hundreds of thousands of dollars a year in revenue, while their employees worked twelve to eighteen hours a day for pennies. Accidental explosions were common and had killed many workers. Despite risking their lives, the factory workers barely earned enough to survive. I accepted these statistics without question.

We then toured a factory, if one could call it a factory. I expected a factory to have equipment: machinery, motors, conveyor belts, and a massive chimney to siphon away fumes. Workers would be wearing white gowns or overalls, gloves, and protective eye goggles. A factory would be clean, efficient, and modern.

I saw only a warehouse, devoid of safety equipment and procedures. Devoid, in fact, of almost any equipment at all. Gunpowder coated everything, creating a monotonous charcoal netherworld where ragged creatures feverishly packed explosives. These labourers squatted in piles of the powder, surrounded by explosives. Their hollow eyes, set in grimy faces, stared back at me. Their lifeless gaze spoke of numbing misery. And yet, I glimpsed a spark of pride. These downtrodden people were the very ones who had joined together, supported by the Mainland Chinese government, and defeated the oppressors who tried to halt the construction of their school. Our presence affirmed their worth.

Only two or three out of one hundred workers were men. They handled the skilled job of mixing the explosive powders while the women packaged them. The workforce of walking skeletons ranged from six-year-old girls to sixty-year-old grandmothers. I had a chance to meet two of them. The fireworks factory union had arranged for us to visit workers' families, in groups of four. A unionist led my group to a slum not far from the factory.

Ah Ping, thirteen, lived with her mother in a wooden hut only six feet tall. Their house was smaller than Mama's bedroom. A plank across the dirt floor served as a bed. Scattered on it were a threadbare quilt and a few shabby clothes. Bowls and chopsticks on a wooden crate and a small earthen stove completed their possessions.

Many families in Macau and in Hong Kong had lost their husbands, fathers, and brothers during World War II. Without their earning power, the women survivors of the family endured the most hardship. Ah Ping had no father and no education. Neither she nor her mother could earn much in Macau. In that city of gamblers, their only options were piecework, such as packing firecrackers, or prostitution. They earned only enough to stay alive for another day. When there was no work, there was no food.

"I can't imagine living like that," Wing Mui choked as we walked away. "What horrible conditions. My mother gives me more for a monthly allowance than the old woman could possibly earn in that factory."

Her heart seemed to be breaking with this discovery. Not only was she learning more about the life of the poor but her own life philosophy was taking shape. And even though I had seen many of the poorest neighbourhoods, these scenes still shocked and disheartened me. "Maybe I haven't worked hard enough to change the lot of the poor," I confessed, resolving to dedicate myself to the cause. Lo had often warned me not to admit weaknesses in front of the others, but I did not care. At this moment, I was overwhelmed by my inadequacy in the face of such extreme poverty. My anguish deepened when we met Grandma Ko, sixty. Firecrackers had blown off two of her fingers. Yet she continued working at the factory. Having lost her husband in the war, she had no family to support her.

"She looks so weak and old," cried Wing Mui. "How I wish I could help her."

Why was the revolution taking so long to change society? What is China doing for the oppressed? What is the Party doing? We're supposed to liberate our people from suffering. But when? Amid the clamour of my thoughts, I barely heard Wing Mui voicing hers: "Kee Ngai ... so depressed ... old and working ... live without hope ... and the young girl ..."

I forced myself to listen. Wing Mui sounded like me at her age, when I had despaired over the beggars on the street. "They don't have the strength to go on living. What can we do? I want to do more, now, but what?" Wing Mui said.

Like my first superior, Leung, I steered my protege toward thoughts of revolution: "We need to sacrifice ourselves …"

"I'm going to save my pocket money for the poor," Wing Mui said. "I need to live more economically and be more generous to others."

I nudged her further. "That's right, but you can only do so much on your own. Only a mass movement can affect real change."

On the ferry ride home, ours was a solemn group. The youthful exuberance of the morning had yielded to melancholy introspection. We were in mourning. "Before today, I didn't know people still live in such poverty," Wing Mui reflected.

Guilt gnawed at my heart. *Had I done enough to help them?* Anxious and doubtful, I examined my record of service. Yes, I had devoted myself to the revolution. None of my comrades or superiors worked as hard as I did, or followed the Party's dictates so exactly. They didn't care for their subordinates as I did. Frustration began brewing inside me. I was growing disillusioned with the Party's slow progress and with my comrades. I sensed the hypocrisy and wondered if there was any other way. The earnest resolve of the students, however, inspired me to continue in my devotion to the revolution. Perhaps I could do more.

The Macau trip had a profound effect on our youth members. They treated each other with more kindness and their parents with more respect. They studied harder. And they kept asking me, "How can we help?"

"Poverty doesn't exist only in Macau," Wei Yee pointed out when I raised the question with her. Our first step was to help Hong Kong's poor. In teams of three or four, our Hok Yau youth visited Aberdeen, where the city's boat people lived. Each team befriended a family there. These families, living on decrepit junks, numbered among the city's poorest. They could not afford an education for their children. Even in our club, members' parents went to extraordinary lengths to send their children to school. The family of one member lived in a large cardboard box in an alley, like the mother and child we had seen by the ferry terminal on our way to Macau. Another member was keenly ashamed that his single mother worked as a prostitute—the only work she could get. These parents scraped together all they could to give their children an opportunity for a better life. The boat people, however, could not do even that. There were government-run elementary schools, but the boat children couldn't attend because they needed to work to help support their families. They had no hope of breaking out of their cycle of poverty.

"Mei Ying's only eight!" In shocked tones, Wing Mui told other club members about the family her team had adopted. The parents took on casual-labour jobs whenever possible. While they worked on shore, Mei Ying, the eldest child, watched her younger brothers and sisters on the boat. "The children can't go to school because they must work, too," Wing Mui continued, thrusting key chains and plastic flowers onto our laps. "Fifty cents per gross—that is, for every 144 of these they put together, they earn fifty cents. And it takes them almost a day to make that many. And you know that a bowl of wonton soup costs *sixty* cents!"

As Wei Yee and I had instructed them, our youth had brought back piecework to do. They would learn how hard it was for these children to earn enough to eat. With the faces of the Macau factory workers fresh in her mind, Wing Mui soon began leading the visits to Aberdeen. This young activist was ready to take the next step. I recruited her to the Youth League and prepared her for battle.

With the Cultural Revolution sweeping China and the December 3 Incident inspiring the locals in Macau, the Party's Hong Kong leaders were eager to ignite a revolution at home. A strike at a plastic-flower factory in Kowloon's San Po Kong district provided the fuse. On April 16, 1967, management at the factory introduced ten drastic rules, with penalties that effectively slashed income for its one thousand workers. After weeks of fruitless negotiations, the union called for a peaceful strike. On May 3, the Chinese factory owner called in the police. When the workers refused to disperse, the police encircled them: public demonstrations—defined as gatherings of three or more persons—were illegal in Hong Kong.

"Go assess the situation," Lo instructed me over the phone. "Prepare a strategy. Then bring all the club's contacts down to the factory in three days." I relayed the message to my subordinates and, after work, visited the strike. A row of common labourers in well-worn coolie pants squatted in the dust, lined up against the factory's wall like ducks awaiting slaughter. This being a silent strike—striking still illegal in Hong Kong—they mutely held signs and banners explaining their reasons for stopping work, and politely requested continued negotiations. I felt sorry for the strikers. They looked doleful, uncertain of what to do next. They were trying their best not to offend the authorities, and the police officers kept a wary eye on the scene from a distance.

In the following days, all branches—the Red Line, the Black Line, and the Grey Line—of the Communist Party's workers' movement in Hong Kong prepared for action, using the strike as an excuse. The Red Line consisted of left-wing schools, unions, and businesses that flew China's flag and displayed Chairman Mao's picture but wouldn't admit to being part of the Communist Party. Despite their refusal to admit their allegiance, the public knew they were left-wing extremists.

The Black Line consisted of groups or individuals who hid their true Communist ideology while working in right-wing institutions. From those who disapproved of Communist principles to those who simply didn't read left-wing newspapers, they were all considered right wing. This included those who worked for the British Hong Kong government, for foreign companies, and for right-wing workers' unions, as well as students in non-Communist-controlled schools. Black Line members tried to obtain positions of authority and influence in right-wing institutions. Behind the scenes, they reported to a

Communist superior. I don't know anything more about Black Line operations, but I did know the leaders of the Red and Grey Lines were part of the secret core, the Hong Kong and Macau Work Committee.

Hok Yau belonged to the Grey Line. We were the underground activists, hidden and silent about our political views. The public didn't know we were a left-wing institution. Although the government suspected that the Party controlled the club, no one knew how far its influence extended. At least, not until the plastic-flower factory clash.

On Saturday, May 6, thousands of students—youth drawn from the Party's contacts in both left-wing and right-wing schools—along with workers' union members converged on the factory. By focusing attention on the strike, the Party planned to educate the public. My orders were to watch, note details, and give a report for those who weren't able to witness it. My group was not to participate or fight.

By the time my contacts and I reached the scene, the openly leftist Red Line activists, left-wing students in their identifying white shirts and blue pants, were already fighting the police. Trade unionists and workers from left-wing institutions such as the Bank of China and other Chinese state-run business institutes were carrying food and water to comfort the striking workers. The unexpected gesture of solidarity touched the strikers, but the police panicked at the sudden influx of supporters. As British Hong Kong police officers tried to disperse the demonstrators, fistfights broke out.

Even though some of the Hong Kong police were Chinese or East Indian, they represented British imperial rule. The sight of them beating back our own people infuriated us activists as well as the crowd of curious onlookers. Many in the crowd joined the fighting. "Down with the British! Down with the yellow-skinned dogs!" Decades-old resentment against the British government and its lackeys erupted.

We saw left-wing activists mingle with the crowd to flush out undercover police officers. They patted people's waists and buttocks, checking for guns and handcuffs. I was repeatedly patted down, too, as my Hawaiian shirt hung loosely over my denim slacks. Despite orders from my superior, my contacts and I were drawn into the fray. Whenever we found an undercover officer, we shouted, "A running dog! Here's another running dog!" as the Red Line activists rushed over to beat him up.

The riot prevention troops soon appeared. Contrary to their name, these men in their distinctive blue caps did not manage to quell the angry mob. Instead, their presence provoked ordinary people to take up arms. The demonstration had now turned into a street battle. The May Riot had begun in earnest.

It was time to step back before things became more violent. Although my group had become separated, we were all keeping an eye on each other, and my contacts were waiting for my signal to retreat. I quickly gathered my group and we left, making our way through the crowd. I took the bus back to the club.

According to newspaper reports, both sides suffered casualties in the incident. In reporting the story, the left-wing *Wan Hui Pao* and *Da Kung Pao* fanned anti-British sentiment among their readerships and mobilized them for war. The right-wing newspapers reported that the Communists had organized mobs to fight the police and incite the riot.

Then came the Garden Road demonstration. From May 19 to May 22, Red Line activists took their places at the front lines of the processions. Clerks, students, bank staff, and workers of the left-wing institutes were among the demonstrators. Thousands marched to the Garden Road house of British governor Sir David Trench, nestled in a prestigious neighbourhood on the Hong Kong hillside. On the exterior walls of his house, they posted signs in Chinese characters, as the Red Guard—Chairman Mao's group of militant youth—had done during its "criticism" campaign in China. Some posters read "Down with David Trench"; others repeated the shouting slogans. The protesters blocked traffic, so that even the governor was confined there for days. They sang revolutionary songs and shouted

Down with British imperialism.
Down with the yellow-skinned dogs.
Down with the white-skinned pigs.
British Imperialism in Hong Kong will be defeated.
Being patriotic is no crime. Fighting against atrocities is justified.

The police drew battle lines along Garden Road. Using tear gas, they attacked unarmed demonstrators. They clubbed protesters on the head. The right-wing newspaper reported that demonstrators fell to the floor as soon as the police closed in and splattered themselves and each other with red ink to fake injuries. However, I saw differently. Hon, one of my recruits, had joined the demonstration with his co-workers. The police beat him until his head was covered with blood and his arm was broken; then they arrested him.

Once a demonstrator was caught, the beating began again with punches and kicks in the transport truck on the way to the police station. Usually two or three police officers continued the beatings in the cell. Sometimes an iron rod or wooden club was used to hit the prisoner's vital organs—the kidneys and liver. Hon was tortured this way, and then jailed for two years.

In the wake of the May Riot, as the leftists dubbed the clash, the government cracked down on all left-wing organizations. On June 8, 1967, we learned from the left-wing newspapers that the police had attacked the Public Works, China Gas, and China Light workers' unions, all headquartered in the same building in Kowloon. The workers resisted, but the police took over the union hall, smashing everything and killing three of the workers and injuring many. The deaths and injuries only further enraged people and so more strikes were planned.

On June 24, the leaders of all left-wing workers' unions called a collective strike. Some twenty unions joined in the action: the workers' unions of Kowloon Bus Company, China Bus Company, Water Works Department, Hong Kong Telephone Company, and those of many wholesale and retail grocer merchants. Prices of daily supplies increased, adversely affecting the lives of many Hong Kong citizens.

According to the British Hong Kong government, the multiple months of rioting in 1967 resulted in 51 dead, 832 injured, and 1936 prosecuted. The striking workers' report said there were 26 civilians dead, and 4979 arrested.* K.K. was caught delivering the *Wan Hui Pao* and was arrested. Fortunately, he received only a light beating, and a former student of his, by then a police officer, saw K.K. at the police station and secured his release.

To increase pressure on the British Hong Kong government, the Party introduced other Red Line leaders; together we organized pre-liberation Communist "flying demonstrations." One of my first demonstrations was planned for the intersection of Nathan and Waterloo Roads, in Kowloon. At 9 A.M., I casually strolled down Nathan Road. Just ahead of me, Wing Mui was window shopping with a few other students from right-wing schools. Across the street, Wei Yee looked like any other housewife going to market. I spotted the familiar blue-and-white uniforms of left-wing students in the throng of shoppers. Students from the Pink Line schools, more openly leftist than the Grey Line and less so than the Red, had also been summoned to the area. Protecting us, I was told, were crews of trade unionists and other Red Line workers. They had armed themselves with knives and clubs in case things turned ugly. For now, though, the weapons remained concealed in newspaper, indistinguishable from the golden thread fish and the green beans the vendors bundled up at the market. All of us milled about, pretending not to recognize each other while we waited for the signal: a banner. As soon as someone unfurled a revolutionary banner, we would rally around it.

---

* *Inside Story of 1967 Riot in Hong Kong* (in Chinese) by Cheung Ka Wai (Hong Kong: Pacific Century Press, 2000), 113. Author Cheung Ka Wai is a reporter for the *South China Morning Post*.

With growing unease, I checked my watch: 9:02. What had happened? Where was the banner? My heart pounded and my breath came quicker. *Should I retreat?*

"Don't expose yourselves or get arrested," Lo had warned. Those were the Party's orders. If the police captured our Grey Line activists, or me, our underground operations would be severely compromised. I understood the risk and danger to my life and that of my subordinates. This was for real, not merely a scene being filmed for a movie. It was a sacrifice we were all willing to make. Demonstrating was not allowed under British rule; we knew if we were caught we could be beaten, tortured, and jailed.

I am a leader. I must stand with my people. I stuffed my trembling hands into my pockets and hurriedly rehearsed a statement in case I was arrested: "I was just walking by. Your officer must have been mistaken. I work for a foreign company. Communist? No, not at all."

As the minutes ticked by, I grew more agitated. Suddenly, one of the students took matters into her own hands. Waving her arms, she ran to the median on Nathan Road and belted out, "Unity is strength!" That was enough. We rushed into the street to join her. Traffic halted. Some drivers cursed, but most gaped. Many passersby applauded us; others simply stopped to watch.

"Down with the British! Down with the running dogs! Oppose British-biased education!" The now-familiar chants rang out as we punched the air with our fists. We marched down Nathan Road in an impressive show of force. "Rise up! Rise up! Purge the city!" "End the corruption! End the oppression!"

Then I saw him. A young officer, Chinese, skinny, and pimply faced. His hands shook violently as he clutched a pistol, its wobbling barrel pointed at us. Other officers came running down the street. By the time they joined him, though, we had melted into the crowd. The slogan-chanting activists were nonchalant shoppers once again. Frustrated, the police arrested a few students, but the rest of us escaped; since we were not wearing uniforms, we could not be identified. The victory, this time, was ours. My heart was beating with pride and excitement.

This was only the first of many flying demonstrations. Public uprisings, particularly by supposedly right-wing students, surprised even British intelligence units. Only the Black Line had remained underground completely. It could not risk joining our flying demonstrations, but instead organized secret teams to hang up banners, plaster posters, and scatter flyers in their schools. Our success inspired us to take bolder steps.

We imitated the "cultural combat teams" of Mao's Red Guards. These teams of Hok Yau students sang and danced to revolutionary songs, put on street plays, and quoted Chairman Mao's teachings on sidewalks across the city. They appeared and disappeared much like the flying demonstrators. However, Grey Line demonstrations were more difficult to organize. The Party didn't want any of our Grey Line students, ones attending renowned government, Catholic, or Protestant schools, to get hurt or arrested. They must be protected but also be given the opportunity to train.

Wing Mui and twenty other students trained for a month in one of the cultural combat teams. They learned Mao's quotations in song, practised musical instruments, and learned a revolutionary dance. They were taught about the dangers of being a demonstrator, how to behave, and how to arrive and leave quickly.

Dong, dong, dong, warned the double-decker tramcar as it travelled down Chun Yuen Street in North Point, Hong Kong. With horns honking from two automobile lanes, hawkers calling from the vegetable and fresh-meat markets, and its many pedestrians, Chun Yuen was a busy street. Behind the street vendors were stores selling salted fish, dried mushrooms, and soy sauce. At 6 P.M., it was especially busy with shoppers picking up last-minute dinner items. To look the part, I bought a few vegetables from a street vendor. I looked at my watch: 5:58 P.M.

The students, arriving separately, began to congregate in front of the designated store. A small flatbed truck drove by slowly, and a few of the students grabbed their musical instruments and other gear off it. The Party had sent ten union workers to the demonstration area to support and protect the students. Two or three were farther down the street, but the majority were here, near the demonstration, amid the crowd. With but a signal from one of the lookouts, the students would merge effectively with the crowd and disperse.

At either end of the street, two or three small trucks—arranged by the Party—were to stall in the intersection and block traffic. This gave the students time to perform and then leave the area. And if the police showed up, their vehicles would also be blocked by the trucks.

It was six o'clock and the students stepped into place on the sidewalk. A drum rolled and a cymbal clanged, like the sounds of a Chinese lion dance, catching the attention of those nearby. Two students held up an eight-foot banner that read: "Students of Government and Private Schools Cultural Combat Team." A student with a megaphone read the banner aloud.

An audience gathered around in a semi-circle, curious. I could see from my position behind the crowd that a few of the students' hands were shaking. Wing Mui's eyes were trained on the ground. A student with an erhu, the Chinese two-stringed violin, began a bright melody. A Chinese flute and ruan, the Chinese alto guitar, joined at a quick tempo. The students began to sing Mao's quotations:

Troops must show concern for every soldier; all people … must care, love, and help each other.
Be resolute, fear no sacrifice, and surmount every difficulty to win victory.

As the audience clapped, the students moved into position for the next presentation. With a drum beating, the music changed to a march and the students sang the "Red Guard's Battle Song," making combat-like moves. The song is about Mao's Red Guards as leaders of

the Cultural Revolution and that they should unite with the people
to go into battle:

> Dare to criticize and repudiate, dare to struggle, never stop
> making revolutionary rebellion.
> We will smash the old world, and keep our revolutionary state red
> for ten thousand generations!

Next, the appreciative crowd was treated to a short play. Students
pretending to be police officers arrested a union worker. Another
worker came to fight off the police, then a drawing of the governor was
set on fire. Finally, the student with the megaphone gave a short
speech denouncing British rule and its "running dogs."

As the audience clapped and cheered for the youths' enthusiasm,
the students, without bowing, dispersed. Again, a flatbed truck cruised
by, and they deposited the gear. A flick of the wrist and a tarp covered
up the evidence. Within seconds, the demonstrators were gone. I
looked at my watch: 6:10 P.M.

In this way, we organized, demonstrated, and rebuked the British
for their role in Western imperialism. In the schools we infiltrated,
many right-wing students joined our cultural combat teams,
rehearsing and conversing with our left-wing students. Increasingly,
Hok Yau was exposing itself as a left-wing organization. The government responded by raiding our premises, searching for evidence
that connected us to the flying demonstrations and cultural combat
teams.

In early August 1967, a unit of police officers and British troops
descended on Hok Yau's North Point premises. The flat was Hok Yau
property, registered under the names of three Communist Party
members, also Hok Yau members. It was a small space, with a tiny
kitchen but a large sundeck. We used the space to organize and
rehearse. At the time of the raid, the only person in the flat was a
Youth League member named Tai. Hearing the beating of propellers,

he looked out the window, only to see a helicopter hovering over the sundeck. Tai quickly escaped to another flat. Government forces surrounded the building and scoured our flat but never caught Tai. Had they, he would surely have been beaten and jailed.

A senior British police inspector wrote of the incident: "Early in the morning on August 4, 1967, from Lei Yue Mun British Army Base to the headquarters of the H.M.S. *Timor* ... in Hong Kong by boat. Then boarded an air carrier at 6:30 A.M. When we arrived, the helicopters were already waiting. We carried with us submachine guns, handguns, dried food, and water. The helicopters took us to North Point and landed on the roof of Kiu Kung Mansion. The left-wing rioters disappeared, no one could be found. However, we did find a makeshift hospital in the building."*

When I inspected the flat later that day, the mess disgusted me. The troops had urinated on our floors and smeared feces on our walls. Papers lay scattered amid the human waste. The whole place stank. Slowly, with anger brewing, our members set about repairing the damage. The next day, Wei Yee issued "A public letter to the Hong Kong Patriot" describing what the British had done to us. It was published in the left-wing *Wan Hui Pao* newspaper. This public condemnation, however, did not prevent the police from returning, a month later.

Wei Yee had called a preparation meeting for another flying demonstration. Thirty cultural combat team members, most between the ages of sixteen and twenty and from the Chinese musical instrument group, gathered at the North Point flat to prepare banners and flyers. Some worked on a press release to give to the left-wing newspapers after the demonstration. I did not attend, but my wife, Wei Yee, did. Just before 9 A.M. on September 1, there was a knock at the door.

---

* In memory of the 1967 riot in Hong Kong, an article appeared in the May 6, 2001, edition of the Chinese newspaper *Ming Pao,* and published on its website at www.mingpao.com, July 11, 2001.

Wei Yee looked through the peephole. "Police," she hissed. "Lots of them."

Bang. Bang. Bang. The officers rapped insistently now. The youths tossed the banners and flyers over the sundeck into the courtyard twenty-four floors below. One fellow slipped the press release into the pocket of the sweater Wei Yee was wearing. My wife glared at him. Everyone noted his act of cowardice.

"Open up," a voice ordered. There was no time to dispose of the letter. Wei Yee slipped it into an inside pocket and swung open the heavy wooden door. A crowd of Chinese police officers along with a British commanding officer stood on the other side of the iron gate.

"What do you want?" asked Wei Yee.

"We're here to search your flat," said an officer.

"Do you have a warrant?" My wife stalled to give the others time to rid the flat of any remaining evidence.

The officer nodded.

"Let me see."

He consulted with the British officer before handing over the papers. After pretending to read the English, Wei Yee swung open the iron gate. The police shoved her aside, and the youths rushed forward to protect her. The officers responded with their clubs and riot shields. Using the shields' pointed centre, they beat everyone back and slammed the door shut behind them.

"Kneel down," they barked. "Kneel down and form a circle, facing inward."

Instead of kneeling—Chinese people hate the submissiveness of kneeling—the members squatted.

"Hold your hands above your heads." Seizing each outstretched hand, the officers smashed everyone's watches. Thirty watches stopped at 9:10 A.M. A few officers herded the boys onto the sundeck and began to beat them with batons and shields, while the girls remained squatting inside. Other officers began to destroy the flat. Folded tables and chairs that were being stored at the apartment had their legs torn off. Banners and music sheets ripped. The music team's instruments—erhu, drum, double bass, flute, and alto guitar—smashed. Our performance stage lights shattered.

As soon as the officers left, Wei Yee called me at home. "Run away, Kee Ngai. They might come for you next." Immediately I rummaged through my drawers and burned photographs and documents that might incriminate me. I could not risk the various photos exposing my contacts and contacts' contacts, and the reports, written on many tiny thin pieces of paper, were enough for the police to arrest me. And if I were arrested, I would no doubt be interrogated, tortured, and jailed. One of my contacts in a workers' union had told me her husband was arrested and interrogated for hours. For her husband, there was no trial, no judge, and no lawyer; he was jailed for two years. Ignoring possible danger, I then rushed over to North Point.

"Ore, it's safe to come in. They've left," said Sai as I arrived at the apartment. He was limping. His slacks were rolled up over a swollen kneecap.

"How are you?" I asked him.

Many of the girls, bruised and terrified, were hugging each other and sobbing. Some of the boys looked dazed. Others lay on the floor groaning, blood on their clothing. I saw Wei Yee, holding her arm. "The police officer was furious when I asked to see the search warrant," she said. "He was angry that I dared to ask."

"They came in and beat up the boys," said Julia. Her father had been killed that June defending the union hall from the police.

As the students told me what happened, I looked at their injuries. The girls were slender and lightweight, each under a hundred pounds. A few had fallen when the police officers pushed them, and two had broken ribs. Wei Yee's shoulder blade was broken. Most of the other students had bruises, and a few of the boys' faces, arms, and elbows were beginning to swell. Relying on first-aid skills I had learned from Mama, I did what I could.

When I finally had a chance to examine the damage, I saw the broken tables and chairs that were scattered around the flat, and the musical instruments, lighting, and other equipment that lay shattered. Even the cooking utensils were broken. The main difference between this raid and those at the union hall was that the police knew most of us were students. A simple beating and threats did the job— no deaths or serious injuries were necessary, or arrests. They had come to search for banners and flyers, and to demoralize us.

I called on my contacts in the Red Line unions for help. Did they know a kung fu master who could set bones and treat torn muscles? I couldn't send anyone to the hospital with injuries because that would require identification cards and police reports, and might lead to arrests and further complications. But nor could I trust any doctors or kung fu masters before I knew their political views; I would only trust one who supported the left-wing movement. I was put in touch with a kung fu master trained to deal with an array of injuries. I accompanied the injured to their first session with the master and arranged for follow-up appointments. For three months, I visited the injured at home, checking with the kung fu master on their recoveries. In the end, the Party paid the master three thousand Hong Kong dollars for the medications and services.

The raids of left-wing organizations continued for months, until early 1968. Meanwhile, Hong Kong's Education Department publicized our influence in the right-wing junior and senior high schools, warning that Hok Yau was a left-wing organization. We had arranged many secret cultural combat teams within Hong Kong University, King's College high school, and other prestigious right-wing campuses. In October, two of our club members attending Queen's College were arrested in front of the entire student body after being caught arranging a long banner on the side of the college building and tossing propaganda sheets to the ground below. By then the whole world knew Hok Yau was a left-wing organization. That labelled us as controversial. *It took us years to build Hok Yau's neutral image in the public's eye, only to have it*

*destroyed overnight. This is a heavy casualty. Is something wrong with
the Party's policy?*

The situation in Hong Kong deteriorated rapidly. Radical members of
the left-wing business merchants association's combat team planted
bombs in public places. In one incident, a bomb was placed on the tracks
to disrupt tram service. Instead, children were killed when they found it
and thought it was a toy. In another incident, a British police officer died
when he tried to remove a bomb he thought was a fake. It had been
wrapped in brown paper and left at a bus stop. On top of the box was
scrawled in red Chinese characters: "Compatriot do not come close."

There were of course many police officers who felt conflicting loyalties, including a traffic constable who was clearing the road for a
motorcade. A youth attacked him with a hand bomb. Although his leg
was injured, the officer did not immediately open fire; he later told a
journalist that he thought the young man was merely acting under the
influence of other people's persuasion.*

Then there was the infamous Lum Bun incident. Lum Bun was a
popular radio talk show host who not only criticized but openly
insulted the left-wing movement in Hong Kong. On his way home
from the radio station with his brother, Lum stopped his car at a sign
indicating road construction ahead. It was an ambush: gasoline was
poured on them and a match lit. They burned to death. Although
many right-wing newspapers and radio stations accused the
Communists of the murders, the police never made any arrests.

The violence took a severe psychological toll on the public. Lum
Bun's murder was considered an attempt to quell free speech in the

---

* *Ming Pao,* May 6, 2001, published on website July 11, 2001. Thirty-four
years had passed since the May Riot of 1967 and a reporter interviewed two
ex–police officers to reflect on history. Officer James A. Elms recollected that on
August 4, 1967, a helicopter was used to raid Kui Koon Mansion in North
Point. Hok Yau Club was on the twenty-fourth floor of this apartment building.
Officer Chow Charm Chiu, a traffic police officer, describes the story of the
youth's hand bomb.

British colony. People genuinely feared that the Communists would take over Hong Kong, and there was great resentment against the troublemakers.

Frightened by the growing militancy of various left-wing groups, many of our politically neutral members fled the club. We lost some of our most useful contacts from right-wing groups, including one fellow who worked for the government's Personnel File Department. Through him, the Party would have had access to private personnel information.

Facing a lack of public support as well as financial difficulties, the Party came under tremendous stress. Left-wing union strikers were able to support themselves by running unlicensed street vending carts and driving minibuses. Because of their involvement with left-wing groups, some people had lost high-paying, stable jobs and were forced to pick up whatever work they could find. Workers tried hard to return to their jobs at major companies such as Star Ferry, Electric Tram, China Motorbus, Hong Kong Telephone, and the Kowloon Bus Company. Without union workers within those companies, the union would cease to exist: they would have no workers to represent.

It was time to change tactics. By 1969, the Party had called on everyone to study Mao's thoughts and challenged union workers to "recover, transform, and change." Regaining the public's trust of Hok Yau was not going to be easy. Because of Hok Yau's tainted name, I began renting City Hall theatre, the city's finest performing space, under my name for our presentations. We were trying to regain Hok Yau's image in the artistic community and among right-wing schools. Though my workload at Associated Timber Industries was heavy, I continued to work diligently for the cause, to enlarge our united front, and to make friends for the club.

For one show, I had arranged for several high-profile music and dance troupes to perform as guest artists. We had on our program the Bow Dance, by the well-known dancer Lau Siu-Ming; Chinese musical instrument pieces; and performances by Hok Yau's own dance club. The interesting and varied program drew a large and appreciative audience, and we had a sold-out house.

The Party commended the club's leaders for maintaining our courage while being persecuted. "Hok Yau," said our superiors, "is a stove for refining ore into steel." Although we had lost some members, we had forged some worthy soldiers. When news of Wing Mui's bravery in a cultural combat team during the May Riot reached our superior leaders—the Hong Kong and Macau Work Committee—they requested, through Lo, a full report from me. The Party published the report in tiny character handwriting on thin sheets of paper and circulated it among its members as an example of how a dedicated right-wing youth could be converted into a useful Communist soldier.

Many of Hok Yau's study groups focused on Mao's teachings and a left-wing view of Chinese history. We sent teams of Party members and leftists, willing to accept re-education, to the New Territories. Our students, both male and female, slept in village halls, ate what the farmers ate, and did what the labourers did. Women always had an easier time than men getting factory work, and many of our female activists found summer jobs in factories to better understand what it was like to be a worker.

During our study groups, students discussed their school curriculum. We believed that textbooks designed by Hong Kong's Education Department distorted important parts of our history: the Opium Wars, unequal treaties, and the British annexation of Hong Kong and its territories. Many aspects of Chinese history, art, and literature were minimized, and instead, British history, English literature, and the English way of life were promoted. It was, we thought, an effective way for the British to encourage pro-Western thinking. We pointed out flaws of the Hong Kong schools and denounced them as tools for enforcing British slavery of the Chinese. In this way, we taught our students to distrust the British.

At the height of the Cultural Revolution and the May Riot, I shouted slogans denouncing British imperialism. Yet I was a textbook case of divided loyalties. Ironically, if I were given a choice to further my dance training in Shanghai or London, I would have chosen London without a second thought. And when I heard "God Save the Queen," or Western classical music, or even a British accent, I didn't think twice about that either. It was as though I had two minds: During face-to-face struggles, I hated the British. They mistreated our people, especially the poor. I felt there was great injustice against the Chinese people. But in daily life, my natural feelings and inclinations made me respect Western culture. My British-biased education had, indeed, affected me, and most likely, many other students in Hong Kong. In my mind, that was not a bad thing.

⚜

After Wing Mui's unsuccessful attempts at finding work in right-wing institutions, she agreed to consider working for a left-wing organization. The Party wanted her to work for the Bank of China in Hong Kong. The Grey Line often supplied graduates as clerks for China's state-owned organizations. Since Wing Mui reported to me, I began to prepare her for the transition to another post and superior. Since it was not my way to order my subordinates to comply with Party directives, I made sure they fully understood and agreed with the rationale for their transfers.

Every week for two months, I reasoned with her, shaping her thoughts, guiding her loyalties. One day, I arranged to meet her at my mother's apartment. Although I no longer lived there—my wife and I had rented a small flat in Wan Chai, Hong Kong, when Father moved back in with Mama—my mother did not object to my using Mei Mei's former bedroom for meetings. Ah Sim raised an eyebrow, but Mama never asked me questions. Wing Mui sat down. Other than our chairs, the only furniture in the room was the desk standing between us. She pulled a handkerchief out of her purse and burst into tears.

"I don't want to go," sobbed Wing Mui. "Why can't I stay with you?" Tears poured down her face. Her intense reaction caught me off guard, but I did my best to calm her. "We can't always stay in one place," I explained gently. "The revolution needs you. As a Youth League member, you must go wherever the revolution requires."

"I can't endure this anymore," she cried, then bellowed, "I'm in love with you."

I let out a long slow breath. *Aren't such intimate confessions usually murmured rather than shouted?* But Wing Mui was always such a bold girl. I tried to hush her. I didn't want to hurt her feelings, but what would Mama and Ah Sim think?

Finally, after draining my glass of water, I did my best impersonation of a father-like teacher. My stumbling response sounded brittle even to my own ears: "Thanks for being honest … I respect … only natural for a girl to fall in love. Nothing to be ashamed of … it takes two." I pointed out I was twice her age—and married. "You're too young to understand love, but you'll understand when you're older."

Wing Mui put both arms on the desk, threw her head down, and sobbed loudly.

"You have a bright future ahead," I added, trying to calm her. "Give it time, you'll be all right."

A few weeks later, she agreed to the transfer.

"You have a way with people," Lo often remarked to me, with more than a trace of envy in his voice. "I really must learn from you."

I was a few years older than him, which seemed to intimidate him. Despite my assurances that I would follow him like any other subordinate, I think he felt inadequate around me. There's nothing to learn," I assured him repeatedly. It was true. I did not capture the hearts of my subordinates by any technique. I simply loved them, honestly and compassionately.

I learned to care for people from Mama. Big Aunt—as Mama was called by her friends and patients—helped many families. She helped find jobs for friends' sons and daughters, she counselled them on

family affairs, and even helped them financially. She was always calm
in the midst of danger, as during the dangerous days of the Japanese
invasion of Kowloon, and passing through checkpoints on the road
of retreat to China. Her circle of family and friends had a saying,
"There was no matter that Big Aunt couldn't solve." Mama seemed
almost superhuman. But she still needed to think about her retirement. Who would support her? Father had given most of his savings
to Mei Mei when she left for Canada. Wei Yee and I never visited to
discuss these things with Mama. The poor and oppressed always had
a greater claim on our time. But Mama did expect help from us; it
was customary for the sons of the family to support the parents in
their old age. Strangely enough, to test the situation, Mama
approached Wei Yee.

"I want you to inherit my apartment. We can divide into two
units," Mama said. "You can stay in one unit, and Father and I can live
in the other. This way, you won't need to pay rent and you can take
care of us in our retirement years."

"I can't take the apartment, I'm a leftist," Wei Yee flatly refused.

Mama was probably not too surprised. Especially after the May
Riot, many leftists became more vocal and open. Although the Hong
Kong public had always disliked left-wing groups because they were
seen as causing trouble, Mama discerned our sympathies and even
supported our efforts to help the poor.

Next, Mama asked K.K., who still worked at Mongkok Workers'
Children School and earned only minimum wage, 360 Hong Kong
dollars a month. It was hardly enough to support his family of four, and
they were living in social housing. But first and foremost was the revolution; his personal life was secondary. He too refused Mama's offer.

Mama finally approached me and asked the same: "Why don't you
take the title on my apartment? We can divide in two and share it. You
won't have to pay rent."

"I'm a leftist, I can't own property," I told her simply, cruelly
refusing.

Being Communist members, my wife and I were proud proletariats and chose not to own property. With the heightened leftist activities after the May Riot, there also came increased criticism within the Party. There would be critique sessions to see who owned washing machines, a piano, or—a serious offence—property. But Mama didn't know any of this, only that we had given away our lives to the Communist cause. How could she get by without any income and no one to depend on? She was heartbroken and disappointed, but she didn't reproach us.

⁂

I was running a meeting at home when Ah Sim phoned. Two months had passed since Mama had offered to give me title of her apartment. "Kee Ngai, you must come over quickly. Your mother tried to kill herself," Ah Sim said.

What? How could this be?

Ah Sim had found Mama trying to hang herself. Luckily, she'd found Mama soon enough and released her while she was still breathing. "I don't know what to do. I called K.K. but no one was home. It is lucky that I found you," Ah Sim said.

I reassured Ah Sim that I was on my way over and quickly dismissed the meeting. When I arrived at Nation Building, I found Mama sitting at the kitchen table drinking a cup of tea. She looked pale and angry and dejected. Before I could speak with Mama, Ah Sim pulled me aside. "You must move back and help take care of your parents," she said. I nodded.

Stunned at seeing Mama like this, I tried to comfort her. I explained, "I will still support you with my earnings. Just because I won't take the title doesn't mean I won't support you."

Mama remained quiet.

"I must continue my work at the Hok Yau Club, but as the saying goes, 'Have rice, will share.' Everything will be all right."

Still no reaction from Mama. I left to attend another meeting. Father was out at the time; I never knew if he was ever told what happened.

For many years, Mama had seen Wei Yee and I work day and night, meeting after meeting, and she got the picture. She could not depend on me. I was crazy and heartless. *How can I explain my attitude and choices?* Even though I was shocked by Mama's suicide attempt, it didn't shake my devotion to the revolution. Consumed with Communist theory and rhetoric, my mind was filled with furthering the revolution and helping those in need. Somehow, that blinkered view did not include taking care of my own parents.

11

SOLDIERS HAVE
NO MOTHERS

1968–1973 Hong Kong, British colony

Peas. Tiny, perfectly round, sweet, tender peas. Chinese farmers did not sell them. Chinese peas grew old and hard long before they reached market. I hated picking the skins of old peas out from between my teeth. Shopping for young peas, though, gave me a pleasurable chill. Only the Dairy Farm, a British-owned supermarket in downtown Hong Kong, sold Western-style peas. I loved its peas.

For days, I had planned to cook peas for my comrades. Lo and his superior, Woon Ling, had called a strategic meeting of the Shadow Core at my home. Wang and Yuk Lin, who had also become Party members, would be here. The struggle against British oppression—the May Riot and its aftermath—had taken its toll on all of us. The Party's demand that we transform ourselves into proletariats drove us to malnutrition and exhaustion. I dreamed of providing my comrades with a hearty dinner, nutritious but not extravagant. Tonight, they would discover the sweetness of tender peas.

Wei Yee and I could ill afford to prepare eggs fried with peas or curried chicken with coconut milk. Barbecued duck, dried mushrooms, beef—these ingredients rarely found their way into our kitchen. But our comrades needed their strength to continue the arduous struggle. We resolved to sacrifice ourselves. We would eat and spend less so that they could enjoy a proper meal.

At the dinner table, I sat back, content to watch the others devour their dinners. Wang and Lo both wore glasses, and when they slurped their soup, their lenses fogged up. They were so intent on shovelling rice into their mouths that, when the clouded spectacles slipped to the tips of their noses, the men didn't bother pushing them back into place.

Within thirty minutes, the platters were bare. Pleased at accomplishing my goal, I cleared away the table and sat down for the meeting. Because Woon Ling served on the Hong Kong and Macau Work Committee at Xinhua News Agency, all of us in the Grey Line were accountable to her. By her joining us this evening, I sensed that it was to be a significant meeting where we would plot how to overthrow the British. Already left-wing schools and organizations had raised China's five-star flag. We expected China's People's Liberation Army to arrive any day to deliver us and institute a free and just society. In good spirits, I leaned forward to catch Woon Ling's instructions. She coughed a slight, hiccupping cough. Her hand covered a burp. In a cotton navy blue cheongsam, Woon Ling looked tall and slim. She seldom smiled, and when she spoke, she spoke with authority. She turned to me.

"Where did you buy those peas? They were so tender. All those dishes must have been very expensive. Do you always eat so lavishly?"

Stunned, I had no response. She was accusing me of living like the petit bourgeoisie, of betraying the revolution. Self-righteously, Lo and the others nodded their agreement. "Be careful," they warned. "You must repent of your bourgeois ways." They cited my love for ballet and Western classical music as examples of how the British imperialists had ensnared me. Only a slave of the British educational system would know where to buy such tender peas.

Instead of an inspiring strategy session, I faced an interrogation on my spending. The hardest part was that I admired Woon Ling. As the leader of the Grey Line and a member of the Communist underground Work Committee, she always seemed to behave like a martyr. I imagined she lived frugally and upheld the Party's convictions. I respected her judgment. This time, however, she was mistaken.

Facing this wrongful accusation, I did not say anything. I had a belief through my study of Chinese classic literature that there was no point in arguing. Right is right, wrong is wrong. At the end of the day, someone would know and understand. All the same, this disastrous dinner only motivated me to work harder for the revolution. I wanted to prove that even a member with a bourgeois background could be a useful tool for the Party, more so than some proletariats. Many Hok Yau students came from the impoverished working classes and could not afford to join the revolution. In tears, my contacts had told me how they longed to serve their country but had to instead support their parents and siblings. They simply could not continue sacrificing, or else their families would starve. Only those of us from the bourgeois classes could afford to devote ourselves completely to the revolution.

Still, the Party did not trust graduates from right-wing schools. It promoted only students from the left-wing schools. Students who grew up memorizing Mao's teachings. Students who blindly followed the Party and asked no questions. Students who depended on the Party to provide them with jobs. The rest of us, although having consciously sacrificed our bourgeois ambitions, were treated with suspicion because we did not depend on the Party for our livelihood. Our superiors' unspoken question was always, "If I had the opportunities he has, why would I give them up?"

The Party preferred operatives such as Fong Yu Ting. We dubbed him Short Guy Fong because he was barely five feet tall. After graduating from a left-wing high school, he worked for years in the covert Double-Grey division of the Grey Line. Members of this division never attended public demonstrations or made contact with organizations in the Grey Line, such as Hok Yau, or with the Red Line, or with anyone else for that matter—only with their Party superior. If these members camouflaged well enough, they might eventually become government employees. Fong had operated directly under his Party contact, apart from Hok Yau. Such isolation, however, was dangerous. Long-time underground workers, according to Party theory, may lose their moral integrity. Without the support and supervision of comrades, operatives may compromise their beliefs. The Party sent Fong to Hok Yau for re-education and training in Communist principles. He needed it.

Physical labour did not appeal to Fong. Moving tables and chairs would have soiled his fashionable slacks and sports jacket. He had taken great pains not to dress like a left-wing graduate, and his wardrobe came courtesy of a comfortable monthly living allowance from the Party. Fong claimed he needed to devote his energy to recruiting more students—he did not have time to work. In contrast, the Party had paid me a limited allowance, merely covering transportation and meals, to work full-time as Hok Yau's secretary. Whenever the club could not afford my salary, I found other jobs; I never drew a full allowance from the Party.

Fong clapped his hand on my shoulder one day. We were at my home, discussing our activists in government and other right-wing schools. He seemed pleased with himself, like a puppy showing off a newly found bone. "Do you know what cadre level we're in?" he asked Wei Yee and me.

The question perplexed my wife. "What do you mean, 'cadre level'?"

"We're in Hong Kong now, but what if we were in China? What official grade would we be at?"

I was annoyed. "What do I care about rankings in China when we're working for the revolution in Hong Kong?"

"It lets you know where you stand in the Party," Fong responded without embarrassment.

"So," Wei Yee asked after a moment's silence, "what grade do you think we ought to be at?"

"Probably about the same grade as a provincial premier …"

Fong's smugness repulsed me. *How can he focus on his own status, rather than our country and the betterment of the poor?* Wei Yee reprimanded him sharply for being status-conscious. Disappointed by our lack of interest, Fong sauntered off. It wasn't right. His way of thinking and acting wasn't right. I looked for an opportunity to guide him back to the proper path of a soldier in the revolution.

"Fong, do you know what people think of you?" I asked him later, with the sincere intention of helping him. He shrugged, averting his face. Undeterred, I continued. "They think you're lazy, that you don't do your share of the physical work. Remember the performance at HKU?" After the Hong Kong University performance, while the rest of the men hoisted scenery into a truck, Fong lounged against a wall and gathered a circle of young girls around him. With a dramatic wave of his newspaper, he had given impassioned speeches about poverty. The boys scowled and grumbled about his laziness but conceded he spoke well. Today, though, he remained silent during my lecture.

"You have many gifts. Use them to benefit the people around you. You must not consider yourself better than others, or rank yourself within the Party. Remember, the people must come first, not you."

Unsure whether Fong had taken our criticism to heart, Wei Yee and I reported his errors to Lo and Woon Ling. Two weeks later, I met with a repentant Fong.

"I am so sorry," he began, wiping away a tear. "I regret that it seemed like I was not putting enough effort into the revolution. I need to learn from you. You're a good role model within our circle." His tears fell faster now. "I see how you sacrifice yourself for the revolution. I always tell my contacts so." Moved by his sincerity, I began to weep, too. I hoped he would be my good comrade thereafter.

With his knack for persuasion, Fong easily recruited many students. His impressive numbers earned him several promotions within the Party. Once the recruits became Party members, they took orders from Fong. But after a while, they refused to talk to him because of his authoritarianism. Fong complained to his superior that he had too many contacts to deal with and that many of them were incompetent. Although this might have reflected poorly on him—after all, he was the one who had recruited them—Fong defended himself by casting the blame on the recruit or the recruit's family. Their having too many house chores, which took away time from studying Mao's thoughts, was just one such excuse.

My wife and I inherited many of Fong's recruits. Several had rebelled against Party directives. The Party was in a dilemma: dumping them meant possible exposure of Fong's circle of contacts if these recruits chose to speak about Fong's underground operation; keeping them was of no benefit to the revolution. The Party resolved to send them to us for re-education. I soon realized the problem was not with the recruits. When I met with Choi, he sat with his face pulled into a tight, angry mask. He refused to look at me. After several stony minutes, he spat out, "So, aren't you going to give a speech?"

"No, I'd rather listen to what you have to say."

"Fong never did."

I learned that Choi's decision to join the Party had been impulsive. Fong had persuaded him with newspaper-based rhetoric. Choi had never given much thought to sacrificing his life for his country or his comrades. After several meetings, I encouraged him to be more patriotic. The major obstacle Choi had was his disagreement with the Party's policies and tactics. He had constantly argued with Fong, who simply ignored him. Instead, Fong gave orders and demanded they be carried out.

The story was the same for all the recruits transferred to us. He had charmed them into signing up for membership. Once they joined, he did nothing to build up their love for their country or devotion to the revolution. Instead, at meetings, he talked for hours about his theories, without allowing his subordinates to comment at all. They felt ignored and abandoned. One fellow worked day and night for the small allowance Fong paid him. Exhausted, and with a heart condition, he finally left the Party. There were many deserters; my job was to persuade the remaining rebel recruits to stay. Wei Yee and I spent hours listening to them, sympathizing with their frustrations and admitting Fong's errors. Although he received all the credit for recruiting so many students, the burden of caring for them fell to us.

Despite his moral lapses and flawed recruiting techniques, Fong continued to climb the ranks. At one point, the Party summoned both Fong and me to report on our right-wing school initiatives in the aftermath of the May Riot. The Hong Kong government had at first cracked down harshly on left-wing organizations. After a year or two of raiding our offices, they switched strategies. Right-wing schools began offering extra-curricular activities that mirrored Hok Yau's many interest groups.

Lo told me that Fong had met with the Party superiors and given his report. Fong had gleaned statistics from the newspapers. Weaving his second-hand data together, he gave an eloquent report on how the enemy was undermining our efforts. His speech quoted policy analysts and political scientists. It sounded impressive but contained no fresh information. After hearing it, the Party wanted direct information from the front lines, not from the newspapers. They were waiting for my details.

I dutifully gathered my data. One by one, I interviewed my subordinates and contacts in schools and prepared a report. In a closed classroom at a left-wing school, I presented my report to Party leaders, members of the Work Committee, and the deputy of Xinhua News Agency. My report was solid. The Party could rely on it to make plans or adjust policy and tactic. No rhetoric or misguided interpretation here. Surely, the Work Committee would appreciate the value of my hard work.

It didn't.

Lo told me later that the Party wanted to promote someone in the front lines of the student movement. That person would provide the Party with up-to-date information on right-wing strategy and tactics.

The Hong Kong and Macau Work Committee would, based on our reports, promote either Fong or me. The answer came a few weeks later.

"Fong is one level up from me now," Lo informed me. He was characteristically detached. Lo did not trust or like me and so was pleased with Fong's promotion. On the other hand, his subordinate had skipped a level and had been promoted above him. That left Lo uneasy, but he was not about to confide in me.

So that's how the Party reacted to my report. By promoting Fong two levels. I shook my head in disbelief. Fong, who had embittered many of his recruits, who never lifted a finger to aid a comrade, who was self-serving and status-conscious, had launched himself two levels up by spouting newspaper dogma. I was stunned. How could the Party be so blind? Personal conduct and dedication, it seemed, should have bearing on one's rank. I cared for the welfare of my people. But the issue was not only that I hadn't received a promotion. For Fong to climb two levels above me raised the first serious doubts in my mind about the Party's values and methods. If the bad guys got promoted to lead the Party, where would the Party be headed?

Despite Fong's promotion, Lo instructed me to book a hall at a left-wing school and summon all of Hok Yau's leftist contacts, both members and non-members, to hear my report. Hundreds of activists came to the hall, listening with full spirit. My report gave them a thorough understanding of how the British Hong Kong government had changed its methods. The May Riot had exposed Hok Yau as a left-wing organization, and we had lost a considerable number of activists because of our extreme-left policy. Now we needed to know our opposition better and cast a new strategy accordingly. The government wanted to isolate Hok Yau—although not necessarily expose it as a Communist organization, since in doing so it would lose a good source of information on Communist activities in the student movement. Although we knew the British Hong Kong government must know that the Communist Party was behind Hok Yau, we also knew that the majority of people in Hong Kong didn't know this: they might know that Hok Yau was left wing, but they did not connect Hok Yau with the Communist Party.

Either way, we needed to break our isolation and merge back into the general public to gain the people's trust. Hok Yau should again become a neutral student organization, at least on the surface, to students and their parents. If Hok Yau could continue to recruit and submerge these new recruits in government departments, then Hok Yau would once again be painted as neutral. My comrades thought the analysis was good and we endeavoured to continue to work for the Party.

However, stories were trickling into the Hong Kong media about Communist wrongdoing in the Cultural Revolution. My uneasiness grew with each report of cruelty and massacre. A right-wing news-paper reported that the Red Guard had arrested Liu Shaoqi, a long-time revolutionary and chairman of the People's Republic of China—second in command to Mao. Liu was a commended expert of underground work and had written a book on his experience. A small Red Guard newspaper in China denounced him as a traitor, Kuomintang spy, and collaborator with the American imperialists. There was no proof, and no trial in an open court. The one-time faith-ful underground worker was left to rot in jail, without food, water, or medical care. *How could Mao treat his comrade like this?* They had fought together against the Kuomintang for two decades. *Had Liu betrayed the Party so badly to deserve such a terrible fate?*

Liu died in prison in 1969.

Then there were stories about Mao's wife, Jiang Qing. She had ordered all the movie stars in Shanghai to go to struggle meetings: meeting after meeting, one after another was accused of being a cultural counter-revolutionary. Some were tortured; many committed suicide. The Hong Kong right-wing press, however, pointed out that Mao's wife had been an actress in the 1920s and 1930s, and that many of those she incriminated were her contemporaries: Jiang Qing attempted to obscure her past by destroying the movie industry.

These rumours did not affect me as much as the common people's stories of suffering. For more than ten years, I read their stories in *People's Literature,* a monthly left-wing magazine published in China. As top Communist leaders struggled among themselves for power, the Party did not have time to censor every publication. There were dreadful accounts of villagers starving as famine swept northern China in the early 1960s. In a small Chinese village, the villagers had lost their yearly harvest because of a drought the year before. The district Party secretary had promised to help with thirty thousand pounds of seeds for the coming season. As planting season approached, the seeds had yet to arrive. When a village representative inquired about the promised seeds, the district Party secretary intimated that before the seeds would be released, he would like a visit from Siu Ling, a beautiful village girl.

Siu Ling worked hard and lived a frugal life. When the villagers told her about the secretary's request, she likely sensed the purpose of the request and refused to go. With the imminent planting season, the villagers grew desperate. For days, they implored her to grant the secretary's request, saying that the livelihood of the village depended on her. Finally, Siu Ling gave in and spent a night with the secretary. A week later, when the villagers went to Siu Ling with the news that the seeds had been released, they found that she had committed suicide.

Another story recounted how some students who were sent north for re-education had fallen in love with each other. When this was discovered, they were punished by separation. Others were falsely accused of rape and executed. Although these accounts focused criticism on local leaders—never the Party, Central Committee, or higher levels—I felt the Cultural Revolution had gone too far and that something was seriously wrong.

Even within Hok Yau, I noticed how irrational the extreme leftist policies had become. Because it considered education a form of foreign enslavement, the Party exhorted students to quit school and devote themselves to the revolution. The Wong girls took this challenge to heart. The three girls came from a wealthy merchant family. They left their home in Hong Kong's exclusive Peak district to experience the worker's life. The two younger sisters found unskilled jobs in a garment factory. The eldest, Mae, who was my contact, worked in a textile factory. To live more authentically, each girl found a worker's family to board with. After two weeks of sharing a wooden hut with a family of five, Mae remained in high spirits. "I was so spoiled before," she gushed. "Visiting the poor can't compare with living with them."

She described the hut as damp in the rain and hot in the sun, offering only flimsy shelter from the elements. The neighbourhood smelled of rotting fish. Rats and flies infested her new home. "We have to chase the cockroaches away whenever we eat," Mae said. "I can't sleep at night because the rats and cockroaches scare me. I must be braver. Besides, I share a bed with the children and their grandma. If I flap around too much, they can't sleep either."

Despite her youthful enthusiasm, I was worried about her welfare. "You don't have to do all this, Mae," I said.

"Of course I do. I need re-education. There is such a huge gap between my family background and the proletariat class."

I knew that, but it saddened me to see how much the Wong girls were sacrificing unnecessarily. Without an education, they would have no hope for the future. *What good would it do to re-educate these students?* As workers, they could do nothing for the student movement or the government. But the Party had already criticized me for leaning too far to the right. It wouldn't do for me to cast doubt on Party policies. All I could say to Mae was, "Consider your health."

I found it even harder to accept the Wong girls' situation in light of how our leaders lived. The Party encouraged us to confess our sins regularly in purification sessions. Criticizing ourselves would keep us honest and humble before our peers. In one of these sessions, Lo had admitted he owned a TV, stereo, washing machine, and piano. He enjoyed the convenience and pleasure of owning these appliances.

After confessing, however, he did not renounce these trappings of capitalism. Instead, he continued to indulge in Western luxuries while condemning the Western lifestyle.

Disappointed by the incompetence and hypocrisy of people like Lo, and doubting the wisdom of Party policies, I began to do as I saw fit. I could not allow the failings of a few comrades, even if my superiors, to hinder the revolution or harm my people.

At Hok Yau, all our materials were subjected to censorship by the Party in Hong Kong and, if deemed necessary, Guangzhou. Every speech, every skit, every song had to be approved before it could be performed. The music group's performances were no exception. When Choi, my contact who headed the group, submitted his program for an upcoming performance, I dutifully passed it up the chain of command. Word came back that two songs, "Blowin' in the Wind" and "Where the Boys Are," were unacceptable. The songs were too Western and would corrupt club members. They were to be struck from the program.

"That's ridiculous," I muttered to myself. "These are wonderful songs about resisting war." Someone above me didn't know his or her music. Ignoring the directive, I granted Choi permission to go ahead with his repertoire.

"That was foolish, Kee Ngai," Lo scolded me. "The Party is greatly displeased that you disobeyed a direct order."

"The songs are harmless," I protested.

"Those students not from left-wing schools are far too familiar with the Western way of life, which would poison our proletariat forces. Furthermore, the songs are bourgeois. You are far too sympathetic toward the enemy. And toward those who are wrong."

It wasn't worth debating the point with him, so I stalked off. *Those who are wrong.* I had heard that one before. Lo had often taken me to task for defending my subordinates. Spoiling them, he said. A particularly ugly situation had developed over Winnie and Keith. She was a young girl, about thirteen. He was eighteen, rode a motorcycle, and was labelled a gangster. He offered her rides to the club every day, and they studied together. At least, *she* studied. Their relationship seemed innocent enough until Wang and Yee-ling interfered. Wang was Winnie's group leader and Yee-ling, a Party member, was the club's resident gossip. Whispers spread throughout Hok Yau about how promiscuous Winnie was. Overnight, she was labelled a slut and he, a crook. Wang and Yee-ling were determined to break up the couple.

When I realized what was happening, I confronted my comrades. Although they insisted Winnie and Keith would spread corruption within the club, Wang and Yee-ling left the teenagers alone after that. The rumours eventually died down, but my fellow Party members bore a grudge after that incident. They accused me of always protecting "those who are wrong." I disagreed. By disobeying misguided directives, I was upholding my oath to serve my country and protect my comrades.

⚓

In 1968, I was laid off from Associated Timber Industries, where I had worked for five years. It was the year after the May Riot, and the height of the Cultural Revolution. I was glad to be free from routine office work so I could dedicate more time to the revolution. My office work schedule had been eight hours daily Monday to Friday, and a half-day on Saturday, with no vacation days. This prevented me from joining many Hok Yau activities, particularly the picnics and camps during the students' Easter, Christmas, and summer holidays. My Party superior had always pointed out the benefit of being a teacher if I was working within the student movement.

After being laid off, I decided to become a teacher, despite the sixty percent pay cut such a position would entail. Hong Kong high schools ran two sessions per day, morning and afternoon classes. I could teach school in the morning and visit students and their families in the afternoon. I could devote more time to the revolution. Wei Yee criticized me for not being practical. I thought she was being selfish while I cared for the good of the revolution. I set about finding a school to hire me; the school would then apply for my teaching licence.

For one year, I taught Chinese history at Roydon House, a private English high school where all classes were in English except for my class and that of Chinese literature. Half the student population was Caucasian—Portuguese, European, Euro-Asians, and British—and the other half was upper-class Chinese. It was not a good source of recruits.

In Hong Kong's education system, the "public" government junior and senior high schools were the best schools, but they were difficult to get into; although it didn't matter if the student was rich or poor, he or she had to sit a standards exam. Students were selected from those who had passed the exam, based on their results. The best candidates for the Youth League were at the government-run and at the right-wing schools, which had mostly Chinese students. I resolved to transfer to one of those schools as soon as I could.

A year later, I joined the right-wing Lock Tao Secondary School, a partially subsidized private high school, teaching economics and public affairs to lower-middle-class students. As a teacher, I was sensitive to the negative criticism given to the young students. At their age, they could accept detention or copying of sentences one hundred times if they did something wrong. But sarcastic attitudes and unjust accusations crushed their spirits.

I treated the students well; I didn't criticize or verbally abuse them. I taught the curriculum, plus practical applications, such as import and export, customs, and foreign exchange, that would be especially useful if these students were going to look for jobs upon graduation. I also talked about the life of the poor and the rich, about gambling, the effects of drugs, how the drug dealer ensnares, and gangster tactics. I wanted my students to analyze a gang member's future: When he reached the age of thirty, forty, or became old and weak, what would happen? What would his family life be like?

I had seen many students become gang members; boys were beaten up, girls were trapped and sold to brothels. Students were often targeted, as they were easily threatened to pay up or join the gang. Gang members carrying long knives often waited outside the school gates, and some of our students were targeted and chased. One boy, Joseph, told me he had been constantly bullied by older students. Wanting to get revenge, he joined a gang. At first, he was excited and proud. The older gang members took revenge on those who bullied him. Each day they treated him to snacks and meals. Before long, they showed him pickpocketing skills and how to carry out robberies. Eventually, he wanted to try his luck at pickpocketing, then robbery. He swore to me that no one had forced him to do it: Joseph had wanted to prove his ability and willingness. The gang members treated him fairly and took care of him as they promised. When he was sick, he stayed in the gang's hut on an apartment roof and they brought him food.

After a few months, Joseph knew he had changed. He had once been polite and gentle; now he behaved in wicked ways. He no longer went home, since his parents had also noticed the change in him and questioned him. Instead, he ate with his gangster friends and slept in the hut. His gang friends continued to take care of him and share their rewards with him. Some nights when he couldn't sleep, he thought about what I had said about the bleak future of a gang member, and he wanted urgently to part with the gang. But he knew it was dangerous to try to leave. The consequences were huge, and his family would have to cooperate. They would have to move far from where they lived now, without giving any reason to anyone. He told me all this after class one day.

Joseph disappeared about a month later, but I never knew if he separated from the gang, as was his wish, or if he had been killed.

⁂

My discontent with the Party continued to grow as my superiors' competency proved untrustworthy. This was how I justified our having a child. When Wei Yee and I married, the Party had told us not to have children because we were undercover student movement activists. We were obedient cadres and had rarely questioned our superiors. As I drew closer to forty, it no longer made sense to put off having children. We had waited eight years; waiting any longer would endanger my wife's health. It was traditional to have children in Chinese culture: just as I was expected to get married, I was expected to have children. It was natural for us to want one. Not knowing what it was like to have a child, we argued that having one would not interfere with our work. After much debate, the Party grudgingly agreed.

"One child. Just one. No more," Lo warned us. "You must put the revolution first. Concentrate on the club."

Our parents did not know the Party's directive forbade child-bearing; they only knew that we planned to have a child. They were happy. A few weeks after Mama's attempted suicide, Wei Yee and I had moved back to live with Mama at Nation Building. Now, with a grandchild on the way, Mama endeavoured to further improve Wei Yee's health. Wei Yee and I agreed that we would give up our flat and move back in with Mama.

Two months before Wei Yee gave birth, she put on so much weight that she had to use a chair as a walker to support herself. When her labour started, we took a taxi from our flat to the Star Ferry in Tsim Sha Tsui and then another taxi to the hospital on the Hong Kong side. She had never experienced such a difficult trip.

Our daughter, Lei Chen, was born in the spring of 1970. At first, Lei Chen lived with us in Mama's flat. Both Father and Mama were fond of her. They took good care of Wei Yee and helped her with Lei Chen. But not long after she was born, Father and Mama had applied for a visa to Canada to see Mei Mei. Mama had been repaid for some loans and now had about ten thousand Hong Kong dollars in savings. A tidy sum, but not enough to live the rest of their lives on. Their disabled daughter was my parents' last hope for retirement life. Mei Mei had always asked them to come to Vancouver. If they liked it, and Mei Mei could support them, they would stay.

Mama again offered to transfer the title of her flat to K.K. and me. But again we refused. Mama sold her flat before she and Father left for Canada, in January 1971.

Meanwhile, the Party had rented a flat for its meetings and now asked Wei Yee and I to take care of the place. With Mama selling the apartment, it suited us perfectly. We would live there as normal residents to cover up the fact that it was a Communist Party meeting place. From then on, we moved our residence approximately every eighteen months to avoid discovery. Given such unstable living conditions and our hectic work schedule, we decided to put Lei Chen in a childcare home. In Hong Kong society, both parents usually worked, especially in the lower classes; the workdays were generally ten to twelve hours without breaks, six days a week. Unless a relative was available to help, it was common to place babies and toddlers at childcare homes, where they stayed overnight. Parents would pick up their children on Saturday night after work and return them to the childcare home on Sunday night.

The Party referred us to the Chows, a couple in their forties who provided childcare services at their home, a large two-level apartment. With two hired helpers, the Chows took care of more than twenty babies. In essence, the Chows became Lei Chen's foster parents while Wei Yee and I concentrated on our work at Hok Yau. While other parents were picking up their children on Saturday night, Wei Yee and I were busy with student activities. We refused to let a baby hinder the revolution. Luckily for us, the Chows adored Lei Chen and didn't mind keeping her on the weekends. Every month when I went to pay the Chows, I took a quick look at my baby in the crib, then rushed back to work.

As the Party had, after the May Riot of 1967, called to "recover, transform, and change," we were urged to study Mao's thoughts. We organized weekly secret study groups in which Mao's teachings were meditated on, memorized, and recited. Our new schedule also included regular trips to China. The Party, with our help, organized five- to ten-day "sightseeing and study" trips to China for their activists and Communist Youth League and Party members. Taking turns, Wei Yee and I led monthly groups to China to visit historical sites, such as Mao's childhood village of Shaoshan, in Hunan province, and Jianggangshan, in Jiangxi province, an important city in the Communists' underground movement.

During the Christmas holiday of 1969, I led a group to Jianggang Mountain in Jiangxi province, where, in the 1930s, Mao had established a guerrilla base to fight the Kuomintang. My group was a combination of senior high school, college, and Hong Kong University students, and young teachers—thirty in all. They took care not to mention their destination to their parents.

The first day of our journey, we took several trains to reach Changsha, in Hunan province, where Mao had studied and taught when he was a young man. There we stayed at a high-end hotel, paid for by the Party. Each spacious room had twin beds and a huge bathroom. And it had central heating—a rarity. Our lavish breakfast consisted of steam buns, congee, hot and spicy pork with cabbage, fried red peppers, and chicken with vegetables. We thanked the Party wholeheartedly for its attention to such luxury as we tucked into our meals.

We travelled by bus to the next province, Jiangxi, where we stopped at the coal mine in Pingxiang municipality. Mao Zedong and his second in command, Liu Shaoqi, had organized workers here in the late 1920s. We stayed in the school dormitory for three nights. As our morning ritual, we went to the school hall to pay homage to Mao: some bowed, some asked Mao for strength, others quoted his sayings, and a few of us stood silently. We attended small group studies of Mao's thoughts and took afternoon naps. In the evenings, we had heart-to-heart talks, during which I tried to deepen the students' understanding of Mao's teachings. We also had recreational time, where we sang revolutionary songs, took part in folk dancing, visited a shooting range, and paid respects to a martyr's family. The son, a soldier in the People's Liberation Army, had died fighting the Kuomintang.

On the third day, we visited Jianggang Mountain. Narrow walking paths led us to the summit, overlooking the border of Hunan and Jiangxi provinces. The grounds and hills around us were barren and dry, the light brown earth devoid of vegetation. Trenches and outposts from the civil war remained, and to the east and west lay miles and miles of roads and paths. We could see how crucial the Communist guerrilla base had been during the civil war in detecting troop movements. The students were seeing the hardships of revolutionary life up close and developing an appreciation for it.

At the end of our trip, the Hong Kong and Macau compatriot hostel, the official hostel for left-wing workers and student activists, hosted an authentic Cantonese farewell banquet for us in Guangzhou. While we drank potent Chinese liquor, local cadres and People's Liberation Army soldiers gave encouraging speeches. As the group's leader, I gave a concluding speech of what we had learned during the trip, and thanked the cadres for taking care of us.

Early the next morning, we headed home. On the train to Kowloon, we separated into groups of two or three and mingled with the other passengers so as not to draw attention to ourselves. We would pretend not to know each other and there would be no more discussion of the trip.

These trips continued until 1972, when the Party decided to stop re-educating leftists and instead concentrate on recruiting more Hok Yau members.

⚓

One day, I ran into Foo, my former superior. As we chatted, he mentioned casually, "I heard your daughter was in the hospital," the way one might say, "I heard you had rice for dinner last night."

I leaned forward, "When?"

"A few months ago. She was running a high fever and the Chows couldn't find you."

"Is she all right?"

Foo shrugged. "Don't know. I suppose so. She was only in the hospital for a few days."

I felt ashamed quizzing him about my own daughter's health. I hadn't spent much time with my daughter in her first year of life. When I shared the story with Wei Yee that night, she felt the same and suggested visiting Lei Chen that week. I agreed, but one week quickly became two. There were so many contacts to see and families to help, we barely had time to eat or sleep. Compared with the poverty and hardship in the resettlement areas or on the boats in Aberdeen, one little girl's now-healed fever did not seem so important. *Children fall ill from time to time. The Chows love her and care well for her. Our daughter is in capable hands.* My guilt faded as I again devoted myself wholeheartedly to the revolution.

When Lei Chen began to walk, the Chows were delighted and called us. We rushed over, saw our daughter walking around the other babies' cribs, and became excited, too. As she walked toward us, the reality of my being a father finally dawned on me. Wei Yee had a similar reaction. We immediately sought to bring Lei Chen home to live with us. To do this, we requested a reduction in workload at Hok Yau. The Party refused our request. We had no choice but to keep Lei Chen with the Chows for the time being.

To support the family, and pay for the additional expenses incurred by having a child, Wei Yee and I both taught at right-wing schools. Our day began with us rushing to our jobs, teaching from 8 A.M. to 1 P.M. Then, after eating our first meal of the day—steamed rice with salt—we again rushed off to attend meeting after meeting, from 2 P.M. to midnight. There were meetings to encourage or reprimand our contacts and to hear their reports, meetings with our superiors, and meetings to organize groups and plan. There were meetings to set vision, to strategize policies, and to implement them. It was never-ending. After the last meeting, I would cook a meal for us. By the time we had washed up, it was usually 2 A.M. We got up at 6:30 A.M. the next morning to catch the bus before the morning traffic jam. There never was enough time or sufficient nutrition, and our non-stop schedules were taking a toll on our health.

My very first contact, Leung, conducted his family life the same way. He was an honest and sincere man and, like me, was insidiously brain-washed and adopted Communists theories. All and everything for the revolution, saving the populace and the world from hardship, liberating everyone until all can enjoy the good life. And our family, our parents, our siblings would be the last to benefit. But I also saw many whose personal interests came first, often hurting other club members and comrades. I struggled with what I was taught and what I saw.

⚜

"Your daughter has chicken pox," Lo announced. "The Chows want you to contact them." Although those were his words, his tone and demeanour said, *I told you a child would get in the way*. But I had grown accustomed to ignoring Lo.

It was 1973. The Chows, having tried to reach us without success, turned to a friend who had Party contacts. We needed to take Lei Chen home immediately to avoid infecting the other children. Wei Yee and I picked up our daughter, covered in blisters, that night. Watching her scratch her rashes roused our guilt. Half-whimpering, Lei Chen protested leaving the safety of Auntie and Uncle Chow's home, but the fever left her too weak to fight off these strangers who were her own parents. She glared at us, her brow furrowed with suspicion. Taking shifts, we watched her through the night. For an entire week, we watched her twenty-four hours a day. This furiously feisty toddler was our daughter. My daughter. How much I had sacrificed for the revolution.

Lei Chen did not return to the Chows' after she recovered from the chicken pox. I continued to teach at Lock Tao Secondary

School, while Wei Yee taught kindergarten near our flat. I took a morning shift, she worked in the afternoons, and so we were able to care for our daughter on our own. During the many evening meetings at our flat, Lei Chen would sit quietly as if listening and watching all that was said and done. Everyone was surprised that a toddler was able to sit still for so long. We were lucky that she was so well behaved, leaving us to devote as much time as we could to our work.

Then the telegram arrived.

Who would send me a telegram? I tore open the envelope. "Mother critically ill. Call 604-872-5555 collect. Urgent. Mei Mei."

Various scenarios flashed through my mind. Had Mama been injured? *Is she dying?* I racked my brain for clues. Mama's last letter had arrived two months ago and it contained nothing unusual apart from grumblings about Father and Mei Mei. Still in shock, I scrawled the date and time on the telegram: April 14, 1973, 7:30 P.M.

Calling long distance was a complicated affair. I called Hong Kong Cable and Wireless Company, located in the Central district, to make an appointment for a long-distance phone call. The earliest it could offer was 8:30 P.M., an hour away.

Weeks had gone by since I last gave my mother a thought. Now I couldn't stop thinking about her. The firmness of her grip on my hand as we marched past Japanese soldiers. The droop in her shoulders after a long day of visiting patients. The pride in her voice when she bought her flat. Then nothing. My memories of Mama had grown sparse in recent years. Soldiers in a revolution have no mothers.

In a tight cubicle at Cable and Wireless, I waited while the operator connected me to Mei Mei in Vancouver. "How's Mama?" I asked the moment my sister came on the line. "How long has she been sick?"

"Mama's in intensive care. She went through four surgeries. I'm very worried."

"What's her condition?"

"She found out that her flat at Nation Building could sell for four times higher now than when she sold it. She was extremely upset. Then she tried—"

"But what's her condition?"

Mei Mei ignored my interruption. She wasn't about to let me rush her explanation. "Then she tried to earn some money to make up for the loss, for selling the flat too cheap," my sister continued. "I told her not to, but she didn't listen to me. She was babysitting and mowing lawns. She only listens to you."

After prodding, I learned Mama had an infection in the gall bladder duct. Years before, she had been admitted to the hospital for a gall bladder infection. Then, some of my students at Hok Yau had taken shifts to help ease my burden of caring for Mama. Her doctor decided to remove the gall bladder to prevent future complications, but the duct had to remain to produce bile. Years later, her gall bladder duct became infected. Again, she went to the hospital, and K.K. and his wife, Ah Sim, and I took care of Mama. This time, however, Mei Mei was alone. Father could only do so much to help her.

"She had to fast before her gall bladder surgery," Mei Mei plodded on with her story. "That gave her an ulcer. She had internal bleeding. The doctor had to operate again to find out what was wrong. He even stopped her transfusion, because he said it was a waste of blood. But I yelled at him, 'Look, my mother is still alive. Why don't you keep trying? There might be a chance.'

"I have to work every day. After work, I have to visit her in the hospital. I'm dead tired, Kee Ngai. You have to come help me. Mama needs you." Mei Mei's voice cracked with the strain.

"I'll come as soon as possible," I promised.

I resigned from Lock Tao Secondary School the next morning. The regular Shadow Core meeting with Lo was set for the following day. I could not wait another twenty-four hours for permission to leave. But I had no choice.

"My mother is critically ill," I told Lo. "I need to see her in Vancouver."

No response.

Pushing ahead with my request, I said, "I also need five thousand dollars for my expenses. Please relay my request to the Party. It's urgent. My mother is dying."

Lo agreed to ask the Party for me. The others, Wang and Yuk Lin, said nothing. Their expressionless faces surprised me. No one asked about my mother's condition or my plans. I broke out into a sweat. *Don't they care?*

Although these leaders showed no concern for my situation, my subordinates did. "When are you leaving?" Winnie asked. "Do you have enough money?" Keith, now Winnie's fiancé, added, "We've saved five thousand dollars for our wedding. Why don't you use it?"

Others echoed their offer. Their compassion touched me. Everyone who was a leftist in the club knew I had no savings. They knew I had donated my earnings to the revolution. The ordinary people were so different from my comrades in the Party; they cared.

"No, the Party will help me," I assured them. "If my comrades were in danger, I would risk my life to save them. I'm sure my comrades will do the same for me." Saying these words reassured me, too. Three days had passed since I submitted my request. Lo told me there was no news from Guangzhou about permission for me to leave Hong Kong or funds for my trip. After another day went by, Lo began dodging my questions.

"May I leave?"

"I don't know ..." Lo's voice trailed off. "I haven't heard anything."

"No permission?"

"Not yet."

"What about the money?"

No answer. Then, "Let's focus on Hok Yau, shall we?"

Panic welled up inside me. And I realized an ugly truth: I could not depend on the Party to take care of me. I had devoted the prime years of my life and all my money to the Party and the revolution it promised. It had devoured me without a conscience. And I had allowed it to happen.

I felt anguished and betrayed, as if an old friend had turned his back on me, a friend I had shown nothing but devotion and respect. I had always cared for my comrades when they fell ill, when they married, when their parents died, when they needed money. Now, for the first time in twenty-four years, I asked the Party for support, and there was none. I was devastated. My stubborn blind trust of the Party melted away. And yet, a large part of me still believed in the cause, if not my fellow comrades. Brushing aside Lo's attempts to change the topic, I declared, "I'm leaving. With or without permission. My mother is dying and I must leave."

Mei Mei and an aunt lent me the money for airfare. My plane left Hong Kong on April 20, six days after I had received the telegram. During the long flight, I mulled over my situation. How naive I had been to believe the promises. *Exert yourself for the Party and the Party will take care of you.* It wasn't true. I had been living a fantasy, in a hollow place with nothing to depend on. Many of my classmates at Chung Chi College held top positions in companies, in government, in universities. I was forty and penniless. The support promised by the Party had proved illusory. *How am I going to take care of my family?*

A stranger smiled at my halting English and directed me to the baggage claim at the Vancouver International Airport. Such politeness surprised me. The Party had always told me "Like the sun at dusk, the Western nations are coming down." But this did not seem like a society on the verge of collapse. The people here seemed pleasant and prosperous.

A thin, dark Mei Mei was waiting for me. "Finally," she humphed, "it's about time you got here."

A fresh breeze greeted me as I stepped out of the terminal. *The air smells sweet here; it's so clean.*

On the way back to her home, my sister vented her frustration. She had borne the burden alone far too long. "Mama won't listen to me. She never does. After her surgery, for instance, she insisted someone stole the diamond ring from her hospital night table. The nurses in the ward searched for it. I told her the ring was at home, but she wouldn't believe me. She never listens to me. I was so scared I would have to handle this on my own. I need you here."

Mama had undergone surgery four times in two weeks. Mei Mei described for me again the gall bladder infection, the stomach ulcer, and her battles with the doctors over the blood transfusion. "I even asked my friend to bring me holy water from Jerusalem," she said. "I gave it to Mama and prayed for her." Whether it was the holy water or the surgeries, Mama had survived the worst by the time I arrived. "She's in intensive care, and still in critical condition," Mei Mei explained, "but they've cleared the infection for now. They just want to prevent further infection and allow her to recover."

"So what do you need me to do?"

"Manage Mama. She's not allowed to eat solid food but insists on having rice. She scolds me every day for not bringing her some from home. But even liquids make her throw up. She can't eat anything. You explain it to her. She listens to you. She'll listen to you more than to me."

⁜

Hospitals the world over smell of soap and antiseptic. Vancouver General Hospital was no exception. I dodged a janitor mopping the linoleum floors as I half-jogged to keep up with Mei Mei. Despite her prosthetic leg, she marched through the halls with no-nonsense speed and determination. Father did not accompany us; he and Mei Mei both agreed he was more useful at home, where Mama wouldn't grumble at him.

Mei Mei disappeared through a door, and I followed. My heart pounded faster and louder at the sight of the tubes sprouting from the childlike form tucked beneath the sheets. *This can't be my mother.* I glanced quickly at the only other patient in the room—no, that wasn't my mother either. Where was her carefully coiffed, jet-black hair? The brittle steel wool that passed for hair had not enjoyed a stylist's touch for months, if not years. Following my gaze, Mei Mei explained, "The nurses needed to chop her hair."

I continued staring, speechless, at the woman in the bed. *This can't be my mother,* I repeated to myself. My mother was beautiful, clever, determined, and strong. This woman was far too short. Her crinkled-rice-paper skin had the translucence of the very old and dying. I couldn't make out much flesh between her bones and the beige parchment stretched over them. *This must be a mistake.*

"Kee Ngai," Mama whispered, then paused for breath. Her eyes rolled languidly in my general direction. Dull, filmy eyes. Those weren't my mother's either. I remembered fierce, shiny black-marble eyes pinning me in their gaze, not clouded fish eyes. It was as if her soul had been taken away from her. Memories of another Mama flashed through my mind. Mama, the gifted doctor, had dispensed advice with confidence. Mama, the negotiator, had outwitted gangsters, Japanese officers, and Communist guerrillas. Mama, my protector, had calmly led me through enemy barricades. Mama, my advocate, had shielded my leftist activities from my right-wing father. Mama, my mother, had continually watched over us and worried about us on the road of retreat and, indeed, all our lives.

Now, I was faced with Mama, the critically ill patient, and deep regret washed over me. All these years, I had failed. I had failed to take care of her, to honour her. When Father and Mei Mei accused her unfairly and complained about her, I had not defended her. Instead, I had ignored her needs for the sake of the revolution. In fighting for justice, I had failed to dispense justice. I had failed as a son.

What could I do now? The Party would not let me stay in Vancouver for long. *If Mama recovers soon, I'll bring her back to Hong Kong. I'll find a high-paying job, take care of her, and still fight for the revolution. If Mama recovers …*

My mother drew the thin line of her lips into a bitter smile and reached for her glasses. Mei Mei helped her put them on.

I reached for her hand. "How do you feel, Mama?"

"Are you tired … from travelling?" Her words came out slowly, as though each were a boulder she had to lift.

"I'm all right, Mama. How do *you* feel?"

"Hungry. I haven't eaten for a long time."

It was true. Mei Mei told me she couldn't remember the last time Mama ate. I looked at the tube the doctors had inserted into her abdomen. A milky cocktail of nutrients flowed into her. It reminded me of an umbilical cord. They had turned my mother into a child again. My eyes misted over and anguish welled up in my heart. "Do you feel any pain, Mama?"

"No, not much."

Yes, this was my mother. She had always endured pain well.

"Water?" Mama croaked.

Mei Mei moistened Mama's lips with a cotton ball. The conversation had tired Mama.

"I'm staying with Father and Mei Mei," I said, injecting cheer into my voice. "I hope you'll recover soon, so we can go for dim sum."

"You better get some rest after such a long trip," Mama urged, sounding more like her old self.

What I thought was, *I love you, Mama, and I'll take care of you*. But all I said was, "I'll see you tomorrow."

12

LOST OPPORTUNITIES

Written on thin, blue airmail stationery—folded up and glued together, letter and envelope all in one, the aerogramme bore a familiar return address: "Wah Tao Building, 42 Wood Road, Wan Chai, Hong Kong." Wei Yee had issued an urgent request to return home as soon as possible.

"How's Mama? Are you coming home soon?" she asked when I phoned her.

"Mama's still in intensive care. I can't come home yet."

Visions of Mama again filled my mind. A web of tubes and wires was holding her captive in a hospital bed. *How could I leave her?* Wei Yee could not possibly understand how I felt. "Lei Chen has the flu, and I'm exhausted." My wife went on to list her responsibilities at home, work, and Hok Yau. In the background, I could hear my daughter crying.

"On top of all that," Wei Yee concluded, "I have to do your work. No one else is covering for you here and no one is helping me."

"I'll come home as soon as I can," I promised.

Unable to convince me to return, Wei Yee finally hung up. I stared at the receiver for a long minute before returning it to the cradle. If Wei Yee saw Mama, she'd understand.

Things hadn't been easy for Wei Yee. With me out of the country, it was left to Wei Yee to finish organizing Hok Yau's upcoming variety show—set for the end of July—on top of her other duties at the club.

What's the right thing to do? Mama needed me. Wei Yee and Lei Chen needed me. The revolution needed me. *Have I failed them all?*

The house was empty. Mei Mei had already left in the car for work and Father had gone for his morning walk. I decided to walk to the hospital. From Mei Mei's home in East Vancouver, it would take me a good two hours to reach Vancouver General Hospital, or VGH, as the locals referred to it. *Good*, I thought, tucking the letter into my pocket, *I need to think.* I closed the door to the house behind me and made my way down the front steps. There were only three steps, but I could see why Mei Mei would find them difficult to negotiate in the winter. Last year, she had slipped on them several times because of the snow and ice. Following the gently sloped walkway, I pictured Mei Mei's prosthetic leg plodding through snow and I could see how dangerous it was for her. With a rush of guilt, I realized how much responsibility had fallen to my sister. *What had I done to share her burden? Nothing.*

Father tried to help her by carrying groceries and other heavy items into the house. He also took out the garbage and shovelled snow. "Even when I'm sick," Father said, "I have to do it. There's no one else. But life is simple and serene here." Father greatly enjoyed life in Vancouver—the fresh air, Mei Mei's quiet neighbourhood. He looked a little younger and had gained weight since I last saw him, four years ago in Kowloon. Unlike other immigrants, he didn't care to read about Hong Kong in the local Chinese newspapers. Instead, he read about vitamins, and how to stay healthy.

"How is she?" he would ask about Mama.

"She's resting and stable for now, but very weak," I told him.

Father shook his head silently in sympathy, but he never visited her at the hospital. One evening, Father had asked me to come to his room. It was quiet and peaceful, with a breeze coming in through the open window. The small room was very neat and sparsely furnished, with only a bed, a desk, and a bookcase full of books, including a few English dictionaries—Father was studying English on his own. Beside the bookcase hung a few *Vancouver Sun* newspaper clippings.

Father wanted to tell me his story, a grievance, which had been weighing heavy on his heart his whole life. "When I was fifteen, I lived with my father's second wife and their children—my siblings. I was a serious and quiet person. After work, I crossed the harbour from Hong Kong Central district back to Hung Hom, Kowloon. At home, I read books whenever I could. Books, all kinds of books that my father—your grandfather—hated so much. Your grandfather had forever bragged about his success with no education. He started his business and it was successful. Within a few years, he branched out to Guangzhou, Shanghai, Guilin, Swatow, and Singapore.

"One day just before dinner, my father—your grandfather—sat resting on his old rocking chair. He noticed me sitting on a stool in the balcony corner reading a book. This offended him.

"'Yick Ting, what book are you reading?' he shouted at me.

"'English grammar.'

"'You are a bookworm; you only know reading books and nothing else.'

"'Bookworm or not, I jumped one grade. If it weren't for you halting my schooling, I should be graduating from high school next year.'

"Then the maid announced that dinner was ready. Everybody— nine of us—sat at a round table. We were in Kowloon, not in the village, so we all ate dinner together, rather than in the Chinese tradition of men eating first. I helped the maid pass out the soup. The first bowl, as always, was for Father to show my respect. Suddenly, he raised his hand and swept the bowl away, soaking me with hot soup.

"'Where are your wages?' shouted your grandfather. 'You only care for your future wife. Remitting all your wages to her. Why don't you give me more money?'

"My wage was only thirty dollars. Your grandfather himself deducted the money. He took twenty-five dollars—twenty for my future wife and five for my room and board. That left me five dollars for pocket money. If he wanted more, he could've taken more, instead of accusing me in front of the whole family. Your grandfather hurt me deeply. I was angry and embarrassed."

Father resolved to leave Grandfather's family and swore not to take a penny from him. He left the family house, moving into the company's backroom in Hong Kong. As soon as he found a job elsewhere, he left altogether.

I thought about my reunion with Father in Vancouver. It was quiet and outwardly dispassionate. As part of our culture, there was no hugging or touching; we kept our feelings inside. But we knew we cared about each other. That talk in his bedroom was the longest I ever had with Father. He couldn't understand why Grandfather had embarrassed him in front of the family. Father experienced rejection by his father. Mama, too, was rejected by her father when she was sold to another family. So even before Father and Mama married, they each had a deep wound.

Deep in thought, I reached busy 49th Avenue and started on my walk to the hospital. Passing a high school, I saw students racing around the track. They looked so strong, so full of life. Heads raised, arms pumping, they reminded me of my younger self. I had always loved how the wind whipped back my hair and the way my muscles rippled on command. A quarter century had passed since I was a high school student. *Had it been so long since I was a teenager soaking up every word of Leung's stories of Communist bravery?* How naive I had been then, and still was.

I thought about my early years in the Youth League. As though in a dream, I watched my teenage self vow to serve my country and people. I had completely trusted the Communist Party's promise to liberate the Chinese people from turmoil, from suffering. For twenty-five years, I had sacrificed everything for the revolution. *Be careful,* I cried, as if trying to caution the Kee Ngai in my dream.

Students chased each other around the field, shoving and teasing good-naturedly. They looked like students from Hok Yau on a field trip to help the poor. *My* students, *my* contacts, such patriotic, idealistic youths. My heart warmed at the memory of each. An entire generation of exuberant youth had followed in my footsteps. These, the revolution's foot soldiers, were the reason Wei Yee needed me so desperately in Hong Kong.

Between 1967 and 1969, the high point of the Cultural Revolution, many of our Hok Yau contacts had left high-paying jobs and prestigious schools to show solidarity with their working-class comrades. In the aftermath of the riot years, however, these activists found themselves in serious debt and under pressure from their families. They could not return to their jobs or schools.

An activist, Wang Wai Jim, who left his job at an export company and became a teacher during the year of the May Riot, had to settle for half his previous salary. Unable to support his family during his two years of teaching, he took out a loan to help make ends meet. After the May Riot, no one in Hok Yau's Shadow Core cared about his problem. He changed jobs, tried to repay his debt, and, at the same time, took evening courses. Instead of receiving help or support for his decisions, he was criticized for seeking personal growth rather than working for the benefit of the Party.

Dorinda Chan graduated from a Catholic senior high school in 1967. She should have attended forms six and seven, equivalent to grades eleven and twelve, in preparation for entrance to Hong Kong University. Instead, she quit school and devoted herself to the Party. After the May Riot, she had to struggle to get into any university. The Party criticized her for caring about her own education. After graduating, she worked even harder for the Party. She put romance and marriage on hold. Now in her fifties, she was still single, and regretted not having married.

Many tried to make up for lost opportunities by taking accelerated courses whenever they could. The extreme-leftist faction of the Party sharply disapproved of anyone attempting to rebuild their lives after the May Riot. Angry and confused, a great number of my contacts wanted to leave Hok Yau and the Party. Even before I received news of Mama's condition, I had been working intensely at the club, trying to help resolve their problems so they would stay with the Party. Wei Yee and I believed our contacts had the right to study, to take accelerated courses, to take care of their families. It pained me to see men without jobs and women losing opportunities for marriage. The sacrifice seemed unnecessary. So we did our best to shield and protect these contacts against the extreme leftists. Convincing them to stay with the Party took all our energy. It was too much to expect Wei Yee to manage all these contacts on her own. I understood why she sent the urgent letter. None of our comrades had assumed my duties as club secretary in my absence. None of them helped Wei Yee with her extra load.

About halfway to the hospital, the exotic scents of Little India wafted into my consciousness. By now, my guilt had given way to frustration, then rage. I recalled the times my comrades had been in need. I had bought them food, clothing, and medication. I had bandaged their wounds and visited them in the hospital. I had made funeral arrangements when their parents died. That was revolutionary friendship: we were a family and had vowed to take care of each other. Where was my family now? Why, when I so urgently needed help, had the Party abandoned me? No one took over my duties, except my overworked wife. No comrade helped her with our daughter. Where was *that* revolutionary friendship?

I pulled Wei Yee's letter out of my pocket and reread it. Lei Chen was staying with her grandmother most nights while my wife attended Hok Yau meetings. It was often past midnight by the time Wei Yee picked her up. To go home, they had to risk taking public transit—

always dangerous at night—or pay for a taxi, which we could little afford.

"Lei Chen is sick again," Wei Yee had scribbled, "and you know my stomach." Wei Yee's health had deteriorated after Mama had left for Canada. At the best of times, Wei Yee was physically weak. Now, it was all becoming too much for her. Some of the girls from Hok Yau were helping Wei Yee with household chores but, of course, they could not take over my Party responsibilities. Our family and our young friends at the club were supporting us with all their heart. But our comrades were not.

I longed to return to Hong Kong to take care of my wife and daughter. Although my frustration with the Party made me want to leave the revolutionary troops, I cared too much about our cause. With so many corrupt and incompetent operatives in the Party ranks, the revolution needed sincere, faithful cadres like me. I could not abandon the revolution. But I could not abandon my mother, either. That much was clear when I saw her frail body still surrounded by tubes and machines.

"Have ... you eaten?" she whispered when I entered the room. I nodded and squeezed her hand. We didn't talk much. Talking took too much energy. Mama seemed content just to have me in the room. Seeing my mother as a sick, old woman made me wince. Where had the years gone? For so long, I had failed to take care of her.

I was in a dilemma. I wanted to make up for those lost years and take care of Mama and Mei Mei. But the revolution needed me in Hong Kong. There seemed to be no solution.

When it was time for me to go home, Mama clutched my hand and whimpered, "Don't leave."

It shocked me. The mother I remembered was invincible. She feared nothing. "I have to make dinner for Father and Mei Mei," I told her. "We'll come back tonight."

"No, don't leave me with her."

"With whom?"

"Your sister. She hates me. She'll kill me."

The strain of being so ill has muddled her mind, I reasoned to myself.

"Don't dwell on nonsense," I said, my hand on her shoulder. "Get some rest."

As I slipped out the door, I pretended not to hear her muttering, "Maybe I deserve to die. Yes, I deserve to die."

On the long walk home, her words haunted me. Father and Mei Mei had always blamed Mama for the amputation. Although I had never defended Mama while she was in Hong Kong, there was even less I could do to protect her from their accusations here in Canada. I wrestled with the conflicting demands as I walked the miles back to Mei Mei's. To *her* home. Not my parents' home, not mine, but hers.

Back at the house, Father was napping. Wanting to be alone, I locked myself in Mama's room, where I was sleeping while she was in the hospital. *I could ask Mama and Father to live with me in Hong Kong. I could give them their own home again.* But how could I afford to on my teaching salary? If I made more money, my parents could live with me in Hong Kong while I continued to support the revolution. Once Mama recovered, we could live together again as a family. I wanted another chance to prove myself a worthy son. I needed this opportunity.

Mei Mei soon added a new twist. "Why don't you move to Vancouver?"

I stared at her. "What did you say?"

"Look around you. Father and Mama are getting old. I can't support them both forever, financially or physically. I just can't. Why don't you immigrate, too?"

Immigration had never occurred to me. I liked Vancouver well enough, but the revolution needed me in Hong Kong. Finding a higher-paying job did not mean abandoning the cause, plus I would be able to adequately care for Mama and Father.

"I—I don't know," I said.

"What's there to know? You've seen Mama. I can't manage on my own."

In the end, I agreed to let Mei Mei apply to sponsor me and my family. Immigration, however, required a second step: I had to apply, and I couldn't do that without discussing it first with Wei Yee and the Party. Although I didn't tell Mei Mei so, my heart was set on taking care of our parents without leaving Hong Kong.

The days rolled by. Whenever I called home, Wei Yee begged me to return. She was too distraught for me to tell her about Mei Mei's request. By my fifth week in Vancouver, Mama was still in intensive care but stable, and thinking more clearly. My tourist visa would soon expire and Wei Yee's situation in Hong Kong was growing more desperate. I booked my plane ticket home for May 24.

⚜

"Mama, I'm going back to Hong Kong tomorrow," I told her gently as I held her hand. "My visa will expire soon. Wei Yee and Lei Chen are sick." I paused as she nodded. "I hope to bring you back to Hong Kong to live with us when you get well."

She nodded again, "That sounds good, but I don't think I'll live that long."

"Don't say such things. Get some rest." I patted her hand.

The next morning, there wasn't much to say. I told Mei Mei to take care of Mama and told Father not to think too much. There were no hugs, just a wave. "If there's any news, I'll send a telegram," Mei Mei promised.

The long flight back home gave me plenty of time to think. *"Trust the Party and the Party will take care of you."* But my belief in the Party had collapsed. It didn't even support me to see my own mother. I began to fear greatly—for my family, for my future. I resolved not to donate any more money to the Party and to get a high-paying job immediately.

Back in Hong Kong, Wei Yee was relieved to see me, and pleased to hear I had decided to find a better job: "See! I told you years ago that you need to think about feeding the family." Indeed, she had often badgered me about retaining money for our own use. I had thought she was not devoted enough to the revolution, but in reality, she was just being practical.

"I thought I could depend on the Party," I said. The explanation now sounded hollow, even to me.

"That's not practical," she said. "When you have a child, you must think about how you're going to support the family." She went on to berate me for being too loyal to the Party: "Look, members from other lines keep their high-paying positions. They donate only whatever they can afford."

I could only nod my head. Then I mentioned Mei Mei's suggestion that we emigrate to Canada.

"I'll be deaf, dumb, and crippled there," she argued, frightened at the prospect of having no status in Canadian society. "How do you expect me to get around or find a job in Vancouver without knowing any English? Why don't you go alone?" Despite all her responsibilities in Hong Kong, she would rather stay here by herself with Lei Chen than go to Canada.

"I can't. We have to apply as a family." As I understood the rules for immigrating to Canada, I had to be either single or divorced to apply on my own. Divorce was not an option. I wanted to keep my family together. I agreed with Wei Yee that it would be better to stay in Hong Kong. That way we could continue working for the Party while taking care of my parents. I was determined to earn enough money to bring my parents home to Hong Kong.

Within weeks of my return, I found a position as head of the service department at Spicers International, a British importer of European printing presses. The company occupied the ninth floor of the American International Assurance Building on Stubbs Road, Wan Chai—a highly prestigious address. As one of only four department heads, I was in charge of the office, service, delivery, and property management for the company. My department was responsible for implementing an inventory system and the move of the company warehouse from the southern tip of Hong Kong to the west side. As usual, my schedule was constantly busy, as I still had Hok Yau's variety show to finish organizing and, on top of that, struggle to attend meetings.

Many of the employees in my department resented my appointment. Some were much older than I. At first, most of my staff ignored my instructions. And everyone, from my secretary to other department heads, continually asked me, "Where's your car?" In the underground parking garage, five parking stalls were reserved for the company's department heads. Four of the stalls were occupied. In status-conscious Hong Kong, my empty stall undermined my authority. So, using my first paycheque as down payment, I bought a second-hand luxury sedan, a Toyota Mark II. For the first time in my life, I had kept the earnings for myself. The Party was not pleased.

"You've changed," Lo accused me at one of our struggle meetings. He peered over his spectacles at me to drive home his point. Then he smirked, as though secretly content at finding fault with me. Wang and Yuk Lin nodded in agreement, silent as usual. Our meetings had become increasingly contentious since I returned. Yes, I had changed, but not in the bourgeois, materialistic sense implied by my comrades. I was, instead, learning to think for myself, to speak up against my corrupt and incompetent comrades. They were incensed.

"My principles have not changed," I insisted. "I'm still teaching ballet at Hok Yau and serving as secretary there. I'm still managing my contacts."

"A Japanese luxury car? A high-paying job serving foreign devils?" Lo said. "Is that what you call sacrifice? Can you call that living purely and frugally?"

"Other Party members own cars and motorcycles, and I need one for my job. And I need this job to support my family. My mother is ill."

Wang cleared his throat. "We all must make sacrifices," he interjected.

I wheeled to confront him. "Sacrifices? What do you know about sacrifices? Are you going to make me pull out Mao's Red Book? Do you want me to quote Mao? Yes, I know his teaching: 'Thousands upon thousands of martyrs have heroically laid down their lives for the people; let us hold their banner high and march ahead along the path crimson with their blood.'"

Aghast at my outburst, Wang could only stare at me. I continued: "Do you remember Kui Fong in your elementary school study group? You wouldn't let her go home at ten o'clock at night when her father was ill. You made her read that quote loudly and forced her to stay. Did you care about her? Did you understand her difficult situation?"

"Really, Kee Ngai!" Wang protested.

"Her father was sick. Had you no compassion? That's why she left the revolutionary troops. Because of your arrogant disregard for her needs."

"Stop this!" Lo ordered.

But I wasn't about to stop now. Weeks, months, years of frustration and doubt welled up inside me. Rage seethed in my chest, churned in my stomach, and twisted into a knot at the base of my skull. "Ever since I came back, none of you have shown the slightest sympathy. My mother is critically ill. She may be dying. Can any of you understand that? Have any of you asked how she is? How I am coping? Do you even care?"

I pointed at Yuk Lin. "And you!"

Yuk Lin blanched. I didn't care about the consequences; my indignation could not be checked. "How dare you sit there and nod? You, of all people, should understand. When your father died, who made the funeral arrangements? Who sat up all night with your mother and your relatives for the overnight vigil? Who bought breakfast buns for everyone first thing in the morning after the wake? Me. And yet, my mother is dying and you haven't uttered a single word of sympathy. What a waste of all that honey I bought you for your sore throats.

"I cared about all of you. Remember, Wang? Remember the clothes I bought you when you first came to Hok Yau? I took care of you. Where were you when *I* needed *you*?"

Lo was becoming flushed and his voice quivered when he interrupted, "Kee Ngai, this is no way to speak to your comrades. What sort of revolutionary friendship are you showing here?"

"Revolutionary friendship? Revolutionary friendship!" I shouted. "What sort of revolutionary friendship did you show when I was in Vancouver? You abandoned my wife and daughter. No one helped Wei Yee. No one took care of my contacts. For twenty-five years I have served the Party. But when I needed help, the first time I ever asked for help, you gave me none. Now, I have to take care of my family and me. Why do I need to find a better job than teaching? Because the Party failed me.

"My parents are old. What if I need to go back to Canada again? And I probably will. My mother is in intensive care right now. I only returned because no one was here helping Wei Yee. I need to go back to Vancouver and take care of my parents. I need to persuade them to come back to Hong Kong with me."

"So that's your plan, is it? You want to move to Canada," Lo sneered, twisting my words.

"I didn't say that."

"At the first meeting after you came back, you said you wanted to emigrate."

"No, I didn't. I said my sister wanted to sponsor me for immigration. We haven't applied yet."

"Why would you let her sponsor you if you're not going to apply? Did you plan this before you left for Vancouver?"

"No, why would I plan to go to Canada? If it wasn't for my mother being critically ill, I would not have to go at all."

"I told you to wait for permission before you went. Why did you ignore my advice?"

"I told you, my mother was dying. Why did you take so long to get permission for me?"

Lo ignored my question and responded with one of his own: "Why didn't you discuss it with your superiors before letting your sister submit the application for immigration?"

"I keep telling you, I haven't decided to emigrate. I have to fly back and forth to Vancouver to visit my mother until she recovers. If the Party pays my expenses and takes care of Wei Yee and Lei Chen while I am gone, I won't have to bring them with me to Canada. I intend to bring my parents home to Hong Kong. Then I can take care of them and continue to work for the Party; that is the perfect solution."

My protests fell on deaf ears, and my comrades did not soon forgive my outburst. Stung by my criticism, they arbitrarily argued with me meeting after meeting, distorting my words and my intentions. I had, they said, betrayed the revolution by leaving for Vancouver without permission. The job at Spicers, the car, my trip to Vancouver—these offered final proof that I was a right-wing sympathizer, a British spy, in love with the bourgeois Western lifestyle. My comrades' decade-long suspicions had finally been confirmed. And with the efficiency and swiftness of a kangaroo court, they found me guilty of Party treason. My sentence? Political execution.

"Is it true?" whispered Mae, one of my contacts. She was almost afraid to ask the question.

I searched her face. "Is what true?"

"Lo says you're leaving the Party."

"Do you believe that?"

"Not really," she said, twisting her fingers together. "You wouldn't leave us because life is better in Vancouver, would you?"

I sighed and tried to reassure Mae the best I could. "It's an unfortunate misunderstanding between me and my comrades. Don't let it bother you."

Here and there, I heard the whispers. Another Party member was taking over my contacts. Directives were bypassing me completely. The Party had ostracized me. Heartsick and unable to sleep, I wandered the streets at night, trying to sort through what was happening. Despite the late hour, the streets were busy. But even the fragrant smells from a wonton stand and a congee restaurant did not appeal to me. I had no appetite. At a sports field a few blocks from my home, beggars slept along the fence under sheets of cardboard. Neighbours had gathered to watch gangster-like kids play soccer. I joined the audience in the stands. My eyes rested on the field without seeing anything. My mind wandered back and forth between memories of Mama—during the war, in Hong Kong, and in Vancouver.

I could not find a solution. *How could I take care of Mama without first going to Canada?* She needed me. Her condition was still critical, Mei Mei had told me during our last conversation. "When are you going to apply for immigration?" she had asked.

I had pretended not to hear. The revolution needed me. My contacts needed me. Although the Party had officially taken my contacts from me, our friendships remained, and many continued to come see me or phone me. I loved them and wanted to protect them from the Party's extreme policies and tactics. Many of them were very young and did not have the finesse needed to deal with people like Lo.

"Why don't you just explain yourself to your contacts?" Wei Yee urged me. Why not, indeed? But they had undergone so much already, why should I draw them into my battle? Many had been criticized in the years of working for the revolution. They, too, had sacrificed their youthful years in the May Riot and the turbulent years that followed, which was detrimental to their careers. And I didn't want to make them choose sides—between the Party and me.

With a sigh, I left the soccer game and continued wandering. Without my realizing, my feet took me to my office building. The security guard waved me through. I sat in my private office overlooking the Happy Valley racetrack. All was silent. The headlights from cars passing by on the streets below assaulted my eyes, but I was so lost in thought I barely noticed. The Party had made me an outcast, like a man with a contagious disease. Several of my subordinates now avoided me.

"If we meet on the street, pretend we are strangers," Leung had warned me when I first joined the Youth League. Now, I was a stranger to my people. What was the point of staying in Hong Kong to protect my subordinates? The Party had cut me off from any position of influence. Like a cult, the Party had brainwashed me into serving it blindly. Now, threatened by my new attitude of independence, my comrades were attacking me through a smear campaign. Ironically, the organization accusing me of betrayal had in fact betrayed me.

Deep inside, my conviction had snapped. The Party was not the saviour I had once thought it was. How could an organization that abused its people like this possibly rescue China from turmoil? The Party condemned me for taking care of my parents and valued cadres like Fong Yu Ting, who was nothing more than a greedy political opportunist. An organization that showed such poor judgment of character could never champion justice.

To lose all hope is a terrible sentence to bear. A man without hope is dead, even though he continues to walk.

I walked, exhausted, into my office the next day. The last thing I recalled was asking a colleague for a file. At her simple response, "I don't know where it is," I slumped to the floor. By the time I regained consciousness, someone had removed my tie and unbuttoned my shirt. The pungent odour of Tiger Balm clung to my temples.

"You're working too hard," a clerk in my department chided me as he escorted me to the doctor. Most people assumed I had collapsed from overwork for the company. Wei Yee knew better. It was neither the overwork in the office, nor the overwork at Hok Yau—in fact, once I started to quarrel with my comrades, my Hok Yau duties were reduced, the Party taking away most of my work there. It was the stress of the struggle meetings, the agony of suddenly realizing the betrayal by my comrades, the dilemma over the future of my family and parents that had caused it.

Some evenings, I listened to Beethoven's *Symphony No. 5 in C Minor* and *Violin Concerto in C Major* to find inspiration. The deep resonating notes gave me courage to wrestle with my difficulties. And I listened to Puccini's opera *Tosca*. It touched me when Tosca was requested to yield herself in exchange for her lover's life. She protests to God, "Now this my hour of pain. Lord, why do you reward me like this?" Tchaikovsky's music expressed such deep sorrow and tenderness. I often listened to *Symphony No. 6 in B Minor, "Pathétique,"* and *Andante Cantabile*. The melodies of compassion and understanding soothed my anxiousness.

Classical music gave me moments of peace but not a solution. Still unable to sleep, I spent many nights wandering the streets, worried about Mama and agonizing over the revolution. All this drained me.

"It's not fair," Wei Yee fumed. "The Party isn't treating you justly. Lies, all lies."

There was not much I could say in response. Instead, I shared with her my decision. "I don't have much choice now," I said. "The Party doesn't trust me. Why don't we go to Canada for two years? We can apply as a family, and I'll work to support us there."

Wei Yee wasn't enthusiastic but understood my desire to care for my parents. Mama was still in intensive care.

"Don't worry. When we come back in two years, I won't have any trouble finding a job." I forced myself to sound stronger and more assured than I felt. At forty, it would not be easy to start over again. The future held so many unknowns.

Wei Yee agreed to apply for immigration, and I focused on continuing to earn enough money to support us. Since returning to Hong Kong, I not only worked at Spicers but also had started my own ballet school. I figured I would have a little more energy and time after Hok Yau's show at the end of July. And now, since the Party had reduced my Hok Yau work, I had even more time to devote to my ballet, plus, I would be able to earn a little extra money.

※

Woon Ling joined us for a meeting of the Shadow Core. She wore her usual grey cotton cheongsam and had left her stringy hair untouched.

Her dull-brown face was not smiling, and her eyes, two shiny, narrow slits, pierced me as though I were a criminal. Her eyes picked me up, inspected me, and tossed me aside like a useless rag.

Lo sat next to Woon Ling. He fawned over her as he would a high official. Whenever she spoke, he nodded energetically.

"Wei Yee, you've agreed to go with Kee Ngai to Canada?" Woon Ling asked.

"Yes, given the situation," my wife said, sounding surprisingly sure of herself. "His sister is crippled, and his parents are growing old. His mother is critically ill."

Annoyed, Woon Ling turned to me. "If you're only going in order to take care of your parents, why do you need to apply for the whole family?"

"Without the Party's financial support, I will have to work in Canada. I can only do that as a permanent resident. The rules say we have to apply as a family."

"Why don't you apply for a student visa?" Lo asked.

Exasperated, I replied, "That wouldn't allow me to work."

"But why do you need to take Wei Yee and your daughter?" Woon Ling persisted, growing even more irritated.

I could not believe this line of questioning. I repeated my complaints about how no one had taken care of my wife and daughter during my last trip. Pointing my finger at each of my comrades, I accused, "None of you cared for them while I left to care for my mother. How can you even claim that, 'The Party will care for you'? What does 'proletariat compassion' mean? I've never had any compassion from my comrades."

I went on to list again all I had done for my comrades over the years. I had lived so frugally, giving every penny to the Party. Few people knew I once ate at back-lane kitchens and at K.K.'s school cafeteria. No one knew Wei Yee and I survived on salted rice so that we could give nutritious meals to our comrades. "How has the Party cared for us? All you've done is spread lies and cut me off from my contacts," I said.

Furious at my attacks, Woon Ling spluttered, "Don't forget we sent you on trips to visit leaders in China. You ate and lived well there."

"You and you," I pointed at Lo and Woon Ling, "are both idiots."

Woon Ling had never been criticized so directly. Enraged, she banged her fist on the table. "What did you say? How dare you accuse me."

My rage now matched hers. I, too, banged on the table. "You don't even know who is a good cadre and who is bad. Many good cadres and activists have left the revolution, and you don't even care. Now that I want to take time to care for my parents, you accuse me of planning this a long time ago. How can you be so sure? All these years, I worked diligently. I am an excellent cadre and served the Party well. The good people are leaving, the bad ones remain, and you have even promoted some. How can the Party be 'glorious, great, and correct'?"

I was furious, yet part of me wanted to give the Party another chance. I decided to gamble. Taking a deep breath, I gave my comrades one last chance to do the right thing. "If you admit I am a good cadre and that the Party needs me to continue the revolution here in Hong Kong, I will not go to Canada," I said.

Woon Ling shook with forced laughter. "The wheel of history will continue to roll forward without you. It doesn't matter who leaves the revolution," she said with a sneer.

I was losing the gamble.

"I'm not leaving the revolution," I corrected her, "the Party can transfer me to the Canadian branch."

"We have no Canadian branch."

That was a lie. I had met a Canadian Communist Party member, a Caucasian, who had transferred to Hong Kong. He played the double bass in a left-wing school orchestra. I had met him backstage after a performance. Even Foo, one of my early superiors, had suggested I learn English in case the Party transferred me abroad. But it wasn't worth arguing over this point.

"Very well, then. I'll come back in two years, after I have settled my family. I want to keep my membership." Even at this late stage, I wanted to convince them that I was a good cadre. Considering I had vowed to dedicate my life to the Party for the liberation of my people, I wasn't going to break my vow—the Party would have to disown me. I also really did plan to return with my parents in two years' time to continue my work. My unit might be dysfunctional, but perhaps other units had dedicated comrades and superiors, and, as far as I knew, there was no corruption in the Party's central circle in Beijing.

"No. When you go to Canada, that's it," Woon Ling tossed back at me with a mocking laugh and left the room.

Lo, face flushed, remained speechless. Wang and Yuk Lin stared at me, their mouths wide open. They could not believe I had spoken like that to a Party official.

It was over. I had reached the point of no return. I would have to leave Hong Kong and the Party.

✣

"Woon Ling asked me to divorce you," Wei Yee told me a few days later.

Hiding my dismay, I raised an eyebrow, "And?"

"And I refused."

I was touched by her loyalty. Ours had never been a romantic marriage, but during this crisis, I came to appreciate my wife's support. Here, in Hong Kong, she would have no difficulty finding a job or even becoming a Party official, but by following me to Canada, she would be giving up everything.

Soon after my quarrel with Woon Ling, she began denouncing me in the Party's network, even though I continued working for Hok Yau, albeit in my reduced role, and was still a Party member. Among the many accusations levelled against me, one was especially hurtful. Back in 1968, Chairman Mao had issued a quota: Class enemies made up five percent of each organization. Leaders had to flush out these enemies. Woon Ling was responsible for finding the five percent within Hok Yau to meet her quota. She turned to the Shadow Core for help in exposing the student spies. We could not think of any. Not long afterward, she claimed to have proof that the enemy had dug a trench into the heart of Hok Yau. The culprit? Yuk Shan Siu, a member of the Light Music Group, which was under Choi's leadership. Choi reported to me. I informed Choi, who, together with other activists, interrogated Yuk Shan Siu and expelled him as a British spy. We had no evidence, just Woon Ling's accusations. Now, years later, Woon Ling was accusing me of wrongfully expelling Siu. I had abused my power, she said behind my back.

The Party asked Wei Yee and me to travel to Guangzhou for an open-forum meeting, where we could voice our opinions to our top superior. I thought of all the tactics the Party had used in the past and refused to go. I had heard of people going to Guangzhou, summoned by the Party, and disappearing, never to be heard from again. One couple I knew, Party members under Fong's supervision, were kind, hard-working people with only a minimum wage allowance from the Party. The wife was asked to go to Guangzhou for political study and self-criticism sessions, which usually last five to seven days. Typically, a person was asked to go if the Party believed he or she had been disobedient and correction was needed.

The husband began to think his wife had been detained when she still had not returned two weeks later. He travelled to Guangzhou, informing his subordinates and other Party members that he was leaving to look for his wife. In Guangzhou, the husband told his superiors that if anything should happen to him or his wife, his subordinates and other Party members in Hong Kong would create an uproar. The Party let them both return to Hong Kong; before Hong Kong's 1997 return to China, the couple emigrated.

Wei Yee and I had been called by the Party many times, especially during the Cultural Revolution, to go study in Guangzhou. In those sessions, we mainly studied Mao's thought and did self-criticism. It was known as "cleaning up oneself." Wei Yee knew this couple's story, too, but she wanted justice and so went to Guangzhou. This time, it was different for Wei Yee. She was allowed to air her grievances. She told the Party what she thought was wrong with the way it had treated me over my unapproved trip to Vancouver—how I had gone to see my ill mother and in doing so was denounced as a traitor. But the superiors in Guangzhou didn't express anything different from what Woon Ling and Lo had accused me of: love of the Western lifestyle, and a secret plan to emigrate to Canada. As with the other couple, the Party knew it could not detain Wei Yee without me causing trouble and creating bad publicity for it in Hong Kong. Wei Yee returned safely to my side.

After failing to trap us in Guangzhou, the Party finally denounced us openly: I had planned to emigrate to Canada a long time ago—my mother's sickness was only a pretext—and I was a traitor, a collaborator with the imperialists, longing for a Western way of life. In my last meeting with the Hok Yau Shadow Core, Lo threatened me: "When you go to Canada, you must behave yourself and do nothing to harm your country. If you do, we, the Party and our people, will pass sentence on you and execute the people's power on you." In other words, they would kill me. I had become the people's enemy.

And because Wei Yee supported me, she too was cut off from her contacts and issued the same threat. She did not accept this punishment quietly but told her subordinates what had transpired. By exposing how the Party had treated us, she triggered a tremendous split. Her contacts rebelled and were ultimately expelled from the Party.

My subordinates, meanwhile, were in a dilemma. They did not believe the accusations against us. They supported me but had never considered rebelling against the Party—or at least as far I knew. Not wishing to distress them further, I ended up assisting the Party in transferring them to another superior by facilitating the meetings. Keith and his wife, Winnie, remained loyal to us because in the past we had protected them against gossip. On the whole, however, I refused to speak to any of my contacts. I didn't know whom to trust, and telling them what had happened would give them only my side of the story. At that moment, they weren't able to discern the truth. I believed that sooner or later the truth would be laid open. Besides, if my contacts sided with me, I didn't want them denounced as traitors and driven out of Hok Yau—that might affect their livelihood in Hong Kong.

To help us know what the Party was saying about Wei Yee and me, one supporter secretly taped a meeting at which three of my comrades—I was not in attendance—denounced me as a "collaborator with imperialism." The title was reserved for traitors and enemies of the revolution. Through these three comrades, Lo, Wang, and Yuk Lin, the Party sent its verdict down the lines of communication to its four hundred contacts in the Hok Yau network, urging every one of our contacts to pass the information on to others. Wei Yee and I stood condemned and isolated.

As the Party cut off contact with us and we gave up our work at Hok Yau, we resolved to enjoy our family life while waiting for immigration approval. With my hefty paycheques from Spicers, we were able to save a lot of money. No more assisting poor comrades, no more donations to the Party. Every day after work, Lei Chen, Wei Yee, and I, a family of three, drove to Repulse Bay for sunbathing and swimming. Sometimes we caught a movie before we dined out at one of Hong Kong's many excellent restaurants. Every weekend we drove to a resort in Hong Kong or in the New Territories. Those family times are one of my happiest memories.

As we waited for our immigration approval, my previous contacts who still kept in touch told me of the false rumours that were spreading. Wei Yee and I, allegedly blubbering with fear, had exposed the Party to immigration officials. Canadian immigration officials had access to Hong Kong government files, and, indeed, we had been summoned for a follow-up interview. In a bare room, an immigration officer questioned Wei Yee and me separately for thirty minutes each. I divulged nothing about my Communist involvement. According to our Party comrades, however, we were traitors—giving out information in exchange for permission to enter Canada. When I heard that, I let out a deep sigh.

All those months, my rage had masked a deep-seated fear. I saw myself as a penniless, middle-aged man facing an uncertain future. Again I thought how foolish I had been to place my trust in the Party all those years. Staring out a taxi window at the crowded tenements we would soon leaving behind, I recalled a Communist painting I had seen when I first joined the Youth League. Students, workers, farmers, soldiers, government officials, and Party members were joyfully marching, hand in hand, celebrating a bountiful harvest. Crops filled one corner of the painting, factories stood in the background. In the centre, waving over them, were the Chinese national flag and the Communist Party flag. How beautiful that picture had looked to me.

As I woke up to reality, I finally learned that the most beautiful promises were created by those who had no intention of fulfilling them.

On July 12, 1974, I boarded a Canadian Pacific Airlines plane with Wei Yee and Lei Chen, headed for Vancouver, Canada. My hands were clammy, and I felt a deep emptiness. My wife slipped her hand into mine. Calm and assured, she smiled at me.

As I held my daughter in my arms, I determined to make up for all the years I had wasted working for the Communists. I would devote myself to my family. I would take care of my mother. Because even soldiers have mothers.

13

MAMA

1995 Vancouver, Canada

Briskly walking along the False Creek seawall in my exercise outfit, I took a deep breath. The early morning breeze and the perfect blue sky refreshed me, cleansing my soul. The waterfront area, south of Vancouver's downtown, was well developed with parkland, residential apartments and townhouses, and Granville Island Public Market. Pleasure boats, cruisers, and houseboats moored at the marinas. Canadian geese pecked the grass.

"Good morning," said an elderly man as he walked by.

I nodded and smiled, "Good morning."

"Great day, eh?" said a young woman as she jogged past me.

I waved and smiled. What a friendly and welcoming place. As I walked, I reminisced. The first two weeks after Wei Yee and I had arrived in Vancouver, we lived at Mei Mei's home, then bought an apartment in East Vancouver. By this time, Mama was much improved, though still weak. I didn't know the streets or the transit routes, but I learned quickly. I searched through the classifieds and soon found a job as an inventory clerk. I didn't like starting at an entry-level position, but I worked hard. And to help me get to work and get my family around town, I bought Mei Mei's car from her. Wei

Yee also found work at a factory, earning minimum wage. Even though we were receiving little pay, I thought, it was better than working for the Communists. Wei Yee's weak health hadn't improved after our marriage. Although she worked and took care of Lei Chen and the household, she was often fatigued and feeling unwell, and I did many of the chores.

I believed it would be difficult for me to get promotions and to advance in a Western company. After two months, I quit my clerk position to start my own business, Ken's Janitorial Services. With minimal investment, I learned the trade of cleaning—how to clean one area at a time and not to walk repeatedly through the same areas. I enjoyed my work and building the business. Some evenings when my janitorial workers called in sick, Wei Yee and I would work until morning, cleaning several offices in one night. My business grew quickly, and six months into it, I had to hire more help. This gave me time to explore other opportunities and be with my family more. Wei Yee by this time was working as a Chinese-language teacher in Chinatown.

A year later, in the summer of 1975, Wei Yee and I had a son. We named him Lin Chen. Mama, now recovered from her infection, stayed with us that year and helped take care of the children. It felt good to have the family together, and I worked furiously to earn money for us, eventually hiring help around the house.

Now, twenty-one years later, here I was enjoying a walk along False Creek before driving the five minutes to Chinatown. At that hour, there were not many pedestrians and plenty of parking spaces. Passing a bakery, I could smell the freshly baked buns and was tempted to buy some. Instead, I hurried into the next store to buy beef, poultry, and fish. Crossing the street, I browsed through the vegetables and fruits, selecting the best. Then I headed over to my parents' apartment a few blocks away.

"Here, Mama, I bought live fish from the market; you'll like these. Here's more chicken and vegetables."

"Yes, these are very good. I'll take this one," Mama said as she chose the fish and the half piece of chicken. After she and Father had selected what they wanted, I took the rest of the groceries home for my family.

Long after Mama's recovery in 1974, Mei Mei and Father continued to have a strained relationship with her. I never intervened. While frantically trying to rebuild my life in this new country, I told both Mama and myself that we would have a good talk once I retired. Now, with a wife and children to support, I did not have time to waste on family politics. Even when I found a vial of black opium in one of Mama's old clothing bags, I said nothing. She had brought it all the way from Hong Kong to Canada: in case she was unable to endure living, Mama had a suicide plan. I was surprised and threw the bottle away, but didn't speak to her about it. Instead, I asked Mama to live with my family and me for a while, away from Father and Mei Mei. I think she enjoyed some happy times. She came on vacation with us to San Francisco, Disneyland, Los Angeles, and Reno. In the summer months, we visited parks and drove to the nearby cities of Penticton and Kelowna. On weekends, we took her to dim sum and elaborate Chinese and Western dinners—Mama's favourite Western dishes were roast beef with fresh peppercorn and spaghetti bolognese.

Sometimes I made Cantonese gourmet dishes and entertained at home. Mama was especially fond of rock cod. I would buy two, each just under a pound—at that size, the fish was sure to be tender. After steaming it for six minutes, I poured a mixture of hot oil, green onion, ginger, soy sauce, and a pinch of sugar over top. Mama always preferred to have the sauce over the fish, while Lei Chen and Lin Chen preferred the sauce with rice. And we all liked crabs in season, cooked either by steaming with garlic and Samshu wine—Chinese rice wine— or fried with hot and spicy sauce, Sichuan style. To top off the menu, I cooked beef with green onion and ginger in a hotpot and, of course, the infamous young and tender peas with fried eggs and curry chicken.

When Mama and Father moved together to a seniors' apartment in Chinatown—Mei Mei having moved into a smaller apartment that she could more easily manage with her bad leg—I visited them often. Father usually liked to stay at home but Mama was more active, so once a month I took her out for lunch or dinner. When Wei Yee, the children, and I visited, Mama bragged to her neighbours, "My son's family is going to take me to a new restaurant for dinner." "Oh, you have such a good son, how lucky you are," the neighbours told her. Hearing this, though, made me feel that I still was not doing enough.

I was looking for a career change and a friend suggested real estate sales. I liked the idea, as it did not require any financial investment. I made plans to sell my janitorial business and began night courses, obtaining, in early 1982, my real estate sales licence. I sold residential properties while continuing with commercial and investment property sales courses. Real estate sales was a difficult occupation for me. By temperament, I wasn't a salesperson. I didn't want to try to persuade people to buy or sell, so instead I told them the information they needed to know and informed them of the market trends. The many immigrants preparing to flee the 1997 Chinese Communist takeover of Hong Kong created a real estate boom in Vancouver, beginning in 1987. I received many referrals from friends in Vancouver, as well as from people in Hong Kong with whom I had kept in touch, and I was able to make a relatively good living.

To unwind in the evenings, I often listened to music. My love of classical composers had never left me. I immersed myself in Strauss's delightful waltz, *Tales from the Vienna Woods,* and Rachmaninov's charmingly captivating "Adagio" from *Rhapsody on a Theme of Paganini.* I appreciated the humour in Mozart's opera *The Marriage of Figaro.* On television, I watched many ballets; I especially loved *Don Quixote,* perhaps because of its happy ending. The choreography by Alexander Gorsky and Marius Petipa required the highest technique from the ballerina and male dancer. Listening to such moving music and melting into the beautiful and gentle lines of the dancers was a welcome rest at the end of the day. And although my daily routine kept me busy, it also left me satisfied that things were well.

⁂

As I was getting ready to head out one Monday morning to visit properties, the phone rang.

"Kenneth, call Mom immediately," Mei Mei said in an urgent voice.

"What's the problem?"

"My call display showed Mom's phone number at 9:45 last night. I was vacuuming and didn't hear the phone ring. I called her this morning."

"So, what did Mama say?"

"She's babbling. I can't understand what she's saying."

"Is she still in bed and maybe not fully awake?" I asked.

"No, I tried three times. I think she should be fully awake by my third call, but her words are unclear. Kenneth, can you go see her right now?"

"Yes, I'll go right away," I replied.

The May sun was shining as I crossed Oak Street Bridge into downtown, joining the morning rush-hour traffic. The hour-long drive from my home in Richmond to my parents' apartment in Chinatown was an anxious one.

All was quiet as I opened the door to my parents' apartment. Father, who could no longer get out of bed on his own, was sleeping in the La-Z-Boy chair in the bedroom. Mama was sitting on the couch in the living room. But there was no trace of her usual smile; instead, her look was one of agony. With garbled sentences and jerky hand movements, she began to explain, with great difficulty, what had happened. "I was exercising … walking the halls … stairs. I was in hall … walking. I fell … my head hit … wooden hand railing. Passed out. When I woke up, I am lying on the floor … no one else there. I didn't know how long … I tried to get up … walk, but fell again. Passed out again. I think … three times it happened."

"How did you get back into the apartment?" I asked.

"I was dizzy … crawled. Phoned Mei Mei but no answer."

The bluish spots on Mama's shoulder and elbow, and lumps and bloodstains on her head, made my heart sink. I phoned her doctor and requested a home visit, but he told me we would have to come into his clinic. I thought moving Mama would cause her more pain, so Mama and I agreed to wait a few days to give her a chance to get some of her strength back. After making Mama as comfortable as possible, I left to meet a client. Father, with his own health issues, was not able to help Mama very much. Besides, Mama wasn't going to ask Father for help. They had not resolved their differences. But he did try to keep an eye on her and said he would let us know right away if anything happened. Mei Mei dropped by for a few hours each day, and at night I slept on their couch. But Mama continued to stumble and fall whenever she tried to walk, and she was still unable to speak clearly.

On the fourth day, in the late afternoon, Father phoned to say that Mama had fallen again and was feeling very ill. Wei Yee and I rushed to the apartment. When I saw Mama lying on the couch, I felt a deep pain. I phoned the doctor and left a message again requesting a home visit. When he finally returned my call that evening, I could sense his annoyance, as if I was wasting his time. He suggested that I take Mama to the hospital. Although angry with the doctor, I followed his advice.

Wei Yee and I followed the ambulance to a downtown hospital. Mei Mei arrived soon after us. After sitting in the waiting room for two hours, Mama was taken into the Emergency ward; we followed. It wasn't until 2 A.M.—four agonizing hours later—that a doctor came to see her. I told him what had happened. Even without my description, the doctor could see signs of delirium in Mama. The doctor checked Mama's eyes, nose, and throat, which made her choke. I asked him to be gentler. He didn't say a word but simply walked away. We waited beside Mama for half an hour, growing more and more impatient when the doctor didn't return. Searching the ward, I found him sitting at a desk reading a newspaper.

I was furious. With great restraint, I asked the doctor in a quiet and polite tone what he intended to do with my mother and what his diagnosis was. He told me that someone would inform us later. I sensed that he was in a bad mood; perhaps something unpleasant had happened earlier. There was nothing for me to do but go back to Mama's bedside.

Soon after, a nurse came to talk to us. Still no diagnosis was given, only promises of a CAT scan and admission to the hospital. An hour later, Mama was admitted to the neurology ward. We hoped that her family doctor would come and give us a diagnosis. He didn't. At the hospital, no one was available for consultation: we didn't get to see the doctor, and the nurses, busy with their own tasks, were unable to answer my question about Mama's condition. We felt helpless.

After five days of observation but no treatment, Mama was discharged. Mei Mei and I questioned the nurses about the promised CAT scan and were told it had not been necessary. The prognosis was that Mama would gradually recover.

Mama continued to have frequent falls after returning home. She couldn't speak clearly and could not even manage her daily life—she couldn't cook, take a bath, have a normal conversation, or even eat a meal. She was often in a state of semi-consciousness. A family friend and I took turns sleeping at my parents' apartment. Helping Mama with her meals, bath, and chores while carrying on our jobs soon left us both exhausted. And still Mama grew weaker and weaker.

On May 19, Father called me at home. Mama had fallen and was unconscious. Father was unable to carry her to the couch. This time, I called my own doctor. He immediately came to see Mama, then recommended we take her to Emergency at another hospital, Mount St. Joseph's in East Vancouver—even phoning ahead to let the hospital know we were coming. Mount St. Joseph's was a small hospital and favoured by many Chinese, in part because it offered a Chinese menu to patients. Every year, Mama put $180 in an envelope and told me to take it to Mount St. Joseph's as a donation.

The doctors at Mount St. Joseph's concluded that Mama had had heart failure and set her up with oxygen and medication. All the doctors and nurses were helpful, warm, and comforting. My own doctor visited Mama every day, as did Mei Mei and I. Although Mama seemed better, she didn't have much appetite, not for the hospital's Chinese menu, nor for the soup and fruits Mei Mei and I brought. Whenever she saw us, though, she smiled.

"How is Father, is he doing all right?" Mama asked slowly.

"Don't worry, Mama. I see Father every day and buy food for him, too."

"How is Wei Yee? Is she all right? And how are my grandchildren doing?"

"Don't worry, Mama. Everyone is okay," I comforted her.

Mama was longing to go home. Finally, on June 28, she was allowed to. Thinking it would help Mama recover more quickly, I took her back to live with Wei Yee and me. I would take care of her from now on, I decided. I had prepared a room for her and rented a wheelchair so I could take her around the neighbourhood. That night, I slept close by her bed in case she needed anything.

But early the next morning, she fell unconscious again. I called the ambulance and asked for Mama to be taken to Mount St. Joseph's. But the paramedics in Richmond could not cross into Vancouver, so they took Mama to Richmond General Hospital, where she was admitted for heart failure. After a few weeks of good care there, Mama could talk a little, walk a little, and her smile was back on her thin, weary face.

The resident doctor asked me, "Has your mother had slurred speech for a long time now?"

"No, not at all, only recently. Before all of this, she was very capable, exercised by walking and taking the stairs, alert," I said.

"She is more stable now. She's able to speak better now than when she was admitted, but her speech is still slurred. I'm just wondering if something happened."

I explained how Mama had fallen three months ago, how we got no diagnosis at the first hospital, and that ever since the original fall she had not been speaking clearly. Hearing this, the doctor ordered a CAT scan. Unfortunately the scan was three months too late.

Mama had a blood clot in the brain that was pressing on a nerve, resulting in slurred speech. The doctor told us she could have minor surgery to remove the clot, and that recovery time would be minimal. I was shocked and dismayed at the news, yet grateful for the discovery. Richmond General Hospital, however, did not handle neurosurgery: Mama would have to be transferred to Vancouver General Hospital. The doctor asked me to make a decision—Mei Mei had already told me to go ahead and make any medical decisions necessary. I was extremely anxious: I did not know whether having a hole drilled in her skull would help Mama recover. Patiently, the doctor explained everything and recommended the surgery, and I agreed to the operation.

On the day of the surgery, I had three real estate deals to close. The neurologist had assured us that the surgery was minor and that I did not need to rearrange my schedule. When I arrived at the hospital later that day, Mama was in the recovery room, awake. The surgery had been routine, only thirty minutes, with no complications.

Within a week, Mama could relay her ideas clearly. She was eating again, and she began walking—albeit slowly—and taking a bath by herself. She fought hard to recover by doing exercises and following the doctor's and nurses' instructions. On August 20, she was released from the neurology ward and transferred to the family ward, where recovering patients stayed while they waited for a room in an intermediate seniors' care home. It was a quiet and safe place, with everyone talking or laughing softly. Mei Mei and I continued to bring Mama soup and rice every day.

After fighting for Mama's life for months, we now relaxed. Mei Mei and I planned to take her out for dim sum just as soon as she was able. And finally, I thought, I will tell Mama that I love her and explain my life to her.

The hospital's administration recommended a Chinese general practitioner in East Vancouver as Mama's family doctor, my own doctor being unable to take Mama on as a regular patient. Mei Mei and I visited the Chinese doctor to discuss Mama's care. "Don't worry, I know what to do," he comforted us, promising that he would see to her quality of life. "After all, she's eighty-six," he said. I didn't understand his statement "after all, she's eighty-six" until two weeks later.

After being in the family ward for two weeks, Mama's health began to deteriorate. We could see and sense it. Maybe she had the flu? The nurse told us that Mama slept most of the day and didn't want to eat or drink, not even Mei Mei's chicken congee. We called the resident doctor, but he was on holiday. The nurse told us that the doctor hadn't been to see Mama since her transfer to the family ward.

Soon, Mama didn't even want to talk to us. She seemed to be semi-conscious. I knew Mama was in pain; she always endured pain without making a sound, keeping it inside. But there seemed to be no doctor taking care of Mama. Mei Mei and I were deeply worried. Several times we asked that any doctor at all in the hospital come see Mama. Two days later, a doctor came, and immediately ran tests. She found that Mama was in critical condition and called her doctor back from his vacation. He came to the hospital the next evening. Mama had kidney problems, he told us. To ease her discomfort, he suggested giving Mama morphine. A kidney transplant was out of the question. The doctor was straightforward: there was a waiting list for kidney transplants, and if a kidney became available, it would be given to a younger person. Mama would live for only three more days.

We were in shock.

"After all, she is eighty-six," the doctor consoled us.

All of us, my wife, my daughter and son, Mei Mei, and two close family friends, Mr. and Mrs. Chan, stood by Mama's bedside. Everyone was told of the doctor's last words, "she'll have three days." It was the evening of September 4, four long months since Mama's first fall.

Mrs. Chan, who was a registered nurse before she retired, offered to stay the first night with Mama. She knew I had high blood pressure and also had to go to work. I thought it would give me a chance to make arrangements so I could stay in the hospital with Mama for her final days.

Early in the morning, September 5, 1995, a nurse called to say that Mama had died. She lived not three days but just twelve hours.

My deepest regret is that I was not there with her when she died.

EPILOGUE

2005 Vancouver, Canada

More than a quarter century had passed since I first stepped onto Canadian soil as a permanent resident. Having only witnessed capitalism in Hong Kong and during the Kuomintang era in China, and since I had never been in another capitalist country, I came expecting to find a morally bankrupt society.

"Capitalism is like a dying person who is sinking fast, like the setting sun beyond the western hills, and soon to be relegated to the museum." This was one of Mao Zedong's many thoughts on capitalism that my superiors had endlessly regurgitated. Communist rhetoric about the debauched, bourgeois life of the West had forged my thinking for decades. I was not easily deprogrammed.

In Vancouver, however, kind, gentle strangers often showed themselves willing to help a newcomer settle in. Neighbours lent a helping hand, showing me how to prune trees and the best way to shovel snow. When my car was trapped in the snow, passersby helped push it up the slope. The courteousness of the officer who stopped me at a roadblock surprised me and gained my respect. I saw bus drivers help the elderly on board. People patiently lined up for theatre and bank cashiers; postal workers delivered registered mail to my door with a smile. I witnessed and benefited from many other small acts of kindness as well, and all have touched me, and contribute toward the high quality of living in this country.

More importantly, here in Canada there is respect for human dignity. I am living in an open society, not in George Orwell's *Nineteen Eighty-Four,* my every move being watched by Big Brother. Here, I discovered an unexpected degree of freedom of thought. People are free to have their beliefs, religion, and political views. They are free to join political parties and unions. No one censures them for their beliefs. People are free to express their opinion about government policies. No one controls anyone else. How unlike the Communist regime, where every act and thought is monitored by the Party.

Having taken my first steps out of the Communist cult, I rapidly discovered many disturbing facts about the Party, which I had either never encountered before or chosen to ignore. Millions of my countrymen died in the famine of 1960 to 1962, a product of the Great Leap Forward, Mao's introduction of communes in an attempt to develop China's agriculture and industry.* The Red Guard and the Gang of Four, led by Mao's wife, murdered millions more during the Cultural Revolution, from 1966 to 1969. I read that, until he died, Mao had kept a harem of thirty young women. I read about the persecution of Marshal Peng Dehuai, who had challenged the validity of Mao's Great Leap Forward and criticized his having a harem. Peng Dehuai was arrested and tortured by the Red Guard. And in 1974, after Peng endured a long illness and he refused medical treatment, his heroic career ended.

I also read about the corruption of rural officials. Farmers were required to pay a multitude of taxes and duties to their village official. In some villages, farmers could pay up to fourteen taxes. When buying and paying for services from farm workers, many of these officials would pay with non-cashable promissory notes, called white slips. However, when these same officials collected taxes and duties, they

---

* "10,729,000 victims in The Great Famine and Retrenchment Period, and 7,731,000 victims in The Cultural Revolution." *China's Bloody Century* by R.J. Rummel (London: Transaction Publishers, 1991), 247, 253.

didn't accept promissory notes, only cash. When there wasn't any, they gave the peasants serious beatings, confiscated their belongings, and even tore down their shelters. The peasants could not run away from the debt because it would only be passed to relatives: any unpaid tax was transferable to the extended family, unless the person owing the debt died. I read about many suicides.

This, and the thousands of students killed on June 4, 1989, in the Tiananmen Square Massacre—wrenched my soul.

More recently, Zhao Yan, a Chinese journalist and a researcher for *The New York Times,* wrote articles exposing Chinese government corruption. Detained in China in September 2004, Zhao Yan was formally arrested in October for "passing state secrets to foreigners, a crime that carries a maximum sentence of death."*

I know ex-Party members living around the world who are afraid to offend the Chinese Communist Party. By telling my story, I not only have given up hope of ever returning to my ancestral home, but I risk my life. Most ex-Party members believe that if the Party wants to find them, it will. They may be killed in what appears to be an accident. The threat is very real.

These same ex-Party members accuse me of betraying my vow to support the Party and never expose it. They've chosen to keep their silence. Yet the Party has betrayed its own vow to serve its country. Worse than the Japanese or the Kuomintang, the Party has systematically killed hundreds of thousands of our own people.

I believe the Party has even betrayed its commitment to Communism. It exerts Nazi-like control on our people in order to serve the bourgeois needs of its leaders. Party officials are divided into grades; the higher the grade, the more perks: automobiles, servants, villas, guards, overseas education for their children, and of course, money—lots and lots

---

* "China Formally Arrests NYT Researcher for Secrets," Yahoo News via Reuters. October 21, 2004. On website: http://news.yahoo.com/news?tmpl=story &u=/nm/20041021/ts_nm/rights_china_reporter_dc_2.

of money. Ironically, the poorest proletariat revolutionary cadres have now become the richest people in the nation. How did officials in Beijing, the centre of power, those supposedly receiving only a few hundred dollars in monthly salary, become millionaires? Corruption is widespread, from the lowest clerk in the poorest village to the highest-ruling official in Beijing. Indeed, corruption in today's China is probably worse than it was during the years under Chiang Kai-shek and the Kuomintang. There is no equality within the ranks of the Party. I was naive to believe that there ever was. Although we had promised to return in two years to work for the Party, Wei Yee and I in the end decided not to.

So much of what I see today in China and Hong Kong reminds me of how the Party operated when I was involved with it. Dishonest and crooked members soar to the top, honest members are left to rot at low-grade positions until they burn out or become disillusioned. And people are used until they drop; the sick and poor left uncared for. Life is extravagant for a few, while millions and millions endure much hardship.

⁂

Sometimes, here in Vancouver, I come across mention of former Party members and contacts. Reading *Ming Pao, Sing Tao,* and *South China Morning Post,* I recognize references to many of my comrades. Some are now teachers, clerks, and bankers; others are government officials in Hong Kong. Curious, I follow what they are up to.

My first contact, Leung, I found out, had in fact already finished high school when he was placed at my school—he had reregistered as a student. He, like me, was sent by the Communist Party to be a recruiter and mentor for impressionable youths. Despite that false-hood, Leung was a dedicated comrade who believed in the cause. After I joined the Communist Youth League, he told me proudly, "I am a proletariat; I have not owned a single property all my life." His wife died in the early 1970s and he died a few years later, sick and poor. His young son was admitted to a mental hospital for autism.

Siu Yuk Shan, whom the Party said I had wrongly accused of being a spy, is now the vice-chancellor of a university in Hong Kong.

I know that Wang and Yuk Lin, my comrades in Hok Yau's Shadow Core, continue to operate under covert identities.

Woon Ling, ironically, was expelled by the Party for corruption. Although it was her husband who embezzled more than a million dollars from the Party, she helped cover up for him for years. While she was accusing me of indulging in luxuries such as tender green peas, she was hiding her husband's criminal activities. The Party sentenced her husband to work in a labour camp, but Woon Ling intervened on his behalf. Today, much older and thinner, she runs a small grocery store in Hong Kong's west end.

Confucius became Guangdong Province People's Representative— an honorary title but a hollow position. Foo told me that Confucius's children received an education abroad. He still lives in Hong Kong.

Foo is now retired from his position as the finance controller for the Hong Kong Federation of Trade Unions. He tries to keep in touch with me by email, Christmas cards, and phone. He says he's just working and trying to stay out of politics. In the early 1990s, before Hong Kong's return to China, Foo, his wife, and the chairman of Hong Kong Federation of Trade Unions visited Vancouver—I didn't know the purpose of their visit. Nonchalantly, Foo told me that Lo had become an official at Xinhua News Agency's Hong Kong's Central district branch, before dying of cancer, in Guangzhou. I no longer keep in touch with Foo.

Since the return of Hong Kong to China in 1997, Fong Yu Ting— status-conscious Short Guy Fong—has been serving as one of the many consultants to Tung Chee-wah, Hong Kong's chief executive.

Keith and Winnie, having become disillusioned with the Party, moved to Canada; we remain good friends. Unlike my former comrades, the many young people I met at Hok Yau have been loyal and supportive to me all these years. I was saddened, however, to hear that many became mentally ill or committed suicide under the Party's regime. They find their years under the Communists too painful to discuss.

In recent years, I learned that Hok Yau Club had created a suicide hotline for students who failed their Hong Kong Certificate of Education Examination, the same one Wing Mui failed years ago and had tried to kill herself over. I did not keep in touch with Wing Mui but heard she was married and continued to work in a left-wing institution.

Hok Yau Club continues to be a non-political student fellowship on the surface. However, the Communist Party in Hong Kong is still up to its old tricks, placing members to work in various institutions. Although there are many political parties in Hong Kong—the Democratic Party, the Liberal Party, the Alliance for the Betterment of Hong Kong, among others—the Chinese Communist Party does not officially exist there, and many people are naively unaware of the Communists' agenda and operations in their city.

Unlike the general population, I'm sure the British government knew about our covert Communist activities, though they tried to suppress it with arrests and jail time. The 1960s was a turbulent time in Hong Kong, and after the May Riot of 1967, the British did try to improve their governing with much more humane policies. In 1969, the title "Royal" had been granted to the police department to become the Royal Hong Kong Police Force. Schools began to allow students to stay after hours and form interest groups. Various departments were formed to support these recreational activities, such as the Art Centre, the Hong Kong Sport Development Board, and the Leisure and Cultural Services Department. The Hong Kong government began a program of social reform that included public housing, student recreational facilities, medical care services, and licencing previously illegal mini-buses to become part of the public transit system. In 1974, the government established the I.C.A.C.—the Independent Commission Against Corruption—and eradicated much corruption from government departments and the police force. Police pay was increased significantly, too. With social law and order re-established, and the efficiency and effectiveness of the government departments maintained, public resentment diminished to a new low. For the majority of Hong Kong people, there was likely a great deal of sadness and more than a trace of apprehension with the lowering of the Union Jack on July 1, 1997.

⁂

Mei Mei and I gradually lost touch, even though we went through so much together during the war and together took care of our parents in their later years.

K.K. spent his entire working life at the Mongkok Workers' Children School. With a record of "deserter" on his dossier, he was never promoted. At the time, I was proud of my brother for dedicating himself to our country by answering the Communists' summons to build a new China. I always remember how good he was—honest, straightforward, helpful to the poor, and able to endure hardship. On the road of retreat, he not only took care of all our luggage but he helped others, too. One winter in Hong Kong, his co-worker's squatter's hut burned to the ground. K.K. gave him his own winter clothing and a cotton quilt. I am no match to his noble character. Nevertheless, K.K. eventually could not forgive me for leading him into a life of poverty, while I lived in apparent prosperity in Vancouver. If it weren't for me dragging him back to Communism by persuading him to teach at Mongkok Workers' Children School, he probably would have operated an electronics repair shop and his life would have been much better. Our communication slowly reduced to a Christmas card each year. When I phoned him, several years ago, he refused to talk to me.

My impaired relationship with Mei Mei and falling-out with K.K. were my fault. In Hong Kong, when I worked wholeheartedly for the Party, I ignored my parents and my siblings, too. This extremely serious consequence will be a burden I carry until I die.

The year Mama died, Wei Yee asked me for a divorce. My belief that love could be cultivated had proved wrong. Part of me was unwilling to break up the family, and part of me was relieved of the heavy burden that I felt I had carried for so long. This was the second time she had asked for a divorce. The first time was in 1982. During the spike in interest rates in 1981, we lost our investments and most of our savings. But we agreed to wait until the children had finished school. In later years, Wei Yee criticized me, saying that sometimes I treated her well and sometimes I treated her badly by neglecting her. At the same time, I did not feel respected or loved either. Though we cared for each other, there was no intimacy between us.

Like traditional Chinese, I always thought my children would live with us until they married. My daughter dropped hints early on that she would move out. I took offence, thinking she didn't like living at home, the home I provided. But later, I understood her need for independence. When Wei Yee and I finally divorced, our children were in their twenties. We sold our house and we all moved out to our own places.

Mama's death struck me hard; I could hardly think about the divorce. I went into a deep depression for a few years, shutting myself at home and not seeing anyone. I felt weak and vulnerable, but I didn't know whom to turn to. I was thankful to a few good friends who called me every other day to make sure I was all right. After pulling out of the depression, I joined personal-growth seminars and read spiritual books, including *Man's Search for Meaning* by Viktor Frankl, Wayne Muller's *How, Then, Shall We Live?* and the Bible. I went to counselling sessions for three years; these helped me get back on track.

When my children were older, they knew I was a leftist, but they hardly understood what that meant. I didn't want to burden them with the knowledge of my Communist membership. Both Lei Chen and Lin Chen graduated from university and went on to good jobs in the technology industry. When they were young, I spoiled them. I didn't often ask them for help with chores; instead, I wanted them to volunteer their help. When they did offer, which was rare, I told them to save their energy for studying. Like most parents, Wei Yee and I wanted our children to have a good education, so I did not demand too much of them other than to be good, honest people, work hard, get good grades, and to be aware that there were always those less fortunate than they.

These days, the children, Wei Yee, and I often have lunch or dinner together, sometimes dining out and sometimes dining at my place or theirs. I love to cook, and to make good food for my family. We get together to celebrate Chinese New Year, Chinese Mid-Autumn Festival, Thanksgiving, and Christmas. I often pick up fresh vegetables and chicken to drop off at Wei Yee's, as I once did for Mama. We talk about our health and our children. I am still grateful to Wei Yee that she came to Canada with me as a family. She would be deaf and crippled in Canada, she said, not knowing English or how to drive. It was a great sacrifice on her part, and I owe her much. Although she did learn to drive and took courses in basic English, eventually becoming president of a club that promoted Chinese ethnic dances, had she stayed in Hong Kong, her life would be much different. Perhaps a traditional Chinese medicine not available here would have cured her from weakness and fatigue, or if she had been an obedient cadre, the Party might have sent her to China for rest and restored her health. Most likely, she would have a good-paying job at one of China's state companies or associations.

Three years after Mama died, Father passed away, on March 6, 1998. We barely knew each other. He was often away from us, but that was how he provided for us. With the high inflation after the war, Father lived frugally and paid for our school fees and boarding expenses. And when I became a father, I was too busy providing for my family to build a relationship with him. Although there was a great distance between us, and I seldom spent time with Father in Vancouver, he knew I respected and cared for him.

In his final years, Father lived quietly without asking for much. I knew the local home-care meals were not his preferred style, but he never complained. He often talked about the events in his life that bothered him the most, such as his father begrudging every penny and preventing him from finishing school. He often murmured, too, that it was his hard-earned money that gave Mama her medical education. Yet, despite his shortcomings and his difficult relationship with Mama, Father was a good and honest man.

⁂

During Mama's last four months, I didn't try to speak to her, thinking that it would be better to wait until she was fully recovered. Perhaps I trusted the doctors too much; I was totally unprepared for Mama's death. I had truly believed that she would recover.

Even though Mama lived and travelled with us for a short time, it wasn't enough. Not only did I not tell her about my life under the Party in Hong Kong and why I didn't give her any of the money I earned, but also, I never validated her. I should have told her I admired her courage and quick thinking during the war, and that Father was wrong, his relatives were wrong, and Mei Mei's leg amputation was not her fault. I should have told her she did a wonderful job of taking care of us.

Because of my preoccupation with my cause, the revolution, I did not try to give my family a better life. But chief among my regrets is how I failed my mother. In my zeal to serve my country and, later, in my drive to make up for lost opportunities, I neglected Mama. I betrayed her by not defending her. There is so much I wish I could have said to her. I am reminded of a Chinese saying: "By the time a son has time to care for his parents, they are gone."

⁂

So now you know the truth, Mama. All those years I neglected you, I thought I was serving my country. I put the revolution first and sacrificed everything. This was my "proletariat passion." That's why I gave everything to my comrades and nothing to my family.

When I look back now, Mama, this was the most terrible consequence of being a Communist. I thought I was a hero, surrendering myself completely. But I sacrificed more than myself. I sacrificed my loved ones. I sacrificed you, Mama. I am so sorry.

For so many years, you suffered from my neglect but you never complained.

I remember the times you made me take you to the beach in Vancouver. It breaks my heart knowing you wanted to fling yourself into the ocean because you blamed yourself for Mei Mei's pain. It wasn't your fault, Mama. Mei Mei and Father didn't understand. Forgive me for not defending you the way you always defended me.

Wherever you are now, Mama, I want you to know I love you. I am so very sorry I never told you that when I had the chance.

This soldier was lucky to have such a mother.

ACKNOWLEDGMENTS

I appreciate and thank the many of you who supported and encouraged me as I wrote this book: Suzanne Bastedo, Ahniko Batskor, Dr. Peter Chan, Valerie Hawick, Betty Hui, John and Jeanie Maggie, Julia Sung, June Swadron, and Tony Yu. Your helpfulness and optimism continually sustained me.

Thanks to Lei Chen and Lin Chen: the time you've spent helping with the manuscript has been immense. And thank you also to Tam Wei Yee, for your ongoing support.

Thanks to Susanna Chu, who laboured through hundreds of pages of transcripts, photos, materials, and emails. Without your initial effort, this book would be impossible.

Special thanks go to Joann Yu, for her many months of writing, editing, compiling, and arranging. Without her continued persistence and belief in this project, and her translating of my story and feelings into words, this book would not have been possible.

Thank you to my agents, Robert Mackwood and Sally Harding, for your hard work and belief in this project.

And to Diane Turbide and Penguin Canada, thank you for your valuable feedback and for realizing the importance of this endeavour.